The New International Telecommunication Regulations and the Internet

Richard Hill

The New International Telecommunication Regulations and the Internet

A Commentary and Legislative History

Springer

Richard Hill
Hill & Associates, Geneva
Geneva, Switzerland

ISBN 978-3-662-52531-9 ISBN 978-3-642-45416-5 (eBook)
DOI 10.1007/978-3-642-45416-5
Springer Heidelberg New York Dordrecht London

Co-Publication with Schulthess Juristische Medien AG

Softcover reprint of the hardcover 1st edition 2014
ISBN 978-3-7255-6935-9. www.schulthess.com
Published by Springer-Verlag GmbH Berlin Heidelberg 2014

Printed on acid-free paper

Springer is part of Springer Science+Business Media (www.springer.com)

The New International Telecommunication Regulations and the Internet: A Commentary and Legislative History

Richard Hill

Did the United Nations (UN) attempt to take over the Internet in December 2012 so as to control it and establish censorship? Yes, according to various specialized blogs, newsletters, and some US politicians. No, according to the author of this book, who has unique knowledge about the International Telecommunication Union (ITU) in general and the 2012 World Conference on International Telecommunications (WCIT-12) in particular.

This book provides a clear and thorough account of the process leading up to the revision of the International Telecommunication Regulations (ITRs), one of the four treaties administered by the ITU. The author's inside view of the events, and his legal analysis of the new ITRs, are different from that what has been aired in most other accounts to date. His systematic approach shows how much of the criticism of the WCIT-12 process, and of the ITRs themselves, is unjustified. This book provides the most accurate view to date of what they ITRs really mean and of what really happened at WCIT-12, which was undoubtedly a key event in the history of telecommunication policy and which is likely to have significant long-term effects.

The book covers in some detail the events leading to the non-signature of the treaty by a significant number of states, outlines possible consequences of that split between states, and offers possible ways forward. The book includes a detailed article-by-article analysis of the new ITRs, explaining their implications, with recommendations for national authorities. It concludes with an analysis of events from the point of view of dispute resolution theory, offering suggestions for how to avoid divisive outcomes in the future.

This book should be of interest to anybody involved in telecommunication policy matters and international negotiations. It provides an account of facts that are not easily accessible elsewhere and thus will be of value for future research. It will be an important resource for academic libraries.

"This is an excellent book, and quite rich and comprehensive. The topic is important and the book will surely be of interest to regulators, diplomats, policy experts, and all those who participated in WCIT. The author is uniquely qualified to write an analysis of the new ITRs and an account of the Conference. This book will be a good reference for the next Plenipotentiary Conference to be held in 2014 which is going to discuss follow-up to WCIT-12." Naser al-Rashedi, United Arab Emirates.

"This is an authoritative expert account of a moment of high significance for vital issues with respect to international networks." Professor Dan Schiller, University of Illinois

"This is an excellent and timely work." Professor Ian Walden, Queen Mary, University of London

" ... interested persons, businesses and governments can draw their policies from the assessments of a telecommunications insider as presented in this book. The manifold arguments enlightening the interpretation of the provisions of the ITRs might become an invaluable guidance for those who apply the ITRs in the future." Professor Dr. Rolf H. Weber, University of Zurich

Richard Hill

Dr Richard Hill was the Secretary, since 2004, for the various ITU groups that discussed the revision of the International Telecommunications Regulations (ITRs). He was the head of the secretariat team dealing with the substantive issues at the World Conference on International Telecommunications (ITRs). He was also Counsellor for Study Groups 2 and 3 at the International Telecommunications Union, that is technical secretary for the ITU groups dealing with operational aspects of service provision, networks and performance, including numbering issues (for example, assignment of international country codes); and charging and accounting matters.

Prior to joining ITU, Richard was Department Head, IT Infrastructure Delivery and Support, at Orange Communications (a GSM operator), responsible for delivering and maintaining the real-time, fail-safe computing infrastructure for the company to support over 300 online agents and related applications such as billing. Richard was responsible for IT Operations, IT Help Desk (support for 1500 PCs), IT Security, Network, Unix, NT, Oracle DB, Tuxedo, Telephony, and Internet and Intranet services.

He previously was the IT Manager at the University of Geneva, responsible for the network, central systems, over 6000 work-stations and PCs, user support, administrative applications, library infrastructure, and audio-visual services.

Prior to that, he worked at Hewlett-Packard's European Headquarters in Geneva, Switzerland. At HP, he had been responsible for world-wide mobile communication strategies and plans; for delivering GSM services throughout Europe; for specifying, procuring, and deploying voice and electronic mail services in Europe; for developing and implementing HP's EDI program in Europe; for operating the IT center supporting operations in the Middle East and Africa; and for providing economic and sales forecasts to HP top management.

From September 1991 to June 1993, Richard was the Western European Rapporteur for EDIFACT, responsible for the organization of the EDI standardization efforts in Europe and for liaisons with other regions working on EDIFACT. He is past chair of EDIFICE, the European Electronics Industry Forum for EDI, and was editor of X.435, the Pedi protocol for EDI and X.400.

Prior to joining HP, he worked as a Research Statistician for the A.C. Nielsen company in Europe, a large marketing research company, and as a systems designer and consultant for a small software company specializing Boston, Mass. that specialized in applications for managing financial portfolios. Prior to that, Richard was Systems Programmer and later Applications Development Manager for econometrics systems developed at M.I.T. and N.B.E.R. (TROLL project). Richard has taught numerous courses and seminars as part of his work and at universities in the US and Europe.

Richard holds a Ph.D. in Statistics from Harvard University and a B.S. in Mathematics from M.I.T. Prior to his studies in the U.S.A., he obtained the Maturita' from the Liceo Scientifico A. Righi in Rome, Italy.

He has published papers on mediation, arbitration, and computer-related intellectual property issues and the standard reference book to X.435.

First of all, I dedicate this book to my friend and inspiring colleague, the late Mr Nabil Kisrawi. But also to all who contributed to the preparation of the revision of the 1988 ITRs, in particular Mr Kavouss Arasteh, Mr Cleveland Thomas, and Mr Alexander Kushtuev. Many ITU colleagues contributed to the Secretariat and there is not enough space to list all of them individually, but I wish to mention Ms Elaine Baron, Ms Doreen Bogdan, Mr Arnaud Guillot, Mr Nelson Malaguti, Mr Preetam Maloor, Mr Mario Maniewicz, Mr Alexander Ntoko, Mr Saburo Tanaka, and Ms Xiaoya Yang. It would be remiss not to mention the Chairman of WCIT-12, Mr Mohamed Al-Ghanim, who worked tirelessly to find agreements whenever possible.

And I wish to thank especially Mr Malcolm Johnson, who as Director of the ITU Telecommunication Standardization Bureau, supported my work on the ITRs, and also Mr Hamadoun Touré, who as Secretary-General of the ITU, graciously allowed me to stay on to complete the work.

And of course my assistant Ms Maite Comas Barnes, without whom nothing would have been possible.

Acknowledgments

I wish to acknowledge the many helpful comments provided by readers of early drafts of this book: Mr. Naser al-Rashidi, Prof. Dan Schiller, Mr Bill Smith, Prof. Ian Walden, Prof. Dr. Rolf H. Weber, and the anonymous reviewers.

Citations

The source of each reference is given in full in a footnote the first time it is cited, but usually without its URL. Subsequent citations use the form "Author (year)". Sources are listed in the References section, with URLs if they are available; however well known treaties and individual ITU conference documents, Resolutions and Recommendations are not listed in the References section.

Table of Contents

Foreword

Aiming at renewing the existing International Telecommunication Regulations (ITRs), developed in 1988, member states of the International Telecommunication Union (ITU), the independent United Nations specialized agency for information and telecommunication technologies, assembled in December 2012 at the World Conference on International Telecommunications (WCIT) in Dubai. Obviously, the telecommunications "environment" radically changed during the last 25 years, the "old" ITRs are lagging behind the technological reality. However, new phenomena such as the Internet encompass not only technical elements, but clearly also social and political issues. Therefore, it was to be foreseen that a consensus about the renewal of the ITRs and the possible intervention of the ITU into Internet governance matters could not easily be reached in Dubai.

Already prior to the WCIT, many non-governmental organizations (NGO) launched different motions, addressing for example the promotion of cyber-security, the increasing role of human rights on the Internet and the principle of multistakeholderism. Indeed, at the WCIT it became particularly clear that a substantial number of countries wanted to get more deeply involved in the current substantively private order of the Internet, mainly by referring to national security interests. These advocates of a "cyber-sovereignty" approach not only raised their voices louder, but also pushed the WCIT delegates to a vote in order to get some "evidence" that the Internet should remain in the competence of national governments including the right to regulate the corresponding activities. Other members of the ITU preferred to have only minor changes to the status quo since market forces and the multistakeholder approach would be the best guarantors for a free and not fragmented Internet.

The outcome of the WCIT is unsatisfactory in many respects: member states of the ITU have been split into two relatively "extreme" positions, not leaving much room for a moderate approach. Many terms of the ITRs are quite vague (for example the term "security") and thereby open to discretionary interpretation. The Internet Resolution, approved by a majority of delegates (contrary to the principle that decisions are to be taken unanimously in the international context) is ambivalent and non-binding. In 2015 some countries will probably apply the new ITRs bringing certain advantages to the consumers, some other countries might deny the application causing an undesirable fragmentation. In such a world of unclear legal rules, it is of utmost importance to have guidance on how to understand and interpret the given regulatory framework.

Richard Hill as expert of telecommunications law in different professional functions for many years has undertaken the not easy task to analyze the history of the development of the preparation of the draft ITRs prior to the WCIT, as well as analyzing the conference proceedings in detail. Whether the answer to the questions raised in the introduction of the book is a "yes" or "no" seems to be of less importance than the fact that interested persons, businesses and governments can draw their policies from the assessments of a telecommunications insider as presented in this book. The manifold arguments enlightening the interpretation of the provisions of the ITRs might become an invaluable guidance for those who apply the ITRs in the future.

Zurich, October 2013 Prof. Dr. Rolf H. Weber, University of Zurich

Introduction

International telecommunications have, since their inception, been subject to intergovernmental agreements in order to facilitate interconnectivity, but also to achieve certain economic effects[1]. However, starting in the mid 1990s, technical developments and a general trend towards liberalization resulted in a major change in the traditional international telecommunications regulatory regime[2]. The main instruments underpinning that regime are the various instruments of the International Telecommunication Union (ITU) and of the World Trade Organization (WTO), see Chapter 1. A key ITU instrument is the International Telecommunication Regulations (ITRs), which was agreed in 1988 in light of the trends towards liberalization and privatization.

However, given the rapid changes in the industry, and the increasing importance of the Internet, starting in 1998 there were calls for a revision of this instrument, in particular so as to reflect appropriately the well-known economic specificities of the telecommunications industry, namely that "competition in the telecom sector results in externalities and gaming which are critical to the development of competition for existing and advanced telecommunication services"[3]. Indeed, questions were raised regarding network externalities at the international level and how to deal with them, as well as how to deal with possible inefficiencies arising from possible significant market power at national and international levels.

As we will see in Chapter 3, given the complexity of the issues, it proved difficult to agree on the scope of the revisions, or even on the need for them, however agreement on the process was finally reached and revisions to the treaty were discussed and approved at the World Conference on International Telecommunications

[1] See for example Ergas, Henry, 1998. "International Trade in Telecommunications Services: An Economic Perspective", in Hufbauer, Gary Clyde and Wada, Erika (eds), *Unfinished Business: Telecommunications after the Uruguay Round,* Institute for International Economics.

[2] See for example Hufbauer, Gary Clyde and Wada, Erika (eds), 1998. *Unfinished Business: Telecommunications after the Uruguay Round,* Institute for International Economics.

[3] Kim, Jino W., 2005. "Economic Theory and Practices: Telecommunication Policy and Regulation for Competition", ITU. This paper was prepared as background for: ITU, 2005b. *Training Workshop on Telecommunications Policy and Regulation for Competition*, 11-15 July 2005.

(WCIT) in December 2012. But consensus was not achieved, so not all countries signed the new ITRs: this was an unusual situation for the ITU.

Thus some questions come to mind. Was WCIT a failure or a success? Is the treaty signed in Dubai on 14 December 2012 by 89 countries an impasse or a way forward? Is it a revolution or an evolution? Why did 55 countries present in Dubai decide not to sign the treaty? What is the significance of the split between the signatories and the non-signatories? What effects will the new treaty have? What are the implications for the Internet and its governance?

In order to answer this, and other questions, we will adopt a systematic approach, explaining first the history of various treaties that preceded the 2012 ITRs, then the background to the calls for revision of the 1988 treaty, the preparatory process leading up to the WCIT, and finally the events that took place at the conference. These are followed by an analysis of the treaty itself, of the Resolutions adopted at WCIT, and of some of the reservations and declarations made at the conference. The book concludes with implications for national legislators and regulators, a list of possible actions to consider, and a postscript on what could have been done better by all involved.

This book is primarily intended for practitioners: it does not pretend to be an academic research work. The purpose of this book is not to argue in favor of one or the other side, nor to criticize or to defend the ITU, but rather to present facts that are not easily accessible elsewhere, and to present an analysis of the facts that attempts not to be tainted by any particular political or economic bias. However, as the author was a senior staff member at the ITU before and during WCIT, it may be difficult to avoid a certain bias. Indeed, the account of WCIT presented in this book differs markedly from certain other accounts.[4] As discussed throughout the book, certain proposals regarding revisions to the 1988 treaty were directly related to the Internet: how could it be otherwise, given that the Internet is a major telecommunications technology, second only to GSM in terms of number of users? Most of those proposals were related to financial matters, some were related to other matters. But, as explained in some detail in the text, the general issue of Internet governance was brought into the conference, and in particular issues of free speech were raised. Indeed, starting at the end of 2011, various specialized blogs and newsletters published alarmist articles to the effect that the United Nations (UN) was proposing to take over the Internet so as to control it and establish censorship. Those articles referred to WCIT. Needless to say, such articles were wildly exaggerated and the mainstream press published accounts which were closer to the reality, namely that neither the UN nor the ITU had any power to regulate or control the Internet, much less to establish new censorship norms.

---

[4] See for example Klimburg, Alexander, 2013. "The Internet Yalta", Center for a New American Security, 5 February 2013; and Dourado, Eli, 2012. "Behind closed doors at the UN's attempted 'takeover of the Internet'", *Arstechnica,* 20 December 2012. This book attempts to show that the views cited above are not correct. A more balanced view, which still differs from that presented here, is given by Crispin, Olivier, 2013. "What Happened at WCIT in December 2012", 14 March 2013. A view similar to that presented here is found in Pfanner, Eric, 2012. "U.S. Rejects Telecommunications Treaty", *New York Times,* 13 December 2012.

In the author's view, bringing the issue of free speech into WCIT was not legitimate, because that issue is exhaustively covered by the ITU Constitution, so nothing in the ITRs can expand or restrict freedom of speech (see p. 40). Be that as it may, the resulting discussions were difficult and, in the author's view, distracted from the economic issues that the conference was primarily intended to address (see p. 65). It is worth noting in this context that a previous attempt to discuss development issues in telecommunications (including economic issues) – at the World Summit on the Information Society (WSIS) – was also distracted by discussions on Internet governance.[5]

Regarding Internet governance in general, some took (and continue to take) the view that it should not be subject to governmental control (see p. 35). But in fact telecommunications networks, including the Internet, have always been subject to political attention and regulation at the national and international levels. As noted above, the purpose of WCIT was to update, and align with the current environment, the 1988 treaty. That treaty had been instrumental in opening the way to liberalization and privatization, and it had facilitated the growth of the Internet, but most of its provisions had become increasingly irrelevant as of 1995.

However powerful economic interests feared that some proposed revisions of the ITRs could be detrimental to them, and powerful nations feared that some proposed revisions could limit some of their actions. Thus arguments that the author considers spurious were put forward in an attempt to derail the negotiations.

Thus the author is very critical of those that brought these issues and arguments into the conference, not because the issues should not be discussed, but because WCIT was not the proper forum for the discussion, and, more importantly, because those that raised those issues at WCIT should have known that WCIT was not the proper forum. While discussions of those issues did not fully derail the negotiations on other issues, the negotiations were only partly successful, in that not all countries agreed to the treaty that was formally approved at WCIT.

Regarding the first question, was the conference a success or a failure, it must be admitted that the conference was a failure in terms of its expected objective, which was to agree, by consensus, a new treaty that would be signed and ratified by all 193 ITU Member States. It also failed to avoid making decisions by voting, despite pleas by the ITU Secretary-General against voting (voting is unusual in ITU).[6]

However, the conference was a success in terms of the ITU's mission to facilitate open and frank discussions amongst its membership, which includes private sector entities as well as governments. As usual in ITU, the production of documents was generally well organized and the conference adopted a structure that facilitated discussions of all issues, whether major or minor. However, the treatment of some documents containing controversial proposals was confusing; there was not sufficient time adequately to discuss the more sensitive issues; there was a fundamental

[5] See Mueller, Milton, 2010. *Networks and States: The Global Politics of Internet Governance*, MIT Press, p. 57 ff.

[6] Part of what follows was originally published in Hill, Richard, 2013. "WCIT: Failure or success, impasse or way forward?" *International Journal of Law and Information Technology*, vol. 21 no. 3, p. 313; the material is included here with the kind permission of Oxford University Press.

difference in the perception of whether or not the conference would or should deal with Internet-related issues; and the ITU's formal rules of procedure are complex and were not fully understood by all participants (for example, it is only through careful reading of the rules that one can understand that there are no hard deadlines for input documents[7]). Some of these issues are explored in more detail in the Postscript.

The conference was a success in terms of bringing into the open the dissensions amongst the members on certain issues, while at the same time reaching consensus on many issues. Indeed, some 90% of the final document was not controversial and was approved by all. It is only the remaining 10% that caused some Member States to defer signing the treaty or to declare that they could not adhere to it.

The non-controversial provisions include the article on charging and accounting which was significantly streamlined and brought into alignment with modern practices; and new provisions to prevent misuse of telephone numbers, to ensure transmission of calling line identification, to ensure transparency of international roaming prices, to improve energy-efficiency and reduce e-waste, and to facilitate use of telecommunications by people with disabilities.

The controversial provisions are the third paragraph of the preamble which recognizes the right to access international telecommunications networks, the replacement of the term "recognized private operating agency" with "authorized operating agency", and the new provisions on encouraging regional traffic exchange points, improving network security and combating spam. Those provisions are contained in 6 paragraphs out of a total of 77 paragraphs that comprise the main text of the treaty. One Resolution adopted by WCIT was also controversial. If that is included, then the controversial text comprises less than 2 pages out of the total 24 pages approved at the conference.

As we will see later, the criticism of the 2012 ITRs appears to be based on a superficial and out-of-context reading of the provisions in question. Be that as it may, objection to selected provisions of a treaty is not usually considered a sufficient reason to refuse to sign the treaty because objections to specific articles can be expressed in reservations.

Indeed it appears that decisions regarding signature of the ITRs may not have been based solely on the legal analysis of the treaty's provision, but also on political and economic considerations. As we will see later, there were important economic and political issues underlying the discussions at WCIT, and the refusal to sign may be more related to a desire to make a statement regarding those issues than to the actual consequences of signing the treaty. In particular, there are ongoing debates about the extent to which national restrictions on freedom of speech should or should not be allowed to restrict communications on the Internet, and there are debates regarding the current funding and pricing model for the Internet. These debates are related to the differences of views between developing countries and developed countries that characterize discussions in many international forums.

A refusal by some countries to implement the new ITRs could deprive their citizens of certain benefits and non-uniform implementation could create difficulties for companies operating worldwide, if different regulatory regimes emerge. In the

[7] The relevant provision is no. 46 of the General Rules.

limit, refusal to implement the new ITRs might result in the development on non-harmonized national practices which might well lead to an undesired fragmentation of telecommunications networks, including the Internet.

One way forward could be to agree on a uniform and non-controversial implementation of the provisions that have been criticized.

One of the main objectives of WCIT was to find an agreement regarding how best to facilitate the rollout of Internet to developing countries. To some extent this was done by modernizing the old article 6, but it was agreed that further discussions should take place.

Such discussions are more likely to be productive in the future if there is a clear separation between the technical and economical issues that have been well handled by the ITU over the years, and the human rights and free speech issues that should be handled elsewhere and that should not be conflated with technical and economical issues.

However, issues related to human rights, free speech, data privacy, and surveillance of telecommunications will not disappear, on the contrary, they are likely to be further discussed in the future[8].

---

[8]See for example Gallagher, Ryan, 2013. "FBI Pursuing Real-Time Gmail Spying Powers as 'Top Priority' for 2013", *Slate,* 25 March 2013; Hamid, Triska, 2013. "The WCIT and the future of internet privacy", *The National,* 29 March 2013; Greenwald, Glenn, 2013. "XKeyscore: NSA tool collects 'nearly everything a user does on the internet'". *The Guardian*, 31 July 2013; Ackerman, Spencer and Lewis, Paul, 2013. "US senators rail against intelligence disclosures over NSA practices", *The Guardian,* 31 July 2013; *Necessary and Proportionate*, 2013; Jungholt, Thorsten, 2013. "Deutscher Datenschutz soll Massstab fuer EU sein", *Die Welt,* 5 August 2013; Gurstein, Michael, 2013. "'Internet Freedom' and post-Snowden Global Internet Governance", *Gurstein's Community Informatics,* 24 September 2013; Schiller, Dan, 2013a. "Whose Internet?", *Le Monde Diplomatique,* October 2013; Kampfner, Jon, 2013. "Prism surveillance: spies thrive in the Internet's legal free-for-all", *The Guardian,* 12 June 2013; Internet Society, 2013. *Statement on the Importance of Open Global Dialogue Regarding Online Privacy,* ISOC, 12 June 2013.

CHAPTER 1

History

From their inception in the middle of the 19th century, modern (that is, electronic) telecommunications networks have been subject to political attention and regulation at the national and international levels.[1]

The purpose of this chapter is not to summarize the history of international regulation of telecommunications[2], but to show how certain international agreements reached in the 19th century have evolved over time and can be considered to be the ancestors of provisions found in subsequent ITU instruments such as the International Telecommunication Regulations (the term "ITU instrument" refers to the treaties agreed by the countries that comprise the ITU).[3]

The Convention of 1865

The purpose of the first international agreements regarding telecommunications was to allow cross-border transmission of telegrams. Such agreements were negotiated amongst European countries starting in 1849.[4]

By 1865, it had become clear that it would be more efficient to replace the numerous bilateral treaties that had been negotiated with a single multilateral treaty. A conference held in Paris in 1865 adopted a treaty (called Convention) which created

[1] See for example Headrick, Daniel R., 1991. *The Invisible Weapon: Telecommunications and international Politics 1851-1945*, Oxford University Press; for an excellent explanation of the issues, the stakes, and the economic and legal frameworks, see Walden, Ian (ed.), 2009. *Telecommunications Law and Regulation*, Oxford University Press.

[2] There are several overall accounts of the development of international telecommunications law and the role of international organizations, see for example Nachszunow, Gregory, 1989. *Development of Telecommunications and International Organizations*, Willy Nachszunow; and Codding, George A. Jr., and Rutkowski, Anthony M., 1982. *The International Telecommunication Union in a Changing World*, Artech House.

[3] A clear and concise overview of the ITU and its instruments can be found in Walden (2009), pp. 728-746.

[4] Headrick (1991), p. 13.

the International Telegraph Union. As stated in the preamble, the purpose of that treaty was to ensure that the telegraphy connections across the signatory states would benefit from simple and affordable tariffs, and that international telegraphy would be improved, while maintaining national freedom of action for all issues not related to the overall (international) service. The signatories were Austria, Belgium, Denmark, France, Greece, Italy, Norway, Netherlands, Portugal, Russia, Spain, Sweden, Switzerland, Turkey, and 6 German states (at the time, the unified German state had not yet been created).[5]

As we will see, many of the provisions of that treaty are found, in one way or another, in ITU's present instruments, or in ITU Recommendations[6]. The key provisions of the 1865 Convention can be summarized as follows (the numbers below do not correspond to the articles of the treaty):

1. Installation of dedicated lines to ensure rapid transmissions.
2. Service between major cities should be available at all times, day and night.
3. Morse equipment would be used.
4. All persons have the right to correspond by international telegraphy.
5. All necessary means would be used to ensure the confidentiality of transmissions and their safe delivery.
6. The contracting states did not accept any responsibilities arising out of international telegraphy services.
7. Use of secret codes was always permitted for official communications between states; secret codes could be used by private parties if it was permitted by their respective states.
8. The message had to be preceded by the address of the recipient and had to be followed by the signature of the sender.
9. Official communications had priority over private communications.
10. Each state was free to determine the routes to be used to transmit messages.
11. If a connection was interrupted, the sending station had to use alternative measures to transmit the message.
12. A state could block the transmission of a private communication that it considered to be dangerous for its security, or contrary to its laws, public order, or good morals, provided that it so informed the sender.
13. A state could suspend the international telegraphy service, either overall, or with respect to certain destinations, if it considered it necessary to do so, provided that it immediately so informed the other signatory states.
14. All messages would be archived for at least one year.
15. The tariffs for communications between any two states would be the same regardless of the origin and destination cities.
16. The actual value of the tariff was set in the treaty (e.g. 3 francs per word between France and certain countries, and 2 francs between France and other countries). There were two types of tariff: a termination tariff for messages

[5] *ITU Convention*, 1865.

[6] ITU Recommendations are non-binding documents that typically contain technical specifications (for example the asymmetric Digital Subscriber Line aDSL) specifications that are used in products that enable Internet connections for many users.

originating or terminating in a country, and a transit tariff for messages that merely transited a country.

17. Detailed rules were given regarding how to count "words" for billing purposes.
18. Each state would credit to the other state a portion of the tariffs collected from the senders of messages to the other state.
19. The inter-state accounts would be prepared at the end of each month and settled at the end of each quarter.
20. Further details were contained in Regulations agreed by the signatory states.
21. The state that had hosted the last conference (France) was responsible for implementing measures arising out of changes to the Regulations.
22. Each state would communicate directly to all other states information concerning interruptions, changes in dedicated international lines, traffic statistics, network maps, and information related to the telegraphy service.
23. The official network map would be published by the French state.
24. Each state reserved the right to make special arrangements of any type regarding matters that were not of general interest, in particular regarding tariffs.
25. Other states could join the Union.
26. Each state undertook to impose, in so far as possible, the provisions of the Convention, on companies that had concessions for terrestrial or maritime telegraphy lines, and to negotiate, if needed, reciprocal reductions in tariffs.

The Regulations contained specifications regarding the format of the official network map, certain characteristics of the sending and receiving stations, the Morse code,[7] the format of the transmissions, and other operational details.

Subsequent Instruments

By 1868, it had become clear that the publication of the network map and related information was very valuable and it was decided (at a conference in Vienna in 1868) to create a permanent international body that would collect the information and publish it. This body was called the International Bureau of Telegraph Administrations and it was the world's first permanent international organization.[8]

Subsequently, conferences took place regularly to decide policy matters. Private companies were allowed to participate, but not to vote, staring in 1872, and countries outside Europe started to join the Union. The two major United States telegraphy companies participated in the work of the Union, but the United States, as a country, did not participate in the telegraphy and telephony work until 1949.[9] US policy, then as now, was heavily influenced by the interests of its domestic opera-

---

[7] The Morse code was later transferred to an ITU-T Recommendation and subsequently to an ITU-R Recommendation.

[8] Headrick (1991), p. 13 and the ITU website at <http://www.itu.int/en/history/Pages/DiscoverITUsHistory.aspx>.

[9] The ITU's published list of Member States indicates that the USA joined in 1908, but this refers to the US participation in the International Radiotelegraph Conference (Berlin, 1908). The USA did not adopt the non-radio treaties until 1949. See *ITU membership list*, 2013; *ITU International Radiotelegraph Convention*, 1908; *ITU Convention*, 1947, p. 90-E; *ITU Telegraph Regulations*, 1949.

tors. AT&T objected, in 1949, to any international regulation, but stated that it could accept weak regulation: "should it become advisable for this Government [the USA] to adhere to some form of international telephone regulations, the AT&T would not object to adherence by the United States to such regulations, provided they were of such general nature as to leave American industry free to carry on their operations under their own standards".[10]

In 1885, an article consisting of five general paragraphs devoted to the "international telephone service" was added to the Telegraph Regulations.[11] These provisions stated that countries could establish international telephone communications that would be charged on the basis of 5-minute increments, and that the tariffs would be set by the interconnected countries. The provisions related to telephony were expanded over time.

In 1932, the Telegraph Convention of 1875 and the Radiotelegraph Convention of 1927 were combined into a single convention embracing the three fields of telegraphy, telephony and radio; the telegraph and telephone regulations were published as separate documents.[12]

The 1932 and 1938 Telephone Regulations did not apply to all countries, but only to European countries and countries that voluntarily chose to join the "European system". The provisions of these Regulations are analogous to the telegraphy-specific provisions of the Convention of 1865, with the addition of provisions related to directories and the omission of the telegraphy-specific provisions regarding how to count "words". The actual tariffs agreed between countries were not included in the treaty, they were published elsewhere.

According to some scholars, the United States did not adhere to the 1949 Telephone Regulations because the ITU set tariffs roughly on the basis of costs, whereas US operators were allowed to exploit their dominant position to set prices well above costs. Further, the US operators used their marketing power to collect more money from their foreign partners than they paid, contrary to the ITU's regulations that called for equalization of charges.[13]

The Telegraph Regulations and the Telephone Regulations were last revised in 1973,[14] at which time they were drastically simplified so that they focused more on general principles, with the more detailed operational provisions being moved to Recommendations.[15] The United States adhered to the 1973 Telephone Regulations with some reservations.[16] The Regulations stated that operators "should comply with Recommendations" and thus the Recommendations were generally considered to be mandatory.[17]

Throughout all these developments, the basic principles dealing with tariffs remained unchanged, including that the rate for a communication between two coun-

---

[10] Hills, Jill, 2007. *Telecommunications and Empire*, University of Illinois Press, p. 51

[11] *ITU International Telegraph Conference*, 1885

[12] *ITU International Telegraph Conference*, 1932.

[13] Hills (2007), p. 52.

[14] *ITU World Administrative Telegraph and Telephone Conference*, 1973.

[15] Hills (2007), p. 91.

[16] Codding and Rutskowsi (1982), p. 53 and p. 220.

[17] Hills (2007), p. 82.

tries would be the same no matter what the route (thus preventing price competition).[18]

The Telegraph Regulations and Telephone Regulations were superseded in 1988 by the International Telecommunication Regulations.

[18] See for example Mestmaecker Ernst-Joachim (ed.), 1987. *The Law and Economics of Transborder Telecommunications,* Nomos, p. 379.

CHAPTER 2

The 1988 International Telecommunication Regulations

The 1988 Melbourne World Administrative Telegraph and Telephone Conference (WATTC) was greatly influenced by the increasingly strong trend towards privatization, liberalization and convergence of services.[1] As a consequence, negotiations were difficult.[2] However, a compromise text was finally agreed upon.[3] The resulting text was called the International Telecommunication Regulations (ITRs) and it replaced both the Telegraph Regulations and the Telephone Regulations, thus implicitly recognizing the decreased importance of telegraphy.[4]

Telecommunications has been considered to be an important industry since its inception, and it currently accounts for 2 to 4 percent of Gross Domestic Product (GDP) in developed countries and 2 to 10 percent in developing countries.[5] Further, some believe that telecommunications is a critical component in economic, cultural and political development.[6] Telecommunication is thus a very important sector of the economy and it is understandable that international agreements which affect the flows of such large sums of money would be considered to be important and sensitive matters.

The ITRs contained a key provision in Article 9, Special Arrangements. Although an article regarding "special arrangements" can be found in all of the ITU Conven-

[1] See for example Rutkowski, Anthony M., 1986. "Regulation for Integrated Services Networks: WATTC-88", *Intermedia*, vol. 14 no. 3, International Institute of Communication, pp. 10-19; Langdale, John V., 1989. "International telecommunications and trade in services", *Telecommunications Policy*, vol. 13 no. 3, pp. 223-232; and Robinson, Peter, 1991. "The international dimension of telecommunications policy issues", *Telecommunications Policy*, vol. 15 no. 2, p. 97.

[2] Hills (2007), p. 91 and pp. 98 ff.

[3] Hills (2007), p. 105 ff.

[4] *ITU World Administrative Telegraph and Telephone Conference*, 1988.

[5] Author's estimates based on OECD and ITU data, see Table 3.2 of OECD, 2011a. *Communications Outlook 2011*; and ITU, 2012. *ITU World Telecommunication/ICT Indicators Database*.

[6] See for example Mestmaecker (1987), p. 43.

tions since 1865, such an article had not previously been included in the Regulations. This is significant because the article found in the Convention stated that any special arrangements should not be in conflict with the Regulations, and the pre-1988 Regulations contained provisions that constrained what private operators could do.[7] Thus it was only in 1988 that, for the first time, private operators were explicitly allowed to use leased lines to provide services, including data services.[8] This provision facilitated the expansion of networks based on the TCP/IP protocol and of the services popularly referred to as the Internet: it did so by removing restrictions that could have impeded the expansion of such services.

The Morris worm, or Internet worm of 2 November 1988, was one of the first computer worms distributed via the Internet and was certainly the first worm to gain significant mainstream media attention.[9] When the WATTC was convened on 28 November, this worm was still a topic of concern. Although the worm itself was not explicitly mentioned in the ITRs, the "avoidance of technical harm" provision of Article 9 is generally considered to have been inspired by a desire to take steps that would prevent a reoccurrence of problems of this type. This is possibly the first cybersecurity treaty provision (if one accepts that cybersecurity includes the security of telecommunication networks).[10] A similar provision was subsequently added to what is now Article 42 of the ITU Convention.[11]

---

[7] See Hills (2007), p. 53 for a discussion of a previous attempt to change the "special arrangements" provision to exempt private operators from international regulation, and the discussion on pp. 92-94. See also Cowhey, Peter and Aronson, P.J. 1991. "The ITU in Transition", *Telecommunications Policy*, vol. 15 no. 4, p. 301, which discusses how CCITT Recommendations limited the use of leased lines; Mestmaecker (1987), pp. 359-363, and pp. 399-402; and Drake, William J., 1988. "Restructuring the International Telecommunication Regulations" *Telecommunications Policy*, September 1988, p. 229.

[8] As stated earlier, the 1988 ITRs were intended to be a compromise between differing views of how the telecommunications sector should be regulated or deregulated. Opinion 1, agreed at the 1988 conference, is an attempt to moderate the possible effects of the new article 9. The USA expressed a reservation regarding Opinion 1 and, in practice, that Opinion has not had any significant effect regarding the consequences of article 9.

[9] Eisenberg, Ted, et. al, 1989. "The Cornell Commission: On Morris and the Worm", *Communications of the ACM*, June 1989, vol. 32 no. 6, p. 706.

[10] As noted in Chapter 1, the 1865 treaty included a provision regarding the use of encryption, and such provisions are also found in later versions. But those provisions were as much about costs (they prevented the use of private short-codes which reduced the number of words in a telegram) as about national security, so they cannot be considered to be security provisions in the modern sense of the term. See Headrick (1991), p. 45.

[11] A detailed discussion of the evolution over time of provisions related to security in the various instruments of the ITU (including the "technical harm" provision of Article 9 of the ITRs) is given in Rutkowski, Anthony M., 2011. "Public international law of the international telecommunication instruments: cyber security treaty provisions since 1850", *Info*, vol. 13 no. 1, p.13.

Contemporaneous Comments

The WATTC-88 participants and those who commented on the ITRs at the time generally took the view that the treaty represented a compromise between those who wanted to install a more liberal regime at the international and national levels and those who favored continued national regulation.[12] For example, the International Telecommunications User Group (INTUG) stated "The new regulations confirm the primacy of national sovereignty and allow for a range of national regulatory options to be applied to the private operating agencies which are providing international services offered to the public. This reflects the existing position today, and does not constrain the future development of more liberal, or more restrictive, regulatory regimes".[13]

Commentators at the time did not attach much significance to the rejection of African proposals to include a prohibition of "economic harm" in the article on special arrangements[14] or to the weakening of the provision regarding application of Recommendations[15].

Nor did they foresee that the developments enabled by the ITRs would soon lead to the demise of the traditional "accounting rate" system[16]. The term "accounting rate" is defined by the ITU as "the rate agreed between Administrations in a given relation that is used for the establishment of international accounts"[17] (an Administration is the entity that represents a country at the ITU, that is, accounting rates were set by governments). The accounting rate system was the traditional accounting regime that had been in force since 1865 for telegraphy, whereby interconnected operators shared their international revenues on the basis of agreements between their respective governments. Since most operators were state-owned monopolies, this amounted to a revenue sharing agreement between governments. Although tariffs were supposed to be based on costs, in practice they often were not: high prices for international connections were used to subsidize national connections.[18] That system came under increasing pressure in the mid-1980's, when it became clear that prices were not declining as fast as costs (the cost declines were largely due to the dramatic technological advances that also resulted in the rapid growth of the information technology industry).[19]

However, some critics of the accounting rate system foresaw, at least implicitly, that its abolition would result in declines in the revenues for developing countries,

---

[12] See Drake (1988); and Pipe, G., 1989. "WATTC Agrees on New Telecom Rules", *Telecommunications International*, vol. 23 no. 1, p. 19.

[13] Hills (2007), p. 112.

[14] Hills (2007), p. 109.

[15] Hills (2007), p. 110.

[16] A clear and concise description, with illustrations, of the accounting rate system is available at ITU, 1996. *Direction of Traffic*.

[17] Recommendation ITU-T D.000 and 2.8 of the International Telecommunications Regulations (Melbourne, 1988).

[18] A good description is given in Cowhey and Aronson (1991), p. 299; in Mestmaecker (1987), p. 381 ff.; and in Walden (2009), pp. 739 ff.

[19] Hills (2007), pp. 133 ff.; see also the good overall account in Chapter 6 of ITU, 1997. *World Telecommunication Development Report (1996/1997)*.

and it was proposed that such declines be compensated by setting aside some portion of the revenue for development projects[20]; but there was some opposition to such proposals because of a perception that telecommunications revenues had not always been used to fund the deployment of telecommunications, at times even being diverted outside of the developing country[21].

The proposals mentioned above foreshadowed much later debates on network externalities. The concept of "network externality" is defined as follows in ITU-T Recommendation D.156: "telecommunication network externalities are benefits, *inter alia*, provided to users of networks in developed and developing countries by users of networks with a strong potential for extension". That Recommendation refers to the earlier work and concludes "that network externalities should be expressed by a premium referred to as an externality premium which is a non-cost element in addition to the cost elements included in Recommendations ITU-T D.93 and D.140". Recommendation D.156 was, and remains, controversial. It was approved at the 2008 World Telecommunication Standardization Assembly (WTSA), but 28 countries expressed a reservation. Subsequent work took place in ITU-T Study Group 3 and the Recommendation was revised. At the 2012 WTSA, it was agreed that, considering the progress achieved in Study Group 3, those Member States concerned may wish to review the respective positions at the WTSA 2008 and possibly withdraw their reservations.[22]

These discussions also foreshadowed discussions at WCIT on proposals whose intent was to allow developing countries to obtain greater revenues from Internet traffic, see p. 31 and 137.

Actual Effects, Relation to WTO

While the 1988 ITRs were a compromise at the time, they turn out, in retrospect, to have been instrumental in facilitating continuing privatization and liberalization of telecommunications markets[23] (by allowing private use of leased lines at commercial negotiated prices, as noted above. It was such use of leased lines that enabled data networks in general, and the Internet in particular). These trends were further facilitated by agreements made in the Global Agreement on Trade in Services (GATS) in 1994 (Annex on Telecommunications) and in 1996 (Reference Paper on Basic Telecommunication Services).[24]

As noted above, the ITRs confirmed the primacy of national regulations. In the-

[20] Hills (2007), pp. 133-134.

[21] Kahai, Simran K., Kahai, Paramjit S, and Leigh, Adrian, 2006. "Traditional and non-Traditional Determinants of Accounting Rates in International Telecommunications", *International Advances in Economic Research*, vol. 12 no. 4, p. 505; Uhlenbruck, Klaus et al., 2006. "The Impact of Corruption on Entry Strategy: Evidence from Telecommunication Projects in Emerging Economies", *Organization Science*, vol. 17 no. 3, p. 402.

[22] WTSA-12 Opinion 1.

[23] Indeed, this was already identified in 1991 by Cowhey and Aronson (1991), p. 306.

[24] A good overall description of liberalization is given in Cowhey and Aronson (1991), pp. 298-310; see also Mestmaecker (1987), pp. 354-356.

ory, countries were free to maintain traditional monopoly regimes for their domestic telecommunications. But, under the pressure of the United States and the European Union, and in recognition of the generally positive effects arising from privatization and liberalization, essentially all countries moved towards privatization and liberalization. And they could do so while being fully compliant with the ITRs.[25]

Around 1980, the United States, under pressure from its domestic financial services industry and other service sectors, started to seek an international forum through which it could promote liberalization of international trade in services.[26] Given that the balance of power in ITU was not favorable to such developments, the US sought to shift responsibility for international telecommunications regulation away from ITU and towards some other institution.[27] That institution eventually turned out to be the General Agreement on Trade and Tariffs (GATT)[28], which later became the World Trade Organization (WTO)[29].

In 1994, the participants in the negotiations regarding the General Agreement on Trade in Services (GATS) agreed an Annex on Telecommunications.[30] This Annex was, as are most international agreements, a compromise.[31] It promoted transparency and liberalization of access to transport networks and transport services, but it also recognized the needs of developing countries and the role of ITU.[32]

The World Trade Organization was created in 1994.[33] A negotiation group on basic telecommunications was established "to negotiate the progressive liberalization of trade in telecommunications transport networks and services".[34] Conflicting commercial interests in various major developed countries complicated the negotiations. The group failed to reach agreement, so it was dissolved and a new group created. An agreement was eventually reached and a "Reference Paper" was published in 1996.[35] This paper contained provisions on competitive safeguards, interconnection, universal service, licensing, independent regulators, and allocation and use of scarce resources.[36] The provisions of that paper could be included in offers under the WTO Basic Agreement on Telecommunications.[37]

The provisions of the reference paper were meant to weaken state-owned monopolies and to foster more foreign competition, in particular through interconnection and independent regulators. Tariffs for interconnection had to be cost-oriented, transparent, and reasonable.

---

[25] Hills (2007), pp. 122 and 125.
[26] Hills (2007), p. 178 ff.
[27] Hills (2007), p. 179 ff.
[28] Hills (2007), p. 186 ff.
[29] Hills (2007), p. 195 ff. A clear and concise description of GATT, GATS, and WTO is given in Walden (2009), pp. 746 ff.
[30] Walden (2009), p. 750.
[31] Hills (2007), p. 195.
[32] WTO, 1994. *Annex on Telecommunications*.
[33] Hills (2007), p. 195.
[34] Walden (2009), p. 751.
[35] WTO, 1996. *Telecommunications Services: Reference Paper*.
[36] Walden (2009), p. 752.
[37] Hills (2007), pp. 197 ff.

The main differences between the traditional accounting rate system and the new international interconnection regime can be summarized as follows.[38]

Accounting rates	**International interconnection rates**
Normally symmetric (accounting rate split 50/50)	Asymmetric (charges may vary between countries)
Bilaterally negotiated	Set unilaterally, but subject to trade discipline
Discriminatory (different rates with different correspondents)	Non-discriminatory (same reference interconnect offer offered to all carriers)
Half-circuit regime (not normally unbundled)	Full-circuit regime (can be unbundled)

The increasing use of international interconnections that were negotiated bilaterally between private companies led to an erosion of the ITU's accounting rate system,[39] and a consequent reduction of the revenues that developing countries derived from international telecommunications traffic.[40] The table below shows a theoretical example of the revenue losses incurred if voice traffic billed under the traditional system migrated to IP-based telephony (commonly called Voice over IP) without a reduction in rates (but in practice the rates were reduced, as discussed later).

	Accounting Rate	IP-Telephony
Operator in Developed country	Collect **US$ 1.00 from user** Pays **US $ 0.55 settlement.** Retains **US $ 0.45**	**Collect US$ 1.00 from user** Pays **US$ 0.30 to ISP for terminating call.** Retains **US$ 0.70**
Operator in Developing country	Receives **US $ 0.55 settlement.**	Receives **US $ 0.02 local call charge.**
Internet Service Provider (ISP) in Developing country	**0**	Receives **0.30 US $ for terminating charge** Pays **0.02 US $ for local call.** Retains **0.28 US $**

[38] The source is various presentations made by ITU staff over the years.

[39] See page 9 for a description of the accounting rate system.

[40] Hills (2007), pp. 133-138 and p. 206; and Stern, Peter A., 1990. *The International Telecommunications Settlement Process: What's Needed? Destroy and Replace It or Adjust It?*, IIC Telecommunications Forum, 25-25 October 1990. A detailed summary of the evolution of accounting rates and the relation to WTO instruments is provided by ITU, 2007. *Accounting Rate Reform undertaken by ITU-T Study Group 3.*

The ITU estimates that, in the period 1993-98, the net flows of settlement payments from developed counties to developing ones amounted to some US $ 40 billion.[41] Due to the shift away from the traditional accounting rate system, and reductions in rates, the net flows of settlement payments from developed to developing countries decreased significantly, and may even have turned in the other direction.[42] In particular, various unilateral actions by the United States were viewed as resulting in a net flow of revenues from developing countries to developed countries, in particular to the US.[43] As one author puts the matter: "the existing economic mechanisms in international communications networks establish the financial flows in favor of the developed countries".[44] Some might view that as taking from the poor to give to the rich; but in fact the historical flow of funds from developed to developing countries did not necessarily benefit the poor: at times it benefited national monopolies or even the ruling elite.[45] Indeed, the tendencies for insiders to benefit from monopoly rents, and for market leaders to be highly profitable, are rather common and may even be observed with respect to the Internet.[46]

In 1997 the US telecommunications regulator, the Federal Communications Commission (FCC), adopted a policy that forced lower international settlement payments. The FCC set a ceiling on the price that US operators could pay to foreign operators.[47] These ceilings were justified as being benchmark rates that should not be exceeded, and did recognize that developing countries might have higher termination costs than developed countries. Many countries objected to this policy, viewing as a unilateral action by one country to impose prices at the international level. Nevertheless, the policy was successful in contributing to the reduction in the cost of international telecommunications.[48]

Indeed, the changes in national regulatory practices resulting from the general trends towards liberalization and privatization resulted in very significant decreases in the cost of international telecommunications. This is illustrated in Figure 1 (SDR refers to Special Drawing Rights, a monetary unit whose value is determined by that of several currencies important to the world's trading and financial systems[49]).

---

[41] See, for instance the analysis in ITU/TeleGeography Inc., 1999. *Direction of Traffic: Trading Telecom Minutes*, ITU, October 1999.

[42] Walden (2009), pp. 741 and 743.

[43] Hills (2007), p. 207; and Walden (2009), p. 744.

[44] Fernàndez González, Juan Alonso, 2011, "Economic sustainability of international telecommunication networks", *Info,* vol. 13 no. 11, p. 6.

[45] Kahai, Kahai and Leigh (2006); Uhlenbruck (2006).

[46] See for example the discussion of ICANN in Mueller (2010), p. 219; and note that one well-known company had, in 2012, some US$ 48 billion in cash and short-term investments and the amount was increasing, see <http://www.google.com/finance?fstype=ii&q=NASDAQ:GOOG> accessed 8 June 2013.

[47] See US FCC, 2011. "In the Matter of International Settlements Policy Reform," notice of proposed rulemaking in IB Docket No. 11-80, (FCC 11-75), 13 May 2011, paragraph 4.

[48] US FCC (2011), paragraph 5.

[49] See International Monetary Fund, 2013. *Factsheet.*

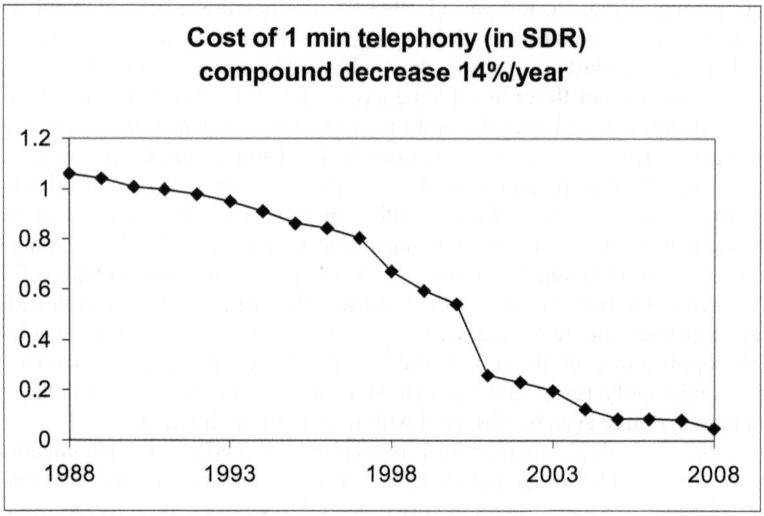

Figure 1: Decrease in telephony costs[50]

However, those decreases must be put into perspective when considering the far greater decreases that occurred in the information technology sector. As can be seen from Figure 2 below, the cost of one common and important information technology component, hard disk storage, decreased by 46% per year, as compared to the 14% per year decrease in telephony costs. Figure 2 shows reductions of the cost of 1 megabyte (MB) of disk storage and of 1 minute of telephony over time, with respect to a normalized cost of "1" in 1988 for both items.

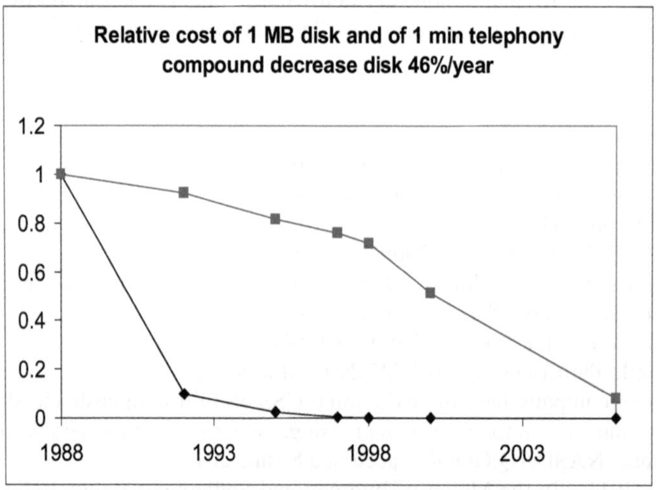

Figure 2: Relative decrease of disk and telephony costs[51]

[50] A more complete explanation is published in ITU, 2011. *History of the ITU-T surveys of accounting rates.*

Figure 3 below shows that the gap between the rate of decrease of information technology costs and the rate of decrease of telephony costs is actually increasing over time. The figure shows the same data as that of Figure 2, but plotted on a logarithmic scale, so that the increasing gap can be clearly seen.

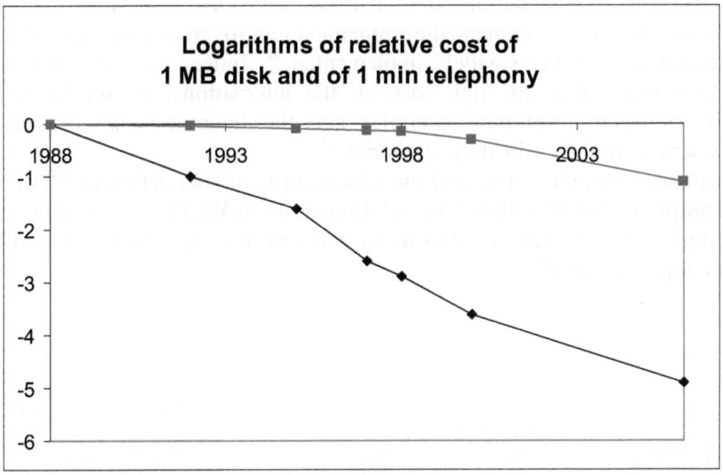

Figure 3: Relative decrease of disk and telephony costs in log scale[52]

International Internet Interconnection

The specific topic of the cost for connecting to the international Internet backbone must be mentioned here. This is a very contentious topic that had long been discussed within ITU-T Study Group 3 (SG3), with little progress.[53]

SG3 started examining the international Internet connectivity issue in the year 1998. The objectives of study were, at that time, to identify the differences between the Internet and the Public Switched Telephone Network (PSTN) costing models. SG3 agreed that the PSTN costing model was inappropriate. Discussion on whether the existing private lease model was the right model highlighted two different views and no consensus was reached within the SG3, which was also unable to develop an agreed set of principles on the equitable cost compensation between circuit providers.

In June 2000, SG3 attempted to gain agreement on a specific proposal but failed due to differing views on policy. That proposal was submitted to the 2000 World Telecommunication Standardization Assembly (WTSA), which, after difficult discussions, approved Recommendation ITU-T D.50. That Recommendation represents a very delicate balance between the various interests. It calls for ar-

[51] Data on disk costs compiled by the author, see for example *Tribune de Geneve*, Saturday 8 March 2008, page 2.

[52] Data on disk costs compiled by the author.

[53] What follows is based on the account at ITU, 2013. *International Internet Connectivity*.

rangements to be negotiated and agreed upon on a commercial basis when direct Internet links are established internationally, taking into account the possible need for compensation for elements such as traffic flow, number of routes, geographical coverage and the cost of international transmission among others when negotiating such commercial arrangements.

Work on that Recommendation continued, and revisions were subsequently approved. However, the Recommendation remained controversial and was not generally considered to have been widely implemented.[54] Indeed, in 2012, it was still generally considered that the high costs of the international circuit for Internet connectivity between developing countries and the Internet backbone networks remained a serious problem for these countries.[55]

As we will see later, this topic, and the related topic of "net neutrality"[56] were the subject of proposals to revise the ITRs and discussions at WCIT. These topics are of course related to the Internet, and thus to Internet governance, which as we will see, is a delicate topic (see p. 35).

---

[54] Indeed, most Internet interconnections are made on a no-cost peering basis, see Weller, David and Woodcock, Bill, 2013. "Internet Traffic Exchange", *OECD Digital Economy Papers*, No. 207, OECD Publishing.

[55] See ITU, 2012e. *Workshop on "Apportionment of Revenues and International Internet Connectivity"*, 23-24 January 2012; Supplement 2 to Recommendation ITU-T D.50, "Reducing the Costs of International Internet Connectivity", May 2013 <http://www.itu.int/rec/T-REC-D.50-201305-P!Sup2>.

[56] See *Network neutrality in the United States*, 2013. Wikipedia.

CHAPTER 3

The Path to Revision

As the effects of liberalization and the shift away from the traditional accounting rate system became visible, certain developing countries started to call for a revision of the ITRs, with a view towards reversing those trends. As noted in Chapter 2, the flow of funds resulting from telecommunications services is very large, and discussions regarding international agreements on telecommunications pricing and accounting are very sensitive. Also as noted in Chapter 2, by the mid-1990s, some countries felt that they could no longer accept the reductions in telecommunications revenues resulting from the shift away from the traditional accounting rate system, and this in particular because they did not believe that such shifts were primarily driven by competitive markets.

Indeed, it is not obvious that full competition can be easily achieved in telecommunications, because it is very expensive to roll out infrastructure and this makes the cost of entry very high for new competitors. Many countries, in particular some European countries, attempt to overcome this barrier to competition through mandatory interconnection prices, facility-sharing provisions, and related measures. But competition at the infrastructure level remains limited, and, according to some authors, full competition is an elusive goal.[1]

In a nutshell, the argument put forth by proponents (influenced by their operators) of revision of the ITRs was the following. If large players dominate certain markets because of limited competition, then they can reap monopoly, or at least oligopoly profits. If the large players are primarily based in developed countries, then developing countries are not benefiting from privatization and liberalization. Therefore it is advisable to introduce some regulation at the international level, so as to ensure a level playing field for developing countries. Indeed, according to this view, state

[1] See for example Mestmaecker (1987), p. 24 ff.; and Stern (1990), p. 14, who predicted in 1990 that competition at the international level would result in an oligopoly with a small number of huge multinational providers dividing the market among themselves rather than competing with each other; the only beneficiaries would be the large users. For a more recent analysis, see Crawford, Susan, 2013. *Captive Audience: The Telecom Industry and Monopoly in the New Guilded Age,* Yale University Press. A summary is provided by Gustin, Sam, 2013. "Is Broadband Internet Access a Public Utility?" *Time,* 9 January 2013.

regulation is important for developing countries, so as ensure access by all to modern telecommunications, including Internet; measures must be taken to ensure that competition is fair and reasonable, in particular for international interconnections; and it must be recognized that the situation in developing countries (which often lack sufficient infrastructure) is not the same as that in developed countries.

Of course the developed countries (influenced by their operators) did not agree with this argument. They pointed out that many developing countries did not have liberalized or privatized telecommunications at the national level, and that their national telecommunications operators were the ones benefiting from monopolistic regimes. Further, they pointed out that liberalization and privatization have had undoubted benefits, resulting in rapid and sustained growth of access to communication services and a great diversification of those services.[2]

Since it was very difficult to collect data to show whether or not monopolistic effects were present in international or national markets, much of the debate was ideological, and it was often difficult to reach any meaningful agreement.

This chapter presents a somewhat more detailed summary of the positions taken by the USA than of the positions taken by other countries. This is because, as we will see later, the positions taken by the USA were instrumental in influencing certain other countries and, ultimately, the outcome of the Conference.

However, we will start by briefly introducing the ITU, for those who are not familiar with it.

A Brief Introduction to ITU

Readers who are familiar with the ITU and its rather complex structure and working methods may wish to skip this section, which is largely based on the material available on the ITU web site[3]. The ITU consists of a General Secretariat and three Sectors, which respectively allocate global radio spectrum and satellite orbits (ITU-R), develop technical standards to facilitate network interconnection (ITU-T), and strive to improve access to telecommunications in developing countries (ITU-D). The organization of the ITU is specified in two treaties, the Constitution and Convention, which documents are hierarchically superior to the other two ITU treaties: the Radio Regulations and the International Telecommunication Regulations (ITRs). The Constitution and Convention are approved by the Plenipotentiary Conference, which normally meets every four years. The Radio Regulations are approved by the World Radio Conference, which also normally meets every four years. The ITRs are approved by the World Conference on International Communications (WCIT), which meets sporadically, as explained in some detail in the next chapter.

The ITU members approve numerous other, non-treaty, texts, in particular Resolutions (at the conferences mentioned above, but also at assemblies of the three sectors mentioned above, and at the ITU Council, which meets annually and handles matters delegated to it by the Plenipotentiary Conference); and Recommendations. In particular, the ITU-T Recommendations are widely known and implemented. Some

[2] Paraphrased from Mueller (2010), p. 260.
[3] ITU, 2013b. *Home Page*.

of those ITU-T Recommendations deal with non-technical issues, in particular financial issues.

Recommendations are developed, and normally approved by consensus, by Study Groups (but ITU-T Recommendations can be approved by voting at a World Telecommunication Standardization Assembly-WTSA). Study Groups usually comprise subordinate groups known as Working Parties, Questions, Rapporteur Groups, Editorial Groups, etc.

The membership of the ITU comprises Member States and private companies. Decision-making is nominally reserved for Member States but, in practice, the non-state members exercise considerable influence, in particular by influencing their governments. Decisions in ITU are usually made by consensus (meaning lack of formal opposition), but (except for approval of ITU-T Recommendations in ITU-T Study Groups) they can be made by a majority vote of Member States, upon the request of any Member State. As we will see later, this was significant for WCIT.

The Evolving Geopolitical and Geoeconomic Environment

It is useful at this point to provide some overall background of general political and economic trends that influenced the discussions in ITU regarding the ITRs.[4]

Empires have always striven to improve communications: early well-known examples are Roman roads[5] and the message system of the Mongol empire[6]. As noted above, with the advent of telegraphy, empires started to use telecommunications, and actively pursued international telecommunication policies that were in their interest.[7]

During the twentieth century, there has been a long-term shift in geopolitical power first from Europe towards the United States and the former Soviet Union, and more recently towards the so-called BRICS (Brazil, Russian Federation, India, China, and South Africa)[8]. That shift resulted in the demise of the former European colonial empires and a rise in the competing ideological and economic empires comprised respectively by the United States and its allies and the Soviet Union and its allies. Following the demise of the Soviet Union, the United States was left as

---

[4] Parts of this section are based on Hill, Richard (2013a) "Internet Governance: The Last Gasp of Colonialism or Imperialism by Other Means" in Rolf H. Weber, Roxana Radu, Jean-Marie Chenou (eds), *The evolution of global Internet policy: new principles and forms of governance in the making?*, Schulthess, Publikationen aus dem Zentrum für Informations- und Kommunikationsrecht der Universität Zuerich.

[5] See *Roman Roads*, 2013. Wikipedia.

[6] See *Ortoo*, 2013. Wikipedia.

[7] See for example Hills (2007).

[8] There is extensive literature regarding the BRICS. We cite here only two: Laidi, Zaki, 2012. "BRICS: Sovereignty power and weakness" *International Politics,* vol. 49, September 2012, pp. 614-632 (an earlier version is Laidi, Zaki, 2011."The BRICS Against the West", CERI Strategy Papers, No. 11, November 2011); and Petropoulos, Sotiris, 2013. "The emergence of the BRICS – implications for global governance", *Journal of International and Global Studies*, vol. 4, no. 2, May 2013, pp. 37-51.

the most powerful military and economic force in the world. Not surprisingly, US dominance is also reflected in today's dominant telecommunications technology, the Internet, and some countries (in particular the BRICS) have consistently expressed dissatisfaction with that situation.[9]

The dissatisfaction of developing countries[10] with respect to the global situation regarding telecommunications is similar to their dissatisfaction with the global situation regarding other industries, in particular pharmaceuticals[11], certain aspects of international intellectual property law[12], certain aspects of public health[13], and international trade in general[14]. Recently, the developed countries have exhibited a tendency to seek bilateral or regional agreements when it appears difficult to find consensus in global forums[15], but even such non-global negotiations can be difficult[16].

It has been argued[17] that the current situation in the global telecommunications sector is a form of colonialism or imperialism. Colonialism can be defined as a

[9] For more details, see Hill (2013a).

[10] We should more properly refer to "governments of developing countries" but of course the same applies to developed countries or even to a specific country. Thus, references to the positions of a "country" should be understood as references to the positions expressed by the government of that country.

[11] See for example Yu, Peter K., 2008. "Access to Medicines, BRICS Alliances, and Collective Action", *American Journal of Law and Medicine*, vol. 3, pp. 345-394; and Bird, Robert C. and Cahoy, Daniel R., 2007. "The Emerging BRIC Economies: Lessons from Intellectual Property Negotiation and Enforcement", *Northwestern Journal of Technology and Intellectual Property*, vol. 5 no. 3, p. 1.

[12] See for example Saez, Catherine (2013). "WIPO Committee To Decide Fate of Treaties To Protect TK, Generic Resources, Folklore" *Intellectual Property Watch,* 23 July 2013; and, more significantly, the breakdown of negotiations at the September 2013 WIPO Annual Assembly: New, William, 2013. "WIPO Annual Assembly Breaks Down; Extraordinary Meeting Eyed for December", *Intellectual Property Watch*, 3 October 2013.

[13] See Dionisio, Daniele, 2013. "WHO Performance Undermined By Inadequate EU Participation", *Intellectual Property Watch,* 23 October 2013.

[14] See for example McClanahan, Paige, 2013. "Roberto Azevedo says that the WTO 'needs a fresh perspective from inside'", *The Guardian,* 3 May 2013; McGregor, Richard 2007. "China blames WTO blockage on US and EU", *Financial Times,* 12 March 2007; Correa, Carlos M., 2013. "Investment Agreements: A New Threat to Health and TRIPS Flexibilities", *Southviews,* no. 64, 27 June 2013.

[15] New, William, 2013a. "USTR Froman: FTAs A Way To Get Higher IP Standards Into Global Trade 'Bloodstream'", *Intellectual Property Watch,* 31 October 2013.

[16] Intellectual Property Watch, 2013. "New Trans-Pacific Partnership Caucus in US Congress", *Intellectual Property Watch,* 30 October 2013; Ermert, Monika, 2013. "Controversial Debate on TTIP Mandate in EU Council of Ministers", *Intellectual Property Watch,* 14 June 2013.

[17] Hill (2013a); Kiss, Jemima, 2013. "NSA furore has roots in US internet imperialism", *The Guardian*, 1 November 2013.

policy by which a nation maintains or extends its control over foreign dependencies. One of the motivations for colonialism is the economic exploitation of the dependencies.[18] It should be noted, however, that the wealth extracted from the dependencies is not necessarily evenly distributed amongst the citizens of the colonizing nation.[19]

Imperialism can be defined as the policy of extending a nation's authority by territorial acquisition or by the establishment of economic and policy authority over other nations. Some aspects of the current telecommunications environment fit well into this definition. For example, developed country companies still largely influence the discussions in the various norm-setting bodies.[20] Regarding Internet, the current environment allows the US to enforce rather easily its domestic policies, at times with extra-territorial effects. For example, the US could easily seize domain names used for well-known poker sites, because those domain names were provided by US entities.[21] The seizure prevented people outside the US from using those sites (the sites were later restored with the stipulation that they could not be accessed from within the US).[22] Another example is provided by the Prism surveillance program, whose implementation was facilitated by the fact that key Internet companies are US entities.[23] (Requests for surveillance of US citizens are subject to

---

[18] There is a vast literature on colonialism and its effects. A pithy and cogent account is given in Morris, Ian, 2011. *Why the West Rules – For Now,* Profile Books, paperback edition, pp. 515-521.

[19] See for example Muller, Jerry Z., 2002. *The Mind and the Market,* Alfred A. Knopf, p. 71, citing Adam Smith. For the Internet, it can be noted that one well-known company had, in 2012, some US$ 48 billion in cash and short-term investments and the amount was increasing, see <http://www.google.com/finance?fstype=ii&q=NASDAQ:GOOG> accessed 8 June 2013.

[20] This can be referred to as "techno-imperialism", Adas, Michael, 2006. *Dominance by Design: Technological Imperatives and America's Civilizing Mission,* Harvard Belknap Press.

[21] See *United States v. Scheinberg*, 2013. Wikipedia.

[22] The existence of a privileged role for the US has been openly acknowledged in an analysis prepared for the US Congress, which raises as a point to consider: "Should the U.S. government maintain its current legacy authority over ICANN and the DNS [Domain Name System], and if so, how can NTIA [National Telecommunications and Information Administration, an agency under the US Department of Commerce] best use this authority judiciously in order to advance U.S. government interests, while at the same time minimizing the perception by other nations (as well as the international community of Internet stakeholders) that the United States has an inappropriate level of control or influence over the Internet and the DNS?" See Kruger, Lennard G. 2013. "Internet Governance and the Domain Name System: Issues for Congress", *Congressional Research Service,* 13 April 2013, p. 20. For an additional analysis, see Hill (2013a).

[23] See Savage, Charlie, Wyatt, Edward, and Baker, Peter, 2013. "U.S. Confirms that it Gathers Online Data Overseas", *The New York Times,* 6 June 2013; it is worth noting that Prism is the successor of a series of increasingly intrusive surveillance programs whose origin dates back to 1898, see McCoy, Alfred, 2013. "Surveillance Blowback: The Making of the US Surveillance State, 1898-2020", *Popular Resis-*

approval by an independent judge, whereas such approval is not required for surveillance of non-US citizens.[24] Thus Prism is an example of the well-known tendency of empires to accord special rights to their own citizens.[25]) A more complete discussion of the impact of the Internet governance issues on WCIT is given in Chapter 3 (p. 35), with references to recent works that review the key issues and the tensions arising from national control of what many consider to be a transnational network. As we will see, those tensions underlaid the discussions at WCIT and were even openly aired, in particular regarding free speech (p. 40 and p. 65).

In light of the shifts in economic power between developed and developing countries, which have not always been matched by shifts in political power, it is not surprising that there was a slow build up of tensions regarding the 1988 ITRs. Various discussions were held in an attempt to defuse some of the tensions, but, as we will see below, they were not particularly successful.

The first such discussions took place at the ITU Plenipotentiary Conference in 1998. This conference took place shortly after the US unilaterally rejected proposals for management of the Internet domain name and addressing systems that had been developed by an ad hoc group convened by the Internet Society. Those recommendations involved creating a truly multi-stakeholder and multi-lateral body, whose participants would sign a Memorandum of Understanding (MoU). The depository for signatures of the MoU would have been the Secretary-General of the ITU.[26]

The unilateral US rejection of those proposals led to the creation of the Internet Corporation for Assigned Names and Numbers (ICANN), and to the adoption of ITU Resolution 101, which explicitly called for the ITU to be involved in Internet matters.

Separately, recognizing that liberalization meant that the importance of Recognized Operating Agencies was diminishing, and that other entities were becoming more important, the 1998 Plenipotentiary Conference implicitly expanded the scope

---

tance, 15 July 2013. An excellent discussion of surveillance and related matters, including cyberwar and cybercrime, in given in Deibert, Ronald J., (2013). *Black Code: Inside the Battle for Cyberspace*, Signal (McCelland and Stewart).

[24] US National Security Agency, 2013. *The National Security Agency: Missions, Authorities, Oversight and Partnerships*, 9 August 2013; and Bowden, Casper, 2013. "The US National Security Agency (NSA) surveillance programmes (PRISM) and Foreign Intelligence Surveillance Act (FISA) activities and their impact on EU citizens' fundamental rights", *Note for the European Parliament*; Ermert, Monica, 2013b. "EU Hearing: War Against Whistleblowers, War Against Journalists, War Against Democracy", *Intellectual Property Watch*, 1 October 2013; see also the presentations made at the *EPFL Congress on Privacy and Surveillance*, Ecole Fédéral Polytechnique de Lausanne, 30 September 2013.

[25] But also to assert jurisdiction over its own citizens even at the expense of the sovereignty of other nations, see Payne, Ed, 2013. "Morales challenges U.S. after Snowden rumor holds up plane in Europe", *CNN,* 4 July 2013.

[26] For a summary, see Hill (2013a); a detailed description and analysis is found in Mueller, Milton, 2002. *Ruling the Root: Internet Governance and the Taming of Cyberspace,* MIT Press; a summary of the work of the ad hoc group is found at *IAHC*, 2013. Wikipedia.

of the ITRs to cover some of these other entities by modifying the ITU Constitution: no. 38 (Art 6.2) of the Constitution provided that the ITRs applied to "operating agencies authorized by Member States". At the time, this change was apparently not viewed as momentous and indeed it did not have any significant practical effects. However, it did affect the discussions in 2012, see p. 64.

In light of the developments outlined above, there were calls to reopen the discussions regarding the ITRs.

Discussions on the ITRs from 1998 to 2006

Consequently, in 1998, the ITU Plenipotentiary Conference decided, in its Resolution 79, to create a balanced group of appropriate experts to review the extent to which the current needs of Member States were reflected in the ITRs and to report to Council 2000.[27]

The group was duly created and reported to Council 2000. It was unable to reach consensus, but agreed to retain four options regarding how the ITRs might evolve:

1. Move provisions of the ITRs, as required, to the Constitution or Convention or to ITU-T Recommendations, and abrogate the ITRs, which would no longer be needed as a separate instrument.
2. Modify the ITRs, with a detailed update of the existing provisions, with a view to keeping the ITRs as a treaty-level text.
3. Further study proposals calling for deferral of any decision regarding whether to review and modify the ITRs.
4. Study proposals calling for new areas of regulation to enable further development and determine which were really appropriate for an intergovernmental treaty-level regulatory agreement.

The first option was favored by European countries, who felt that they no longer needed the ITRs, given that the European Economic Community (later European Union) instruments (in particular, Directives) had replaced the ITRs for what concerned intra-European telecommunications, and that no particular international regulations were needed for what concerned telecommunications between Europe and the rest of the world.

The second option was favored by those developing countries that felt that the shift away from the traditional accounting rate system had resulted in a loss of revenue for developing countries.

The third option was favored by the United States, which was very satisfied by the regime that had arisen under the 1988 ITRs and the GATS/WTO instruments.[28]

The fourth option was a compromise: it called for study of the measures that might be proposed by developing countries in order to determine whether they really were appropriate.

---

[27] Fahmi, Alaa M., 2000. *Council Working Group on the ITRs: General Overview*; and ITU, 2011a. *Past work on ITRs*.

[28] Indeed, as stated by L.S., 2012. "A digital cold war?", *The Economist,* 14 December 2012, "no other country benefits as much from the status quo in the online world. …. America's internet firms also capture most of the profit pool of the online industry".

As we will see, many discussions took place from 1999 to 2009, with essentially no progress: each of the camps defending one of the three options remained adamant.

The matter was considered at sessions of Council subsequent to 2000, and the Council duly reported that to the 2002 Plenipotentiary Conference (PP-2000). That conference, in its Resolution 121, decided that the ITU should continue a process of reviewing the ITRs and instructed Council to establish a working group to study the matter and to report to PP-2006. Council duly created that working group and presented the group's report to PP-2006.[29] As mentioned above, no significant progress was made: the group reported that no consensus had been reached and that there were three views on how to proceed:

a) Leave the ITRs unchanged.
b) Amend the ITRs, this will include adding new provisions.
c) Terminate the ITRs and transfer certain provisions to the CS, CV and ITU-T Recommendations.

Option (a) was a more explicit formulation of the old option (3) and it was staunchly defended by the United States who argued that the ITRs had served the telecommunications industry well since their adoption in 1988, so there were no reasons to envisage any changes. In particular, the United States staunchly defended the three-month deadline for settlement of accounts found in Article 2 of Appendix 1 of the ITRs. This provision allowed its operators to defer payment of amounts due, thus defeating the provisions of ITU-T Recommendation D.195 which had been developed in 2003 in order to shorten the payment cycle, in recognition of the widespread adoption of computerized billing systems. It should be noted here that the three-month deadline in the 1988 ITRs was identical to that found in the 1865 Convention and its successors (and to which the US had not agreed until 1973), see page 3.

Option (b) was the old option 2 and it was put forth by certain developing countries who contested the US view and argued that, on the contrary, the developments since 1988 clearly indicated that a new international regulatory regime was required.

Option (c) was the old option 1 and it was staunchly defended by the European countries who took the view that any required treaty-level provisions should be found in the Constitution or Convention, so that the ITRs were no longer needed as a separate treaty.

However, the group did more than just rehash the old positions. It also compiled a list of specific proposals for changes to the ITRs, in the form of a table that presented, for each article of the ITRs, any proposed changes and a summary of the positions expressed by Member States regarding those proposals.[30] That table would later prove to be the basis for further work.

Discussions on the ITRs from 2006 to 2010

The 2006 Plenipotentiary Conference considered the group's report and inputs from the Member States and decided, in its Resolution 146, that a review of the ITRs

---

[29] ITU, 2007a. *International Telecommunication Regulations.*

[30] Document C05/EP/11 <http://www.itu.int/md/S05-CL-INF-0011/en> accessed 6 October 2013.

should be carried out and a World Conference on International Telecommunications (WCIT) would be convened in 2012. The ITU-T should undertake a review of the existing ITRs and the fourth World Telecommunication Policy Forum (WTPF) should consider emerging telecommunication policy and regulatory issues, with respect to international telecommunication networks and services, for the purpose of understanding them and possibly developing opinions as appropriate.

The discussions at the Plenipotentiary Conference were difficult and the outcome was viewed as a breakthrough, because, for the first time since the discussions had started in 1998, there was a consensus to hold a conference to revise the ITRs. That consensus was achieved by agreeing to separate the review of the existing provisions of the ITRs from consideration of possible new or emerging issues, with separate processes to be used, on the one hand to review the existing provisions, and on the other hand to consider new or emerging issues. The consensus was also made possible because the agreed process for consideration of new or emerging issues, the WTPF, had a fundamentally different nature from other ITU processes: in essence, it was not a decision-making process and its output did not bind the ITU membership in any way.

In accordance with the decisions of the Plenipotentiary Conference, an expert group to review the ITRs (ITR-EG) was duly created in May 2007. That group reported its work to Council 2009.[31]

The WTPF was held in Lisbon in 2009[32] and it adopted, inter alia, Opinion 6 on the International Telecommunication Regulations: New and emerging issues referred to in Resolution 146 (Antalya, 2006) on Review of the International Telecommunication Regulations.

Council 2009 considered the report of the ITR-EG and Opinion 6 of the WTPF. Pursuant to Resolution 146, it created the Council Working Group to Prepare for the World Conference on International Telecommunications in 2012 (CWG-WCIT12) with terms of reference that provided for discussion of proposals for revisions to the existing ITRs, including proposals for suppressions of provisions and/or abrogation as appropriate, and of proposals relating to new and emerging issues.[33]

In March 2010, the United States dramatically shifted its long-standing position, which had been that there was no need to make any changes to the 1988 ITRs. Indeed, as late as March 2008, the US had stated: "Since the ITRs were adopted there has been a significant growth in international telecommunications traffic. As the United States noted in its contribution to the initial meeting of the ITR Expert Group, Geneva, October 10-11, 2007, very large traffic volumes worth billions of dollars are settled each year relying upon the ITRs. Carriers who today are carrying traffic across the world's regions have in place large numbers of correspondent agreements that rely on contractual agreements based on the ITR provisions; reliance upon this treaty level document provides certainty and predictability in the negotiation of these agreements. Although some have suggested that the ITRs are outdated or are not widely used, the United States disagrees. U.S telecommunications carriers regularly reference the ITRs (often referenced as the "Melbourne Agreement" or "Melbourne Convention") in their bilateral operating agreements

[31] ITU, 2011b. *International Telecommunication Regulations.*

[32] ITU, 2009. *WTPF 2009.*

[33] ITU Council Resolution 1312.

with other international carriers and in resolving or preventing disputes that may arise under such agreements. Such timely resolution of disputes between carriers is critical for providing uninterrupted telecommunications service for consumers. The removal of the ITRs would risk causing unnecessary uncertainty and confusion in these traffic arrangements which could adversely impact the delivery of services".[34]

But in March 2010 the US stated: "Considering market liberalizations and corresponding regulatory transformations experienced by a significant majority of the ITU's Member States as well as technological innovations in telecommunications achieved since adoption of the ITRs in 1988, the United States believes that there is no longer a need for a treaty covering the subjects governed by the current ITRs. For example, according to the most recent statistics available, during 2008 only approximately 6% of the international telephone traffic billed in the United States was settled following provisions outlined in Article 6 of the ITRs, compared to 86% during 1998".[35] So the US shifted from option (a) to option (c), the one favored by the European countries. In the author's opinion, this shift was due to the fact that the US was isolated in proposing no changes to the ITRs, so it had no choice but to align with other countries, and abrogation of the ITRs was more acceptable to the US than adopting a revision that covered many new issues.

However, in the meantime, some European countries had softened their support for option (c) and were willing to envisage option (b), the one favored by some developing countries. So the US change in position did not significantly alter the balance of power: it came too late to do that.

CWG-WCIT12 reported its work to the 2010 Plenipotentiary Conference. The United States attempted to change the scope of the work so as to exclude any consideration of new or emerging issues[36], but it could not muster enough support, since most countries felt that it would not be appropriate to convene a conference to revise a treaty without being able to consider new issues that had emerged in the 24 years since the treaty had been adopted.

Having considered the report of the CWG-WCIT12, and contributions from Member States, the 2010 Plenipotentiary Conference confirmed the previous decisions of Council, thus confirming that the WCIT-12 would indeed take place as planned, that proposals regarding new and emerging issues would be considered, and that CWG-WCIT12 should continue its work to prepare for the Conference in 2012.[37]

At that time it appeared that the key issues to be considered when revising the ITRs would include:

- Security in use of ICTs and spam
- Misuse of numbers
- Application of certain ITU-T Recommendations
- Quality of service
- Right of access/non discrimination
- Taxation

---

[34] Document ITR-EG – C 10.

[35] Document CWG-WCIT12/C – 14.

[36] Addendum 6 to PP-10 Document 15.

[37] PP-10 Resolution 171.

- Provisions regarding accounting
- Market-based costing

All of these issues were discussed throughout the preparatory process and at the conference itself. A discussion of these, and other, issues is provided on p. 57. But we introduce here the key points. Security and spam were sensitive issues because some took the view that measures should be taken by states to improve security and to combat spam; whereas others took the view that it would be more appropriate for such measures to be taken by the private sector (perhaps with the assistance of civil society) – because that would be more efficient, effective, and flexible, whereas state intervention could have unintended consequences including on freedom of speech (see p. 40).

Telephone numbers were being increasingly used for purposes other than the ones for which they had been assigned, and this in order to perpetrate various kinds of fraud or to avoid high termination fees and certain types of taxes (see p. 96 for more details). While there was general agreement that such practices should not be allowed, there was no agreement on how best to achieve this. Further, there were concerns that a provision regarding numbering misuse might be applied to the Internet, and some felt that this was highly undesirable (see p. 35 for a discussion of the sensitivities regarding Internet). The question of whether or not to include a provision on transmission of calling party identification was also raised.

Some felt that the change agreed in 1988, to weaken the commitment to apply CCITT Recommendations (now called ITU-T Recommendations) had had negative effects on quality of service and financial matters, so they sought to give greater weight to at least some of those Recommendations. Others took the view that, in a privatized and liberalized environment, it was not appropriate for states to impose implementation of Recommendations that were developed with the expectation that their implementation would be voluntary.

The quality of service issue was related to the one outlined above: namely whether certain Recommendations should be made mandatory.

The right to access/non-discrimination issue was raised by certain countries who had specific complaints about actions by other countries that blocked their access to all or certain Internet sites. The countries that did the blocking justified it either under UN Security Council Resolutions (for example for blocking directed against Sudan), or simply on the basis of national interests (for example for blocking directed against Cuba). This issue also led to references to actions taken by certain states to block access of their citizens to information, in particular through the Internet. Western countries tended to be critical of such actions. As we will see later, these discussions significantly affected the conference (see p. 65).

The taxation issue arose because of concerns that 6.1.3 of the 1988 ITRs (which concerns taxation) was difficult to understand and to interpret in the current telecommunications environment. Although the topic was discussed in some depth, it turned out to be difficult to agree on any new text, so in the end the existing text was retained. However, in the author's view, the discussions did help to clarify how to interpret the text, see the discussion under 8.3.1 in Chapter 6.

As noted above, financial issues were at the heart of discussions regarding revisions of the ITRs, and this included the discussion on market-based costing, and on the prices charged to end-users for international mobile roaming services.

Discussions on the ITRs from 2011 to 2012

At the end of August 2011, the USA submitted its comments to CWG-WCIT12 regarding the various issues.[38] In essence, the USA firmly stated that it was opposed to any significant strengthening of the ITRs. According to the USA, the treaty should remain essentially unchanged or, better, be watered down.[39] This was of course a reversion to the historical US policy since 1865 of not participating in any treaties related to non-radio matters, see page 3. Some of the arguments advanced by the US to justify its position didn't sit well with many other delegations. For example, the US stated that bilateral agreements should be the preferred method to ensure consistent implementation of international telephone numbers, and this in light of well-documented widespread misuse of such codes.[40] And the US stated that the taxation provision of the ITRs should not be clarified to state that international double taxation should be avoided because "it is not clear what is intended by the term double taxation".

In mid-September 2011, the United Arab Emirates (UAE) submitted proposals to CWG-WCIT12, including a proposal to eliminate certain overlaps between the ITRs and the other ITU treaties (in particular the Constitution and Convention) by deleting the overlapping provisions in the other treaties and retaining them in the ITRs. In addition, in light of a general agreement reached at the 2010 Plenipotentiary Conference to revise the Constitution so as to make it more stable and less prone to frequent revision, the UAE proposed moving certain provisions from the other treaties to the ITRs, and to delete them from the other treaties.[41]

Also in mid-September 2011, Germany, on behalf of a group of European countries, submitted a paper pointing out that the purpose of a treaty is to record agreements between parties subject to international law (in particular states) concerning obligations that they undertake regarding national or international matters. Noting that some of the language of the current version of the ITRs referred to private parties, Germany proposed to revise such language, and to agree that revised ITRs contain only provisions regarding obligations of Member States, and not direct the activities of private parties.[42]

At the same time, Portugal, on behalf of a group of European countries, submitted detailed comments regarding the various issues. While basically consistent with

---

[38] Document CWG-WCIT/C-45

[39] For example, the USA proposed that the ITRs include language to the effect that none of its provisions should be interpreted as modifying rights or obligations of signatories under any other treaties.

[40] For example, operators in certain countries were able, without infringing national laws, to divert international telephone numbers assigned to certain island nations in the Pacific Ocean for use within those nations. These diverted numbers were used in particular to provide access to domestic (that is, not Pacific Island-based) so-called value-added services: in practice sex-talk lines. (The 900-series numbers should be used for this, but they are often blocked, so using an international number for a national call allows more customers to be reached.)

[41] Documents CWG-WCIT/C-51 and 52.

[42] Document CWG-WCIT/C-53.

previously expressed European views[43], this contribution indicated a certain willingness to envisage negotiations regarding some issues that were not covered by the 1988 ITRs, namely spam, cybersecurity, misuse of numbering resources, and transmission of calling party identification. It also indicated a willingness to discuss revision of existing provisions on quality of service, access, and taxation.[44] Not surprisingly, the European contribution reflected a certain lack of consensus within Europe and was, on some points, internally inconsistent.[45]

Discussions at the September 2011 meeting of the preparatory group were limited to procedural matters, that is, there were no substantive discussions. Regarding the procedure, the United States, supported by Canada, proposed that each individual proposal be listed separately and presented as a separate option. It was pointed out that, since there were some 300 separate proposals, some consolidation of the proposals would be necessary prior to the treaty conference itself, otherwise the conference would simply not have enough time to consider the proposals.[46]

The subsequent meeting of the preparatory group took place at the end of February 2012. By then, countries had started to coordinate regional positions and it had become clear that Europe would align with Africa, Arab States, and the Regional Commonwealth in the field of Communications (RCC – mostly composed of countries that had previously been part of the Soviet Union) regarding certain issues, in particular imposing treaty obligations on all operators (called Operating Agencies in ITU's terminology), adding new provisions regarding transparency of mobile roaming retail prices and countering spam. However, the European position was more closely aligned with that of the United States for other issues, such as the status of ITU-T Recommendations and tariff matters. Several countries consistently supported the US, in particular Australia, Canada and Japan. However, the US did indicate that it was willing to envisage references to certain ITU-T Recommendations.[47]

---

[43] In particular an insistence that other international instruments, in particular WTO agreements, take precedence over the ITRs and constrain what could be agreed in the ITRs.

[44] Document CWG-WCIT/C-54.

[45] For example, arguing that certain provisions were not sufficiently strategic to warrant including in a treaty (the ITRs), while not noticing that very similar provisions were included in internal European Union treaties or WTO agreements. Or arguing that, for the same reason, certain provisions should not be included in the ITRs, but should be retained in the Constitution.

[46] Indeed, if only 10 minutes were devoted to discussion of each proposal, then discussion of 300 proposals would require 50 hours, that is 10 working days (each working day is about 5 hours, due to limits on the working times of interpreters and lunch and coffee breaks). The conference was expected to last 10 days, with 1-2 days required for opening and closing formalities and administrative discussions.

[47] In its contribution CWG-WCIT12/C-76, the US proposed the following language for paragraph 1 of Appendix 2: "Administrations should comply with the relevant ITU-T Recommendations and any Instructions forming part of or derived from these Recommendations, when establishing and settling accounts under this Appendix." But paragraph 2.3 of that Appendix provided that references to "administrations" shall be read as "accounting authority" for what concerns appendix 2,

The Internet Society (ISOC) presented a contribution[48] that made various statements regarding supposed differences between "the Internet" and all other forms of telecommunications. It is the author's opinion that some of those statements were extravagant. For example, ISOC stated that "any endpoint of the Internet can address any other endpoint, and the information received at one endpoint is as intended by the sender, wherever the receiver connects to the Internet". But in fact most end-devices that use the TCP/IP protocol are located behind firewalls and/or Network Address Translators (NATs) and cannot be addressed directly by another end-device. In contrast, most end-devices that use other telecommunications protocols (in particular circuit-switched voice protocols) can be addressed directly by any other end-device. That is, any telephone in the world can dial another telephone, but a user's PC can only receive information if the end-user has allowed that, typically by requesting that information be sent to it.

ISOC also stated that "there is no central authority that designates or permits different classes of Internet activities". But ICANN and the Internet Assigned Numbers Authority (IANA) are central authorities that designate domain names and IP addresses. No Internet activities can take place without such names and addresses, which are centrally controlled; for domain names, there is even a central database which must be used by anybody who wishes to resolve a domain name to an IP address. Contrast this to telephone numbers, which are designated and administered at the national level, and for which there is no central database that can be used to resolve telephone numbers (which are "names") to the physical addresses required to complete a call. No innovation with respect to domain names is possible without the permission of ICANN. Contrast this with telephone numbers, where new numbering ranges can be created by national decisions (a good example being the introduction of 800 numbers in the USA before there was any international standard regarding freephone numbers).

The ISOC paper contained many other statements which raised the eyebrows, if not the hackles, of other participants.

Although no proposals had been submitted by Member States regarding consolidation of related proposals, the group accepted the Chairman's suggestion to start simplifying the list of proposals by identifying issues on which there was agreement in principle and attempting either to agree a consensus text, or at least a reduced number of options to be further discussed.

Regional preparatory meetings[49] too place starting in March 2012, and proved very valuable in progressing the work of the group. At its meeting in April 2012, the group was able to agree a draft structure[50] for the revised ITRs and to prepare a document[51] containing a reduced set of option to be submitted to the WCIT. A

---

and paragraph 2.1 provided that any entity could be designated as an accounting authority. Thus the US proposal implied that any entity designated as an accounting authority should comply with the relevant ITU-T Recommendations.

[48] CWG-WCIT12/C-74.

[49] ITU, 2012a. *Regional Preparatory Meetings*.

[50] Document CWG-WCIT12/TD 53.

[51] Document CWG-WCIT12/TD 54

summary[52] of preliminary regional positions indicated significant support for including in the new ITRs several issues not covered by the 1988 treaty, such as (these issues are briefly explained at the end of the previous section):

- Misuse
- Calling party identification
- Transparency of international mobile roaming prices
- Price of international mobile roaming services
- Security
- Countering spam

Inputs to the June 2012 meeting, which was the last meeting of the group, reflected a certain convergence on the one hand towards the views of the developed countries regarding economic issues in general (that is, limited or no intervention in commercial matters) and on the other hand towards other proposals that did not fit well with the prevailing "hands-off" views of most developed countries. In particular, there were African, Arab, and Latin American proposals regarding the price of international mobile roaming; and proposals from Arab States, a Latin American country, and a group of European operators regarding principles for international connectivity, as well as African and Arab proposals regarding general economic and policy issues. It is worth noting that some of the Latin American proposals were inconsistent with the views of the USA, so that for many key issues there was not a coordinated regional American position.

A significant development occurred at the eighth meeting: for the first time, a group of operators (ETNO-European Telecommunications Network Operators) submitted a proposal to add new provisions to the ITRs. The intent of that proposal was, on the one hand, to prevent governments from restricting differentiated quality of service offerings for Internet connections and, on the other hand, to establish the principle of sending-party-pays for Internet traffic. The underlying reason for these proposals was to attempt to obtain revenue from the large Internet content providers, such as Google, Facebook, etc. In ETNO's view, these companies were transmitting ever increasing volumes of data over the network, forcing operators to invest in new infrastructure, but the operators were unable to generate new revenue from the increased traffic.[53] Needless to say, these proposals drew outraged criticism, with some going so far as to characterize them as "a tax on the Internet".[54] (See also page 38.) The original ETNO proposal was not adopted by any Member State and so it was not submitted to WCIT (only Member States can submit proposals), but a variation whose intent was the same was submitted by several countries. See p. 137 for a discussion of those proposals and the final outcome concerning them. It is worth noting that there has not yet been any significant commentary on the recent

---

[52] Document CWG-WCIT12/TD 60

[53] See AT Kearney, 2010. *A Viable Future Model for the Internet*, December 2010. Related efforts by newspaper publishers to limit use on the Internet of the titles of their newspapers were somewhat more successful in at least one country, Germany, see Ermert, Monica, 2013c. "German Parliament Votes to Protect News Snippets from Republishing", *Intellectual Property Watch,* 22 March 2013.

[54] McCullagh, Declan and Downs, Larry, 2012. "U.N. could tax U.S.-based Web sites, leaked docs show", *CNET,* 7 June 2012.

G20[55] decision to address the tax challenges of the digital economy, which could include measures regarding the attribution of value created from the generation of marketable location-relevant data through the use of digital products and services and collection of VAT/GST with respect to the cross-border supply of such goods and services.[56] Nor has there been significant commentary on US plans to allow taxation of online shopping.[57]

Another significant development at the eighth meeting was the submission of proposals concerning two totally new issues: energy efficiency (to mitigate climate change), and accessibility (making ICTs useable by the disabled).

Since the group did not have the mandate to resolve differences, the various proposals were compiled and submitted to WCIT.[58] Those proposals were made public by a decision of Council 2012, which also authorized the Secretary-General to set up a mechanism to collect public comments online.[59] See the more detailed discussion on transparency on p. 48.

At the end of CWG-WCIT, there was consensus on the following points:

1. Retain current structure and titles of articles except possibly title of art. 6
2. Replace "member" with "Member State"
3. Replace CCITT with ITU-T
4. Update references to Administrative Council, IRRB, etc.
5. Replace "Convention" with "Constitution and Convention"
6. Preamble
7. Existing definitions (except for Arab proposal regarding "telecommunications/ICTs")
8. Article 7 (Suspension of services)
9. Delete 6.3.2 (coefficients gold franc/SDR)
10. Minimize incorporation of provisions of the Constitution and Convention (CS/CV)
11. Do not change definitions found in CS/CV

There were no disagreements in principle, only drafting issues regarding the following items:

12. Existing provisions of article 5 (Safety of Life and Priority of Telecommunications)
13. Article 8 (Dissemination of Information)
14. Article 10 (Final Provisions)

---

[55] *G20*, 2013. Wikipedia.

[56] G20 Leaders, 2013. "Tax Annex to the St. Petersburg Declaration", *G20*, 6 September 2013, Annex, Action 1. In this context, it is worth noting that one of the Italian political parties has proposed to tax online advertising by requiring that some portions of the business be carried out by local companies, see Jones, Gavin, 2013. "Italy eyes 'Google tax' to help fix public finances", *Reuters*, 4 November 2013.

[57] Reuters, 2013. "Online sales tax bill moving ahead in U.S. House", *Reuters,* 12 September 2013; Nesto, Matt, 2013. "Are You Ready for a Federal Online Shopping Tax?", *Yahoo! Finance*, 29 August 2013.

[58] See CWG-WCIT12/TD-64.

[59] ITU, 2012b. *Landmark decision by ITU Council on proposal for public consultation and open access to key conference document.*

The following items were supported in principle by most countries, but no exact language had been agreed, and the items were opposed by some countries (primarily the US and its allies):

15. Replace "recognized private operating agency" with "operating agency"
16. New provision on misuse
17. New provision on calling line ID
18. New provision on roaming price transparency
19. New provision on security
20. New provision on countering spam

There was divergence between Africa/Arab/RCC[60] versus Asia/Europe regarding the following items:

21. Make certain ITU-T Recommendations binding
22. Refer to Recommendations of the ITU in certain provisions, as opposed to ITU-T Recommendations
23. Use of terms such as "shall ensure" versus "should encourage"
24. New definitions
25. New provision on transparency of routing
26. Replace/augment existing article 6 with new general principles for Economic and Policy Issues, including new provisions on cost-based pricing (including for roaming), pricing transparency, dispute resolution, etc.
27. New provision regarding fraud
28. Including prevention of "financial harm" and "security" in article 9
29. Scope of new security provision

There was no clear majority view regarding the following items:

30. Provision on taxation
31. Appendix 2 (Maritime Telecommunications)
32. Appendix 3 (Service and Privilege Telecommunications)
33. Existing Resolutions, Recommendations, and Opinion
34. New Resolutions

The following significant items had been raised by only one or two regions or countries or operating agencies:

35. Retain existing article 6 (Charging and Accounting) and the related Appendix 1 (RCC)
36. New provision on harmonization of emergency numbers (RCC)
37. New provision which is a generic version of D.50 (Arab and Paraguay)
38. New provision on energy efficiency (Ghana)
39. New provision on accessibility (Hungary)
40. New provision to subordinate ITRs to all other treaties (USA)
41. New provisions on inadvertent roaming, billing units (Brazil)
42. New provision on control of routing (Arab) (also naming numbering)
43. Network neutrality and sending party pays (ETNO)

Some of these issues continued to be discussed through WCIT itself, see p. 57.

---

[60] RCC is the Regional Commonwealth in the field of Communications, comprising the Russian Federation and other countries formerly associated with the Soviet Union.

Following the last meeting of CWG-WCIT12, a number of regional preparatory meetings took place.[61] In preparation for these meetings, and during the meetings themselves, various countries and regions made their views known to the other countries and regions. In particular, the USA made it clear that it was opposed to any text on security in the ITRs and to any text that might affect the flow of funds for Internet traffic. The USA was successful in modifying the position of some European and Asian countries, with the result that proposals from those regions were relatively in line with the US position (but not for all issues). However, the USA was not successful in modifying the positions of some Latin American countries, most African countries, most of the countries in the Regional Commonwealth in the field of Communications (RCC – countries that were formerly associated with the Soviet Union) and most Arab countries. In particular, Brazil submitted proposals that were in direct contradiction to the US views, going so far as to submit one item that had been originally submitted by the Russian Federation, but had been withdrawn by the Russian Federation due to lack of support. As a result, there were strong differences of views going into the conference. As we will see below, it proved impossible to reconcile some of these differences.

The views expressed by the USA contained what the author considers to be some internal contradictions. For example:

- At first strongly supporting retention of the accounting rate system, then proposing that it be abolished (see page 25).
- On the one hand, stating that the ITRs do not apply to the Internet, on the other hand opposing specific proposals on the grounds that they might have negative effects for the Internet.[62]
- Opposing a proposal for a provision on network security that was almost literally copied from a US Presidential declaration.[63]
- Arguing strongly that certain proposals related to Internet flow of funds would reduce access to Internet by residents in African countries, while not recognizing that Internet penetration in Africa was very low, so the real issue was how to increase access to Internet in Africa.
- Opposing various provisions on the grounds that they might affect freedom of speech, while not recognizing that no WCIT provision could have such an effect because, in accordance with Article 34 of the ITU Constitution, countries have the right to cut off, in accordance with their national law, any private telecommunications which may appear dangerous to the security of the State or contrary to its laws, to public order or to decency. Indeed all countries limit speech on the Internet, albeit in different ways and to a different extent (with the US being one of the least restrictive).[64]

---

[61] ITU (2012a).

[62] See document WCIT-12/9.

[63] See document CWG-WCIT12/C-60 for the proposal, and CWG-WCIT12/TD-62 for the US opposition, expressed as "Cybersecurity should not be included in the ITRs in any way, shape or form." The proposal is CWG/4/225 in the publicly-available document ITU, 2012c. *Draft of the future ITRs*.

[64] For example, Internet gambling is not permitted in the USA; various forms of hate speech and political speech are not permitted in many European countries;

- On the one hand, admitting that both security and flow-of-funds issues were very important issues that deserved discussion, while on the other hand stating that such discussions should not take place in ITU, but should take place in various other forums that many countries considered not to be truly global.[65]

The Internet Governance Issue

Starting at the end of November 2011, a series of articles and speeches were published by US sources (including a Commissioner of the Federal Communications Commission – FCC) to the effect that many countries "would like to use to significantly expand the jurisdiction and legal authority of the ITU, even potentially giving this United Nations agency greater influence over internet governance". The citation is from the first such article, written by David Gross and Ethan Lucarelli of Wiley Ryan LLP, a US law firm; Gross was representing a group of companies.[66]

These articles and speeches drew immediate support in the US. As a noted scholar had prophetically noted (but without reference to WCIT): "Mention global governance in the context of Internet and [some in the US] hear only 'the UN wants to take over the Internet' or 'some other state we don't like (China, the EU, whatever) wants to regulate the Internet.'"[67]

Internet Governance can be defined as "the development and application by Governments, the private sector and civil society, in their respective roles, of shared principles, norms, rules, decision-making procedures, and programs that shape the evolution and use of the Internet".[68]

Although the ITU had long had a role in norms and decisions that shaped the evolution and use of the Internet (including the 1988 ITRs; standards for modems, ADSL, and backbone links; allocation of frequency spectrum allowing the development of WiFi and other technologies used to facilitate wireless access to Internet services; the X.509 standard that underpins HTTPs, etc.), there was considerable controversy regarding a possible extension of ITU's role to the management of

---

copyright violation is not permitted in most countries; pedophile material is not permitted in most countries; etc.

[65] See for example CITEL document OEA/Ser.L/XVII.4.1/CCP.I-TIC/doc. 2700/12.

[66] Gross, David and Lucarelli, Ethan, 2012. "The 2012 World Conference On International Telecommunications: Another Brewing Storm Over Potential UN Regulation Of The Internet", *WhosWhoLegal,* November 2011. Subsequently, Gross listed himself as representing the "WCIT Ad Hoc Working Group, an industry-led coalition with broad representation from the communications and information sectors including AT&T, Cisco, Comcast, Google, Intel, Microsoft, News Corporation, Oracle, Telefonica, Time Warner Cable, Verisign, and Verizon" (see testimony before the US House subcommittee on communications and technology of 31 May 2012, <http://energycommerce.house.gov/sites/republicans.energycommerce.house.gov/files/Hearings/CT/20120531/HHRG-112-IF16-WState-GrossD-20120531.pdf> accessed 28 July 2013).

[67] Mueller (2010), p. 263.

[68] Proposed by: Working Group on Internet Governance, 2005. *Report*.

Internet domain names and addresses, a function carried out by a private company (the Internet Corporation for Assigned Names and Numbers – ICANN) under certain arrangements with the US government.[69]

Those issues were discussed extensively[70] during the World Summit on the Information Society[71] and the spin-off groups created at that Summit, namely the Working Group on Internet Governance[72] and the Internet Governance Forum.[73] The matters were also extensively discussed, from 1998 through at least 2012, in various ITU bodies, such as the Plenipotentiary Conferences (which regularly revised Resolutions 101 and 102), Council, and certain Council Working Groups.[74] The discussions reflected fundamental differences between countries regarding the proper role of governments with respect to telecommunications in general, the Internet in particular, and broader issues such as freedom of speech.[75] Several scholars have provided good accounts of the various issues underlying discussions on Internet governance, including the tensions regarding national control of what many view as a transnational network.[76]

Thus a statement to the effect that the WCIT might be used to make certain decisions regarding certain aspects of Internet Governance was sure to attract attention, even if in fact no specific proposals had been submitted by February 2012 regarding matters related to Internet domain names and addresses (with the exception of a non formulated proposal by the Russian Federation stating that ITU should be involved in some way in the allocation of IP addresses, a proposal that had been made before and extensively discussed in ITU[77]).

The November 2011 article went so far as to state that "some of the proposed changes to the ITRs could position the ITU as a supra-national regulator", despite the fact that there were no proposals to establish any supra-national agencies with regulatory powers. There were proposals to the effect that countries should harmonize their national legislation/regulation in certain areas, and the national regulatory authorities would then be expected to enforce those national laws and regulations. The article correctly noted that the ITU did not have legal authority directly to regulate either retail or wholesale international mobile roaming rates, but stated that

---

[69] A good account of the policy and other issues related to ICANN's creation and the sensitivity of ITU's role in this area can be found in Mueller (2002).

[70] A pithy and cogent account of how the focus of WSIS was shifted from development issues to Internet governance issues is given in Mueller (2010), pp. 57 ff.

[71] ITU, 2005. *World Summit on the Information Society*.

[72] ITU, 2005a. *Internet Governance*.

[73] Internet Governance Forum, 2013. *Internet Governance Forum*.

[74] See Hill, Richard (2014). "The Internet, its governance, and the multi-stakeholder model", *Info*, vol. 16 no 1 (forthcoming).

[75] See Hill (2013a). Those differences of views persist and may have been exacerbated by the revelations regarding the US Prism surveillance program (p. 21), see news24, "Brazil to host internet governance summit", *news24,* 10 October 2013.

[76] McKinnon, Rebecca, 2012. *Consent of the Networked: The Worldwide Struggle for Internet Freedom*, Basic Books; Mueller (2010); Goldsmith, Jack and Wu, Tim (2006). *Who Controls the Internet: Illusions of a Borderless World*, Oxford University Press.

[77] For the previous discussions, see ITU, 2012d. *IPv6*.

"WCIT could expand the ITU's authority over international roaming, especially regarding wholesale rates", again, despite the fact that no such proposals had been made (again, the proposals addressed possible actions by national regulators, not the creation of a supra-national regulator).

The November 2011 article did, however, correctly note that a significant issue for WCIT would be the proper role of governments regarding the regulation (or not) of telecommunications. As noted above, a number of governments did take the view that the 1988 ITRs were too liberal and that government control should be reintroduced in certain areas, for example to prevent the misuse/hijacking of telephone numbers.

On 21 February, 2012, the Wall Street Journal published an opinion piece by FCC Commissioner McDowell.[78] This article repeated in a shriller and more alarmist tone the messages summarized above. It was widely read and was cited by many other commentators. But the evident exaggeration in the article was picked up by several commentators, who noted that the actual proposals made to CWG-WCIT12 were not consistent with the fears expressed by McDowell.[79]

On 28 February 2012, speaking at the Mobile World Congress, McDowell warned against decisions that might "balkanize" the Internet by creating a world where the Internet might be partitioned between countries that live under an intergovernmental regulatory regime and those who decide to opt out of that regime.[80] The "balkanization" theme was picked up at the same conference by Eric Schmidt, Chief Executive Officer of Google.[81]

It is not exactly clear what was meant by "balkanization" of the Internet, because the term in English means to divide something into a number of smaller and often mutually hostile units, as was done in the Balkan Peninsula in the late 19th and early 20th centuries. Despite various claims to the contrary (see the discussion above of ISOC's contribution C 74 to CWG-WCIT), the Internet was divided into somewhat mutually inaccessible islands by its users, for example through firewalls used to improve security, network address translators (NATs) to minimize the need for IP addresses, and content in languages other than English (by 2012, the majority of Internet users were non-English speakers and extensive non-English content was hosted on the World Wide Web). Further, all countries had prohibitions on certain types of Internet content, usually matching prohibitions on printed media, for example, prohibition of child pornography, online gambling, promotion of racial hatred, etc. Those national prohibitions varied widely, and were enforced either through technical means (so-called national firewalls or filters) or legal actions.[82] And there

[78] McDowell, Robert, 2012. "The U.N. Threat to Internet Freedom", *The Wall Street Journal*, 21 February 2012.

[79] See for example Hruska, Joseph, 2012. "FCC fires FUD at the idea of a UN-controlled internet", *ExtremeTech*, 23 February 2012.

[80] Fulton, Scott, 2012. "FCC Commissioner: Ending ICANN could lead to an 'Engineering Morass'", *ReadWrite Mobile*, 28 February 2012.

[81] See 35:45 of the video at <http://wn.com/eric_schmidt_at_mobile_world_congress?orderby=published&upload_time=all_time> accessed 30 June 2013.

[82] For example, a significant legal action was the 2011 US action against online gambling sites, see *United States v. Scheinberg* (2013); for a more systematic

were differing rules regarding registration of domain names in country code top-level domains (ccTLDs), and differing regional rules regarding allocation of IP addresses.

In his intervention at the Mobile World Congress, Schmidt replied to a question regarding the high cost of Internet access in Nigeria. He squarely admitted that there was a problem and said that the solution was to improve access, but he did not give concrete suggestions regarding how to do that. As noted above, the high cost of international Internet connectivity had long been a controversial subject in ITU, with Member States taking differing views on how best to reduce such costs (another example of an "Internet Governance" issue that was squarely within the ITU's scope).[83]

At the time, network operators around the world were dissatisfied with the split of revenues of Internet traffic, feeling that they bore the brunt of the costs (network infrastructure) while the majority of the revenues went to content providers or service providers such as Amazon, Apple, Facebook, Google, etc. Some network operators were proposing to institute differentiated charging schemes for differentiated quality of service, but these proposals were opposed by the content and service providers.[84] It is possible that calls against "balkanization" of the Internet were actually calls to oppose the introduction of new tariff and revenue models that would result in lower profits for content and service providers and higher profits for network operators. Indeed, in testimony before a US Congressional committee, McDowell stated: "They [developing countries] see an opportunity to charge some web sites or application providers, Google or Facebook, to charge them on a per-click basis and that have money flow to sometimes state-owned telephone companies."[85] And he reiterated this statement, in more detail, when he testified in front of the US Congress on 31 May 2012, stating that foreign governments had told him that they would "use international mandates to charge certain Web destinations on a 'per-click' basis to fund the build-out of broadband infrastructure across the globe. Google, iTunes, Facebook, and Netflix are mentioned most often as prime sources of funding."[86] (See also the G20 declaration referred to on p. 31.)

One commentator stated that under the current unregulated peering system, foreign Internet Service Providers (ISPs) pay US ISPs a fee to carry internet traffic, which means that US companies profit from foreign access. If Internet servers were truly decentralized – a possible "balkanization" – then US ISPs would end up paying considerably more money to their foreign counterparts and derive less profit from

---

discussion of national actions regarding Internet, see Goldsmith and Wu (2006) and Hill (2014).

[83] See ITU (2013) and ITU (2012e).

[84] Much of the debate took place under the rubric of "network neutrality", see for example CWG-WCIT12/INF-5.

[85] Hearing regarding the FCC budget, 19 March 2012 <http://mms.tveyes.com/Transcript.asp?StationID=200&DateTime=3%2F19%2F2012+10%3A04%3A00+PM&Term=International+Telecommunication+Union&PlayClip=TRUE> accessed 3 March 2013.

[86] McCullagh, Declan, 2012a. "U.N. takeover of the Internet must be stopped, U.S. warns", *CNET,* 31 May 2012.

Internet traffic.[87] Indeed, subsequent analysis of the proposals made during the preparatory process stated that the conference was likely to focus on financial issues.[88]

In the author's view, there is no reason to think that "the Internet" – or even fundamental principles of free speech and free enterprise – would suffer from the introduction of different charging and traffic management principles that might better fund future infrastructure.

It is also possible that calls against "balkanization" were merely another example of the well-known US tendency to resist any international agreements that didn't conform exactly to its own views on a particular matter.[89] Indeed, the US opposed all proposals regarding new ITR provisions that would harmonize national measures to improve cybersecurity, and this despite the fact that such provisions would surely have reduced "balkanization". Presumably the US resistance was due to fears that internationally harmonized solutions might not be identical to existing US national solutions. (See also the discussion regarding the Prism surveillance program on pages 21 and 42.)

Indeed one commentator stated that any attempt to create an international system of internet governance would weaken the efforts of US content producers (such as record labels and film studios) to strengthen copyright protection measures. Some proposed US legislation to that effect was aimed at restricting and controlling foreign Internet traffic, which could only be done effectively if such traffic were flowing through the US. If Internet control were to shift towards nations that favored fewer copyright restrictions, Internet access as a human right, and limited punishment for piracy, it would be a serious threat to content distributors.[90]

In this context, it is worth noting that the US telecommunications regulatory framework in place in 2012 dated back to 1996 and made a distinction between "traditional" telecommunications and "the Internet" that was not found in the regulatory frameworks of most other countries. The Telecommunications Act of 1996 defined "telecommunications service" as the offering of telecommunications for a fee directly to the public.[91] It defined "information service" as the offering of a capability for generating, acquiring, storing, transforming, processing, retrieving, utilizing, or making available information via telecommunications, including electronic publishing, but not including any use of any such capability for the management, control, or operation of a telecommunications system or the management of a

[87] Hruska (2012).

[88] Krishnatrarok, 2012. "UN 'Internet takeover' about subsidizing phone companies", *DSLReports,* 21 June 2012.

[89] See for example Chomsky, Noam 2000. *Rogue States: The Rule of Force in World Affairs*, South End Press. Although Chomsky exaggerates and extrapolates at times wildly, he does document well the US tendency to wish to impose on the rest of the world its own views regarding many topics. More recently, see New, William, 2013b. "United States Chided as TRIPS Scofflaw at WTO", *Intellectual Property Watch*, 16 March 2013. According to this article, the US has been accused of ignoring WTO dispute body decisions regarding a Cuban rum trademark and online gambling services offered by Antigua and Barbuda.

[90] Hruska (2012).

[91] Paraphrasing of 47 USC 153 (53).

telecommunications service.[92] And it provided that when an operator (called "telecommunications carrier" in the Act) was providing "information services", it was not subject to the rules and regulations that applied to "telecommunications services".[93] This is significant because the Act included certain regulatory provisions regarding "telecommunications services", but those did not apply to "information services".

Thus "traditional" telecommunications services were regulated in the US, while services offered through, or based on, "the Internet" were not.[94] This situation became increasingly controversial as more and more services migrated to common infrastructures (which often used the TCP-IP protocol), a trend often referred to a "convergence".[95] However, various attempts to reform the US regulatory regime failed[96], and the 1996 regime was still in place when the ITRs were revised in 2012. Those attempts failed for various reasons, including the desire of those who benefited from the status quo to maintain it, and the desire of the unregulated companies (such as information service providers) to avoid the possible imposition of new regulations.[97]

The apogee of the US campaign against any significant changes to the ITRs came in May 2012, when a Congressional hearing[98] was held. The background memorandum[99] prepared by the Congressional staff grossly mischaracterized the proposals submitted to CWG-WCIT12, stating that "Proposals by Russia and China to establish an "information security" regime are of particular concern. They: 1) appear to enshrine an international cybersecurity regime; 2) could serve as a justification for countries to engage in Internet censorship in the name of national security; and 3) seek to authorize regulation of the Internet by an international governmental body within the ITU, replacing the multi-stakeholder model that has served the Internet

---

[92] Paraphrasing of 47 USC 153 (24).

[93] 47 USC 153 (51).

[94] A good account of the significant of this situation is given in Mueller (2010), p. 56.

[95] See for example Cooper, Mark and Kimmelman, Gene, 2001. "The Digital Divide confronts the Telecommunications Act of 1996: Economic Reality versus Public Policy", in Benjamin Compaine, *The Digital Divide: Facing a Crisis or Creating a Myth*, MIT Press; and Atkin, David, Lau, Tuen-Yu and Lin, Carolyn, 2008. "Still on hold? A retrospective analysis of competitive implications of the Telecommunication Act of 1996, on its 10th year anniversary", *Telecommunications Policy*, vol. 30 no. 2, pp. 80-95.

[96] See for example Crandall, Robert, 2005. *Competition and Chaos: US Telecommunications since the 1996 Telecom Act*, Brookings Institution Press;

[97] Gattuso, James, 2005. "House Telecom Rewrite Needs a Rewrite", *The Heritage Foundation,* 23 September 2005.

[98] US Energy and Commerce Committee, 2012. US House of Representatives, *Hearing on International Proposals to Regulate the Internet,* 31 May 2012.

[99] US Majority Committee Staff, 2012. "Hearing on International Proposals to Regulate the Internet", *Memorandum to the Committee on Energy and Commerce,* 29 May 2012.

and the world so well." It is the author's view that there were no proposals that could be construed to do (3).

It is article 34 of the ITU's Constitution which authorizes stoppage of any telecommunications, including Internet, which appear dangerous to the security of the State or contrary to its laws, to public order or to decency.[100] Thus, in the author's view, there were no proposals submitted to CWG-WCIT that could be construed to do (2).[101]

Be that as it may, various blog posts and articles referred to WCIT as posing a threat to freedom of speech[102], and this did affect discussions at the conference, as we will see in Chapter 4 (p. 65).

Regarding (1) above, it is possible to describe as "proposals to enshrine an international cybersecurity regime" the various proposals calling for increased cooperation to improve cybersecurity.

Indeed, one analyst took the view that the true nature of some of the proposals was to limit state-sponsored cyberattacks and/or cyberwar.[103] A careful analysis of some of the proposals supports this view. One proposal was: "Member States shall ensure unrestricted public access to international telecommunication services and the unrestricted use of international telecommunications, except in cases where international telecommunication services are used for the purpose of interfering in the internal affairs or undermining the sovereignty, national security, territorial integrity and public safety of other States, or to divulge information of a sensitive nature."

Art 34 of the ITU Constitution provides that Member States reserve the right to cut off, in accordance with their national law, any private telecommunications which may appear dangerous to the security of the State or contrary to its laws, to public order or to decency.

One thing that is immediately apparent is that the scope of the proposed ITR provision is in one sense narrower than that of the Constitution. The Constitution applies to *"any private telecommunications"* which obviously includes domestic telecommunications. The ITR proposal applies to *"international telecommunica-*

---

[100] The article provides that Member States reserve the right to cut off, in accordance with their national law, any private telecommunications which may appear dangerous to the security of the State or contrary to its laws, to public order or to decency.

[101] We note in passing that mentioning the Russian Federation in this context appears incongruous to this author because that state is bound by the European Convention of Human Rights, and the judgments of the European Court of Human Rights, which set high standards, and enforceable standards, for human rights and free speech.

[102] See for example Kerr, Dara, 2012. "Amendments to UN treaty could censor the Internet", *CNET*, 24 June 2012; Kays, Laurel, 2012. "WCIT-12: A Threat to the Free and Open Internet, *Digital Liberty*, 19 November 2012; Center for Democracy and Technology. "Civil Society Must Have Voice as ITU Debates the Internet", *CDT Policy Post*, 6 March 2012.

[103] Mueller, Milton, 2012. "Threat Analysis of the WCIT Part 4: the ITU and Cybersecurity", *Internet Governance Project*, 21 June 2012.

tions", which obviously excludes domestic telecommunications. So the ITR proposal would not affect censorship of national telecommunications.

On the other hand, the proposed ITR provision is broader, because it applies to all telecommunications, not just *"private telecommunications"*. That is, the Constitution applies only to private telecommunications, while the WCIT proposal would also apply to non-private telecommunications.

The term *"Private telecommunications"* is not defined in the ITU instruments, but one might define it by analogy to "private telegram" which is defined in the Constitution as *"telegrams other than government or service telegrams"*. *"Government telegrams"* include telegrams originating with any members of a government.

Regarding the exceptions to free access, the wording in the Constitution appears to be much broader than the wording in the ITR proposal. Under Art. 4 of the Constitution, the Constitution prevails if there is an inconsistency between the Constitution and the ITRs. So, for what concerns *"private telecommunications"* the broader wording of Constitution would prevail over the narrow wording of the ITR proposal.

But the ITR proposal would apply to non-private international telecommunications. As worded, it would not prevent a Member State from attempting to send such telecommunications into another state, but it would authorize the receiving Member State to attempt to block such telecommunications. And it would bind all Member States to cooperate to prevent the transmission of such telecommunications.

This could, conceivably, be construed as an attempt to create an international cybersecurity regime whose intent would be to attempt to prevent state-originated cyberattacks or cyberwarfare.[104] And it is conceivable that some states did not wish to agree to a treaty that would have such an effect.[105]

Indeed, in the author's opinion (and that of others[106]), the revelations in 2013 of the US Prism surveillance program[107] cast a new light on the US refusal to accept treaty text calling for cooperation with respect to telecommunications security. As noted on page 21, apparently no judicial approval was required for surveillance of

[104] In this context, see the proposed "International Code of Conduct for Cybersecurity" submitted on 12 September 2011 to the United Nations by China, Russia, Tajikistan, and Uzbekistan. Article 2 of that text explicitly restricts cyberwarfare. The text is available at <http://www.fmprc.gov.cn/eng/wjdt/wshd/t858978.htm> accessed 28 July 2013.

[105] For example, the United States, which reportedly conducted hundreds of offensive cyber operations, see Gellman, Barton and Nakashima, Ellen, 2013. "U.S. spy agencies mounted 231 offensive cyber-operations in 2011, documents show", *Washington Post,* 31 August 2013; Schneier, Bruce, 2013. "Has U.S. Started an Internet War?", *CCN,* 18 June 2013.

[106] Gurstein (2013).

[107] See Savage, Wyatt and Baker (2013); Hruska, Joel, 2013. "The NSA's Prism leak could fundamentally change or break the entire Internet", *Extreme Tech,* 10 June 2013; Karimi, Faith, 2013. "Facebook, Microsoft disclose information on user data request", *CNN,* 15 June 2013; CNN staff, 2013. "Holder: leaks damaged U.S. Security", *CNN*, 14 June 2013; Barabas, Emily, and Bankston, Kevin, 2013. "It's Not Just About the US: How the NSA Threatens Human Rights Internationally", *Center for Democracy and Technology,* 12 June 2013.

non-US citizens. Presumably, this would have had to be revealed in the context of cooperation, and could have been found objectionable by some countries, thus potentially limiting the US surveillance. As one article put the matter: "It is now clear that the issue before WCIT was not one of authoritarian regimes destroying the freedom of the Internet; but that no limit should be placed on the US intelligence agencies' 'right' to hack the global Internet infrastructure."[108]

We note here that, after the revelations regarding Prism, the US expressed a willingness to cooperate with the Russian Federation regarding security matters[109], whereas it had staunchly opposed treaty text calling for international cooperation, in particular by citing the Russian Federation as a country that might rely on such treaty text to restrict freedom of speech.[110] The position taken by the US at WCIT may create some backlash in light of the Prism revelations[111] and even lead to

---

108 Purkayastha, Prabir and Bailey, Rishab, 2013. "How NSA is Hacking the Whole World", *Frontline,* 12 July 2013.

109 US White House Press Office, 2013. "Joint Statement by the Presidents of the United States of America and the Russian Federation on a New Field of Cooperation in Confidence Building", *The White House,* 17 June 2013.

110 For example, see the statement cited above in US Majority Committee Staff (2012). During the debate prior to WCIT on a House Resolution, Ms Eshoo of California said: "In addition to proposing new regulations on broadband services, several nations, including Russia, are set on asserting intergovernmental control over the Internet, leading to a balkanized Internet where censorship could become the new norm"; see Rizo, Chris, 2012. "Int'l proposals for U.N. Internet regulations draws bipartisan rebuke", *FierceOnlineVideo,* 20 June 2012; and US Congress, 2012. *Congressional Record*, vol. 158, no.116 (Wednesday, August 1, 2012), House, pp. H5599-H5602; when he testified before the US Congress on 5 February 2013, FCC Commissioner Robert McDowell stated "In fact, last year, China teamed up with Russia, Tajikistan and Uzbekistan to propose to the UN General Assembly that it create an 'International Code of Conduct for Information Security' to mandate 'international norms and rules standardizing the behavior of countries concerning information and cyberspace.' Does anyone here today believe that these countries' proposals would encourage the continued proliferation of an open and freedom-enhancing Internet? Or would such constructs make it easier for authoritarian regimes to identify and silence political dissidents?" <http://www.fcc.gov/document/commissioner-mcdowell-congressional-testimony> accessed 28 July 2013.

111 See for example statements by Brazilian Foreign Minister Antonio Patriota as quoted by Bosco, David, 2013. "Brazil Wants UN to Help Safeguard Internet", *Foreign Policy,* 8 July 2013; Naughton, John, 2013. "Edward Snowden's not the story. The fate of the Internet is", *The Guardian,* 28 July 2013; Morozov, Evgeny, 2013. "The Price of Hypocrisy", *Frankfuter Allgemeine* (24 July 2013); Rousseff, Dilma, President of Brazil, 2013. "Statement at the Opening of the General Debate of the 68th Session of the United Nations General Assembly", United Nations, 24 September 2013; Koot, Matthijs, 2013. "Dutch govt position concerning U.S. spying for economic purposes + answers to Parliamentary questions re: Snowden/Le Monde", *notebook,* 28 October 2013.

renewed discussions on Internet governance[112] (see p. 35 for a discussion of Internet governance in the context of WCIT).

Other items in the background memorandum presented to the US Congress that the author considers to be blatant inaccuracies included stating that [The ITRs] "govern the international operation of traditional telephone service." This is not correct. The 1973 Telephone Regulations did that. The 1988 ITRs coverall all technologies, data and voice, and indeed the Internet would not exist without article 9 of the ITRs. So the 1988 ITRs already "governed" the Internet because they allowed the peering agreements that underpin international Internet connections.

The background memorandum stated that the US should "oppose any treaty provisions at the WCIT that expands the jurisdiction of the ITU to cover the Internet". But the ITU already "covered" some aspects of the Internet, see for example Plenipotentiary Resolutions 101 and 102 (which even refer to the domain name system), not to mention all the ITU-T Recommendations that enable the Internet (xDSL, fiber optic, cable modem, compression, X.509 certificates, etc.). And, as stated above, the current ITRs covered the Internet because they made it possible.[113]

According to the background memorandum, [The 1988 ITRs] "specifically addressed voice telephony, not data processing capabilities, and resulted in large payments from U.S. communications companies to telephone companies in foreign, mostly developing, countries." It is the author's view that none of that is correct. The 1988 ITRs were technology-neutral and addressed both voice and data. They resulted in reductions, not increases, in the payments from US companies to others, as shown above (see page 10). Those reductions were the main reasons why the US did not wish to see changes to the ITRs.

Further, the memorandum failed to note that there were several proposals (with significant support) to suppress the old settlement provisions (article 6) altogether, which suppression would enshrine the new commercial approach that had become prevalent after 1988.

As computer specialists are fond of saying, "garbage in, garbage out".[114] Given the input, it was inevitable that the US Congress would adopt a Resolution which included statements such as "proposals have been put forward for consideration at the 2012 World Conference on International Telecommunications that would fun-

[112] Ermert, Monica, 2013d. "A New Model for Internet Governance Is In The Air", *Intellectual Property Watch,* 23 October 2013, according to which the Brazilian foreign minister referred to the US surveillance as a key reason to move towards a new model for Internet governance. And Ermert, Monica, 2013e. "At IGF, Glimpses of Future IP Governance Overshadowed By Mass Surveillance", *Intellectual Property Watch,* 28 October 2013; Nothias, Jean-Christophe, 2013, "And Now the Second Battle of the Internet", *Huffington Post Blog,* 13 June 2013; Internet Society et al., 2013a. *Montevideo Statement on the Future of Internet Cooperation,* AFRINIC, ARIN, APNIC, IAB, ICANN, IETF, ISOC, LACNIC, RIPE NCC, W3C, 7 October 2013.

[113] A more complete discussion of the ITU's role, and the controversies surrounding it, is provided in Hill (2014).

[114] *Garbage in, garbage out,* 2013. Wikipedia.

damentally alter the governance and operation of the Internet". Congress resolved that US authorities "should continue working to implement the position of the United States on Internet governance that clearly articulates the consistent and unequivocal policy of the United States to promote a global Internet free from government control and preserve and advance the successful multistakeholder model that governs the Internet today".[115] Presumably this resolution refers only to keeping the Internet free from the control of governments other than that of the United States, because the US continued to maintain its control over the Internet Assigned Names and Addresses (IANA) function and the US executive branch has indeed exercised that control when it re-delegated ".edu" on its own initiative.[116] And of course US courts continued to enforce various laws and measures such as the ban on online gambling.[117] The US government even went so far as to impose a cap, in November 2012, on the price charged by Versign for registration under the domain name ".com".[118]

Needless to say, the initial press reports on this hearing did little more than to echo uncritically the alarmist view expressed by McDowell. The significant influence that the US holds over the running of the Internet was largely ignored. Nor was there any mention of the various proposals to increase transparency of end-user prices, in particular for mobile roaming, nor of the proposals to control the prices for mobile roaming—and this despite the fact that the existence of such proposals had been publicly disclosed by the ITU Secretariat[119] and by European Member States[120].

Presumably the discussions in the US Congress, and the related press coverage, would have been significantly different if correct information had been presented, namely that the purpose of WCIT was to modernize the international framework

---

[115] <http://thomas.loc.gov/cgi-bin/query/z?c112:H.+Con.+Res.+127:> and <http://www.govtrack.us/congress/bills/112/hconres127/text> accessed 6 October 2013. During the debates, statements were made such as "In addition to proposing new regulations on broadband services, several nations, including Russia, are set on asserting intergovernmental control over the Internet, leading to a balkanized Internet where censorship could become the new norm" (by Ms Eshoo of California), which of course did not reflect the actual proposals that had been made.

[116] *.edu*, 2013. Wikipedia.

[117] And indeed when it was proposed that similar language be included in a law, there were strong objections, and the language limiting the role of governments was removed. See Mueller, Milton, 2013. "An Internet 'Free From Government Control': A Worthy Principle", *Internet Governance Project,* April 14, 2013; and the bill itself, H.R. 1580 <http://www.govtrack.us/congress/bills/113/hr1580/text> accessed 28 July 2013.

[118] See McCarthy, Kieren, 2012. "Verisign loses dot-com piggybank", *.nxt,* 30 November 2012; and US Department of Commerce, "Department of Commerce Approves Verisign-ICANN .com Registry Renewal Agreement", *Press Release,* 30 November 2012.

[119] Hill, Richard, 2012. "World Conference on International Telecommunications", ITU, 19 April 2012.

[120] da Costa Cabral, Manuel, 2012. "Revising the International Telecommunications Regulations", CEPT ComITU, 19 April 2012.

underpinning international telecommunications (the ITRs) and to find ways and means to share revenue so as to ensure continuing investments in, and roll-out of, infrastructure, in particular in developing countries. And presumably the public perception in the US would have been different if it had been mentioned that reduction in international roaming prices was one of the key topics to be discussed at WCIT.

The frenzy in the US specialized media resulted in vehement calls for the ITU to make public the proposals made to WCIT[121]. However, before the ITU could even consider how to deal with such requests, the summary of proposals made as of April 2012 was leaked and published.[122] Although some commentators interpreted the actual proposals as confirming threats to the Internet, other commentators took the view that, as stated by the ITU Secretary-General, there were no proposals "to take over the Internet" or to impose censorship[123]; there were, however, proposals that, if accepted, could have a significant effect on the flow of funds for Internet traffic[124]. However, as pointed out above (see page 15), this topic had long been under discussion within the ITU, so it was not surprising that it would be discussed at WCIT. A Canadian academic published a very thoughtful and accurate analysis of the various outcries concerning WCIT[125], but that analysis was not picked up by other commentators.

The blog frenzy continued, with many alarmist articles, but the main stream press tended to take a more moderate view. In November 2012, just prior to the conference, an Indian academic published a thorough analysis of some of the key issues[126], stating that "a careful examination of the proposals would show that the hype of ITU taking over the Internet is very much a creation of certain groups who have other interests". He pointed out that the Internet is not independent of "telecommunications" and that it is only under the peculiar US regulatory regime that a clear distinction is made between the two. He surmised that the purpose of the anti-WCIT campaign was to promote an international telecommunications framework in which

---

[121] Multiple authors, 2012. "Letter to Secretary-General Dr Hamadoun Toure", Center for Democracy and Technology, 17 May 2012; and Mueller, Milton, 2012a. "We Want TD64! ITU Transparency Begins at Home", *Internet Governance Project,* 5 June 2012.

[122] Mueller, Milton, 2012b. "TD64 for Breakfast", *Internet Governance Project,* 6 June 2012.

[123] Goldberg, Mark Leon, 2012. "Proof that the UN Does Not Want to Control Your Internet", *UN Dispatch*, 6 June 2012; and Mueller, Milton, 2012c. "Threat Analysis of WCIT Part 2: Telecommunications versus Internet", *Internet Governance Project,* 7 June 2012.

[124] Mueller, Milton, 2012d. "Threat Analysis of WCIT Part 3: Charging You, Charging Me", *Internet Governance Project,* 9 June 2012; and Pfanner, Eric, 2012a. "Debunking rumors of an Internet takeover", *New York Times,* 11 June 2012.

[125] Winsek, Dwayne, 2012. "The ITU and the Real Threats to the Internet, Part IV: the Triumph of State Security and Proposed Changes to the ITRs", *Mediamorphis,* 19 June 2012; see in particular parts i, ii, and iii which are cited in part iv.

[126] Purkayastha, Prabir, 2012. "Is ITU Really Threatening the Internet?", *Newsclick,* 8 November 2012.

there would be no role for ITU (or a very limited role), akin to the US situation where "information services" were not subject to regulation. And he went on to point out (as had other academics) that the various proposals submitted to WCIT regarding security would not threaten human rights, although they might create difficulties for states that wished to practice cyberwarfare (in this context, see the discussion regarding the Prism surveillance program on pages 21 and 42).

On the basis of the Congressional Resolution and the campaign outlined above, the US successfully lobbied, at a high level, other governments in order to convince them to align their views with those of the US. And the US restated its clear position against any significant changes to the ITRs in its contribution to WCIT of 3 August 2012 (WCIT/9). The USA proposed to modify articles 3 and 6 to reflect the fact that interconnections are based on commercial arrangements and it proposed to limit changes to other articles to minor editorial correction.

Further, the USA stated: "The United States also notes, however, that the Internet has evolved to operate in a separate and distinct environment that is beyond the scope or mandate of the ITRs or the International Telecommunication Union." This statement seemed to ignore the fact that all Internet traffic was covered by Article 9 of the ITRs (special arrangements), so at least the carriage of Internet traffic internationally was indeed within the scope of the 1988 ITRs.

Regarding the mandate of the ITU, the US statement appeared to ignore the fact that Plenipotentiary Resolutions 101, 102, and 133 (amongst others) established a clear mandate for the ITU regarding "the Internet" and it also seemed to ignore the fact that the Internet could not work without relying on numerous ITU-T Recommendations (for matters such as compression, cable modems, xDLS, fiber optic backbone links, and security[127]), not to mention the Radio Regulations (which enable WiFi), or the development programs of ITU-D. And the statement regarding "a separate and distinct environment" appeared to ignore the phenomenon known as convergence.[128]

The formal US position was, not surprisingly, identical to the position advocated by the US companies that had been lobbying since November 2011. Their spokesman David Gross stated in August 2012[129] that there were no international rules with regard to the terms for commercial agreements between carriers for Internet interconnection, thus apparently ignoring Recommendation ITU-T D.50 which deals with exactly this matter. Gross went on to characterize a proposal from the European Telecommunications Network Organization (ETNO) as requiring ITU and governmental intervention into those agreements, and requiring that the negotiations follow a certain format and include the possibility of having "sender party pays". The ETNO proposal did indeed mention "sender party pays", but it was in reality a proposal that governments agree to refrain from regulation and intervention, because

[127] The Secure Hypertext Transport Protocol (HTTPS) relies on Public Key Infrastructure (PKI) encryption, which is specified in Recommendation ITU-T X.509.

[128] See *Convergence*, 2013. Wikipedia.

[129] See Couts, Andrew, 2012. "Interview: US Ambassador David Gross Explains UN 'Takeover' of the Internet", *Digital Trends,* 9 August 2012.

the ETNO proposal[130] stated that differentiated quality of service should be allowed, which was not in line with various network neutrality[131] regulations that were under consideration in various countries at the time.

At the time, the author was of the view that the media campaign criticizing WCIT was mostly meant to prevent adoption of the financially-related proposals that could have harmed the economic interests of certain companies, in particular the providers of Internet services (the so-called "Over-the-Top" or OTT). However, in light of the revelations regarding the Prism surveillance program (see p. 21), the author is now of the view that the media campaign was also meant to justify the US refusal to accept any treaty text calling for cooperation to improve network security, because such cooperation could hinder the current unilateral US actions (see p. 42).

The Transparency Issue

The issue of the ITU's transparency, or rather its perceived lack of transparency, was raised by many of the critics referred to above (and by many civil society organizations[132]) and it was the subject of much discussion at the 2012 session of the ITU Council.

The ITU had a practice of publishing all its documents on its web site, but with password protection, so that they were available only to its membership. This practice had developed over time: it was not explicitly defined in the ITU's basic texts.[133] In fact the matter of using electronic means to disseminate ITU documents was discussed at least as early as 1989, when the Nice Plenipotentiary Conference adopted Resolution 60, calling for increased automation of document processing, and Resolution 62, calling for remote access by the membership to the ITU's information systems. The Geneva Plenipotentiary Conference of 1992 adopted Resolution 14, which resolved that all documentation available in electronic form be made available electronically to the ITU's membership. This decision was reconfirmed in Resolution 66 of the 1994 Kyoto Plenipotentiary Conference, and the revisions to that Resolution agreed at the 1992 Minneapolis, 2002 Marrakesh, 2006 Antalya, and 2010 Guadalajara Plenipotentiary Conferences.

Some Member States were of the view that the ITU was sufficiently transparent and open, because any organization can become a member of the ITU and have

---

[130] The key parts of the ETNO proposal stated "to ensure an adequate return on investment in high bandwidth infrastructures, operating agencies shall negotiate commercial agreements to achieve a sustainable system of fair compensation for telecommunications services and, where appropriate, respecting the principle of sending party network pays" and "best effort delivery should continue to form the basis of international IP traffic exchange. Nothing shall preclude commercial agreements with differentiated quality of service delivery to develop." See CWG-WCIT12/C 109.

[131] See *Network Neutrality*, 2013. Wikipedia.

[132] See for example the letter of signed by many organizations: Multiple authors, 2012a. "Letter to the ITU Secretary-General and to the Chairman of WCIT", Access Now, 9 December 2012.

[133] See 3.8 of Council document C12/31 Rev.2

access to its work, and because it is the duty of the individual Member States to consult their citizens through their national consultation mechanisms. In particular, any Member State could allow public access, on its web site, to any ITU document, as it considered appropriate.

Other Member States were of the view that, given the trends towards open government,[134] freedom of information laws,[135] and the increasing involvement of civil society[136] in certain policy discussions, the ITU should become even more open and transparent, in particular by allowing public access to the WCIT documents.

It should be noted that some European Union countries were among the strongest proponents of increased transparency, while the European Union itself does not practice such transparency with respect to treaty negotiations.[137] It should also be noted that the US was also a strong proponent of transparency, while it does not itself practice such transparency with respect to certain treaty negotiations.[138]

Council 2012 agreed to allow public access to the main output of CWG-WCIT12, the document containing the reduced set of proposals to be further discussed (Addendum 2 of document WCIT/4). It also agreed that the Secretary-General should set up a website[139] where all stakeholders could express their views and opinions on the content of that document or any other matter related to WCIT. Very few comments were submitted and they spanned a full range of views.

However, Council did not agree to allow public access to the more detailed compilation of proposals (Addendum 1 of document WCIT/4), and this of course resulted in continuing criticism of ITU's perceived lack of transparency, despite the fact that that detailed compilation was only of historical interest and would not be used at the Conference itself.[140]

The United Arab Emirates had proposed to publish all CWG-WCIT documents on its own web site.[141] But this proposal was challenged both by those who felt that it was not useful to publish all the documents; and by those who did favor such publi-

---

[134] See *Open government*, 2013. Wikipedia.

[135] See *Freedom of information legislation*, 2013. Wikipedia.

[136] See Weber, Rolf H., 2010. "New Sovereignty Concepts in the Age of Internet?", *Journal of Internet Law,* August 2010, p. 12; *Civil society*, 2013.; and *Nongovernmental organization*, 2013. Wikipedia.

[137] See Ermert, Monica, 2013f. "European Court Upholds Confidentiality in International Trade Talks", *Intellectual Property Watch,* 20 March 2013. This article refers to *Sophie in 't Veld vs European Commission*, 2013. European General Court T-301/10, 19 March 2013.

[138] New, William, 2013f. "Wikileaks's Release of TPP Chapter on IP Blows Open Secret Trade Negotiation", *Intellectual Property Watch*, 13 November 2013; Kaminski, Margot, 2013. "Capture, sunlight, and the TPP leak", *Concurring Opinions*, 14 November 2013.

[139] The website is at <http://www.itu.int/en/wcit-12/Pages/public.aspx>.

[140] See for example Rangnath, Rahhmi, 2012. "Public Knowledge Disappointed that ITU Documents Remain Closed to the Public", *Public Knowledge,* 12 July 2012; and Wong. Cynthia, 2012. "ITU Gives a Nod Towards Transparency; Still a Long Road to Full Civil Society Participation", Center for Democracy and Technology, 16 July 2012.

[141] See document C12/71 Rev.1

cation, but felt that it had to be done by the ITU itself, not by an individual Member State. And indeed, there are views to the effect that a Member State should respect the confidentiality request of another Member State.[142]

However, it is worth noting here that the World Intellectual Property Organization (WIPO) is considerably more transparent than the ITU, and that the negotiations in 2013 for a treaty regarding copyright exceptions for the blind were conducted with full transparency, to the satisfaction of all concerned.[143] Thus it cannot be said that full transparency is necessarily a disadvantage.

Continuing the critical campaign mentioned above, a US Representative (Ms Bono Mack) stated that the discussions concerning the ITRs had "been going on in secret', thus apparently ignoring the fact that all ITU members had access to all the documents and discussions and that the US government would provide, upon request, any ITU document to any US citizen that request it.[144] (It is also worth noting that the US routinely conducts truly secret treaty negotiations.[145])

Just prior to the conference, the supposed secrecy of the proceedings was exploited by Google – whose financial interests were at stake as outlined above (see page 31) – to attack the ITU as an institution by claiming that negotiations between closed doors would lead to increased censorship.[146] This was apparently the first time that a private company attacked a UN institution *per se*, as opposed to decisions, or lack of decisions of a UN body. The ITU Secretariat, in an unusual move,

[142] See *Sophie in 't Veld vs European Commission* (2013). Paragraph 126 of that judgment states "As to the applicant's argument that, in essence, it should have been possible for the Commission to disclose the various positions taken in the negotiations without identifying the negotiating parties defending those positions, it must be held that, in the context of international negotiations, unilateral disclosure by one negotiating party of the negotiating position of one or more other parties, even if this appears anonymous at first sight, may be likely to seriously undermine, for the negotiating party whose position is made public and, moreover, for the other negotiating parties who are witnesses to that disclosure, the mutual trust essential to the effectiveness of those negotiations. As the Commission emphasizes, establishing and protecting a sphere of mutual trust in the context of international relations is a very delicate exercise."

[143] See Flynn, Sean, 2013. "WIPO Treaty For The Blind Shows That Transparency Can Work (And Is Necessary)", *Intellectual Property Watch,* 26 June 2013.

[144] Burstein, Dave, 2012. "ITU Secrecy Disappearing as U.S. ITAC Open to All", *Fast Net News,* 7 August 2012.

[145] See for example New, William, 2013c. "USTR: IPRs Amongst 'Most Challenging' Issues as TPP Talks Accelerate", *Intellectual Property Watch*, 14 March 2013.

[146] <http://www.google.com/intl/en/takeaction/> accessed 15 January 2013; Franzen, Karl, 2012. "Fearing Web Restrictions, Google Launches Campaign Against U.N. Conference", *TPM,* 20 November 2012; and Ackerman, Elise, 2012. "The U.N. Fought the Internet The Internet – And The Internet Won; WCIT Summit in Dubai Ends", *Forbes,* 14 December 2012.

replied to that attack[147], rebutting a number of the statements by Google, in particular pointing out that the ITRs could not override higher-level instruments that exhaustively determine freedom of speech; that is, pointing out that the ITRs could not increase censorship.[148]

Apparently influenced by such propaganda, the European Parliament adopted a Resolution that, in addition to legitimate statements of European positions, recited some of the criticisms mentioned above.[149] Again, the ITU replied, this time in the form of a rebuttal written by the author of this book.[150]

In order to address the alleged lack of transparency, WCIT-12 agreed, at its opening plenary, to make all input documents available to the public: this was an unusual move for the ITU, which has traditionally taken the view that transparency is best achieved at the national level, that is, that it is the responsibility of national governments to make ITU documents available to their citizens and to conduct national consultations. Furthermore, in keeping with past precedents, WCIT-12 agreed to allow public access to its decision-making sessions (meaning plenary session and sessions of Committee 5, the group dealing with the actual text of the treaty[151]) and to webcast those sessions publicly.[152]

As a consequence, WCIT was, to the author's knowledge[153], undoubtedly the most transparent treaty-making conference that had ever taken place (however, as noted above, a subsequent WIPO treaty-making conference was far more transparent).

[147] The ITU Secretary-General, in many speeches, stressed that WCIT was not about Internet governance, that ITU had a long tradition of making decisions by consensus, and that he did not expect that any decisions would be made by voting. As we will see later the Secretary-General's expectations were not fully met.

[148] Conneally, Paul, 2012. "The Google Campaign - An ITU View", *ITUblog,* 23 November 2012.

[149] Falkvinge, Rick, 2012. "European Parliament Unanimously Passed Resolution Against ITU Asserting Control Over Internet", *Falkvinge & Co.,* 22 November 2012; and European Parliament, "Joint Motion for a Resolution" *B7-0498/2012, B7-0499/2012,* 20 November 2012.

[150] Hill, Richard, 2012a. "EU Parliament Resolution on WCIT Flawed", *ITUblog,* 26 November 2012.

[151] The other WCIT-12 committees dealt with procedural issues such as accreditation, the budget of the conference, the time plan, etc.

[152] But there was one significant innovation: in the past, only the non-interpreted original statements made at meetings had been publicly accessible, due to intellectual property restrictions imposed by the interpreters. At WCIT-12 all six UN languages were publicly webcast.

[153] Private communications with various experienced international treaty negotiators. Compare also to ACTA and ongoing negotiations for other treaties, see for example Masnik, Mike, 2013. "Yes, You Can Have An Open and Transparent Treaty Negotiation for Intellectual Property", *TechDirt,* 27 June 2013; *Anti-Counterfeiting Trade Agreement*, 2013. Wikipedia; New (2013f).

CHAPTER 4

What Happened at WCIT

It is necessary to explain in some detail what happened at the conference in order to understand the outcome and its implications. Unlike other ITU conferences[1], this one failed to achieve consensus and the final treaty text was not signed by a significant number of countries.

In a way, this was predictable, given the strong positions taken by the two sides: the USA and its traditional allies, versus developing countries (including Arab states) and Russia and its allies.

In essence, one side was of the view that there should be no (or very little) regulation of new telecommunications technologies[2], and in particular no regulation of Internet, while the other side was of the view that some regulation was needed. An analogy to radio matters is instructive. Few seriously question the need for international coordination of radio frequencies[3], because it is understood that this is the only way to avoid harmful interferences; such coordination amounts to regulation, and it is accepted that national governments will enforce the international regulations. This is accepted because it is generally understood that the benefits of avoiding interference outweigh the disadvantages of regulation. In contrast, there are serious questions regarding the extent to which governments should regulate non-radio telecommunications, and the questions arise both at national and international level. As outlined above in Chapter 1, the ITRs trace their origin back to the times when telecommunications were primarily provided by state monopolies, but this is no longer the case, so indeed such questions are appropriate. In particular, it is appropriate to question whether competition at the international level is adequately provided by privatized and liberalized regimes, or whether additional measures should be taken to promote competition and to ensure efficient markets at the international level.

---

[1] But in keeping with other recent conferences, such as the WIPO 2013 Annual Meeting.

[2] Indeed this has long been the view of the United States, see p. 3.

[3] Provided in the ITU Radio Regulations, which is a very long and detailed technical document. This document is a treaty, but in many countries it is not subject to ratification by parliament, rather it is enacted by executive decree.

Europe, Brazil, India and other non-aligned states could have been expected to be a moderating force, able to help to achieve a compromise. But the US was able to influence many European countries, so that, during the conference, Europe was mostly aligned with the USA.

Nevertheless, the final compromise text proposed by the Chairman did reflect many European positions and it was an attempt to provide a solution that would be acceptable to the developing countries and to Europe.

Thus it came as a surprise that European countries refused to sign the compromise text. Indeed, given that only 6 paragraphs out of the 77 paragraphs of the main treaty text were controversial, one could have expected countries to sign while expressing reservations.

The meetings of the European Union states were open only to those Member States, and during the conference there was no public information available regarding the discussions. However, subsequently published information shows that a majority of the European Union states were willing to sign the treaty[4], but some countries (led by Sweden, UK, and the Netherlands)[5] took the view that the treaty should not be signed and the European Commission argued that it could not be signed until further study regarding whether it contradicted some elements of the formal decision of the Council of Europe (see p. 74).

Therefore the members of the European Union, plus Norway and Switzerland, decided as a block not to sign the treaty at the end of the conference and to consider subsequently whether or not to sign it. (At the time of publication of this book, the matter was still under consideration.)

Thus, on the last day of the conference, 89 Member States signed the treaty, while 55 did not.[6] Of the 55, a majority stated that they needed to conduct further consultations before deciding whether to accede, whereas the others[7] stated that they could not envisage acceding to the treaty.

As noted above, the compromise text attempted to cater to the positions expressed by the majority of the European countries, albeit not to the more extreme positions of some of the European countries, so the conference leadership team and many non-European countries were disappointed when the European countries stated that they would not sign the treaty.

---

[4] See Council of the European Union, 2013. Document DS 1335/13, 24 February 2013, "Outcome of the World Conference on International Telecommunications (WCIT)", publicly available at <http://www.hill-a.ch/wcit>.

[5] Various private communications.

[6] The split was along the same lines as those seen in other intergovernmental discussions, that is, the US and its allies versus other countries. See for example New, William, 2013d. "WIPO Folklore Talks Stalling; Work Continues On New Draft Text", *Intellectual Property Watch*, 18 July 2013; and New (2013).

[7] In the author's understanding of the declarations made during the last four plenary meetings, only the US and Canada stated that they could not consider acceding to the treaty. Other non-signatory states reserved their position pending further consultations.

Conference Structure and Work

Before analyzing the compromise text that was proposed by the Chairman, formally approved by the Conference, and signed by 62% of the Member States present and accredited to sign, it is necessary to explain the structure and working methods of the Conference.

A large number of individual proposals for revisions to the 1988 ITRs were submitted by Member States: 1275[8] in total. And there were over 1400 delegates from 151[9] Member States. Obviously it would be impossible to discuss 1275 proposals in a room with 1400 participants. Thus discussions were broken down, in accordance with ITU practice, by topics. In accordance with ITU rules, there were four statutory committees dealing with procedural issues (such as time planning, accreditation, the budget for the conference itself, and editorial alignment in six languages). Committee 5 was created by the conference to deal with the substantive issues. Again, in accordance with ITU practice, a hierarchical approach was adopted: two working groups were created under Committee 5, one to deal with article 6 (financial matters) and related proposals, one to deal with all other proposals. These groups were proposed by the membership and formally approved by the conference in accordance with ITU procedures.

However, recognizing that some issues were more controversial, while others were less so, the management team (Chairman and Secretariat) had prepared a finer subdivision, allocating each individual proposal by topic and each topic to a sub-working group. The initial plan provided for 18 sub-working groups (the topics being, for example, numbering misuse, calling line identification, spam, etc). The overall plan was not published, rather, as issues were discussed in the working groups, sub-working groups were created, in accordance with the usual ITU working practices. Thus the actual number of sub-working groups was not identical to that originally planned. Nevertheless, the original planning proved valuable because it allowed sub-working groups to be scheduled so as to minimize overlaps. Despite the planning, there were overlaps, and some delegations complained about that, in particular at the end of the first week of the conference.

Preparation of documents for the sub-working groups was greatly facilitated by the proposal management database that ITU has been using and developing for the past several years. Each individual proposal (that is, each proposal to change a particular provision, or to leave it unchanged, or to delete it) is coded with the reference number of the provision, the source of the proposal and other fields. At WCIT, each proposal was also allocated to a sub-working group. The proposal management system is capable of automatically producing the agenda (which references the source documents for the proposals to be discussed) and the input document (compilation of all proposals to be discussed) for each sub-working group.

Certain issues had been identified as being relatively non controversial. Those issues were dealt with directly by the plenary sessions during the first week of the Conference. Thus, some parts of the ITRs were already approved during the first week.

---

[8] Source: ITU.

[9] Not all Member States were accredited to sign, hence the discrepancy between the 151 participating Member States and the 144 accredited to sign.

With the agreement of the Conference, certain key issues were dealt with in a sub-group chaired by the Chairman of the Conference. Other issues were first introduced in the working groups, then discussed in detail in sub-working groups, then brought back to the working group to resolve any outstanding issues. In ITU practice, text that is not fully agreed is shown in square brackets. So sub-working groups would present to their parent group text which might contain square brackets.

It was originally planned that issues shown as square brackets would be resolved in the working parties, or, failing that, in Committee 5. The working party dealing with non-financial issues was able to resolve a certain number of issues, but many remained. Once the working groups had finished, given the time pressure, and the interactions between various issues, the conference agreed to the Chairman's proposal to discontinue Committee 5 well before the end of the conference and to discuss all remaining issues in Plenary.

And the conference agreed to the Chairman's proposal that, in order to facilitate the work, he submit a consolidated draft for discussion by Plenary. The Chairman prepared that draft by compiling the provisions that had been approved during the first week with the outputs of the various sub-working groups, working groups, and Committee 5. However, the compilation was selective, in that proposals were excluded if it seemed clear that no consensus could be reached. The next section shows in detail which proposals were contained in the Chairman's draft and which were excluded.

In order to determine the proposals for which consensus could be reached, the Chairman and the Secretary-General conducted informal consultations, that is, they held meeting which were not part of the formal time plan of the conference.

Proponents of full transparency have criticized these meetings because they were not open the public. But it is a fact of life that, at times, sensitive negotiations have to be conducted outside the public view, and this is commonly accepted[10], so long as the outcomes of such negotiations are subject to public scrutiny and approval.

And indeed such meetings are normal practice in ITU. At WCIT, three such meetings were held.[11] The first was held by the Chairman on 10 December. That meeting was open to representatives from the regional groups[12], but there were no

---

[10] See for example *Sophie in 't Veld vs European Commission* (2013). Paragraph 119 of that judgment states "Secondly, it cannot be denied, and the applicant herself admits in the reply, that the negotiation of international agreements can justify, in order to ensure the effectiveness of the negotiation, a certain level of discretion to allow mutual trust between negotiators and the development of a free and effective discussion. As the Commission points out, any form of negotiation necessarily entails a number of tactical considerations of the negotiators, and the necessary cooperation between the parties depends to a large extent on the existence of a climate of mutual trust."

[11] The author acted as Secretary for all three meetings. The account that follows is based on the author's contemporaneous notes.

[12] Meaning representatives of Member States. ITU does not put any limitations on who can represent a Member State and indeed many Member State delegations included people who were not government employees. For example, the US delegation contained many employees of private companies or civil society organizations.

limits on participation (apart from the size of the room) and about 150 people were present. At this meeting, the following key issues were identified as being difficult[13]:

1. Internet and proposed definitions including ICTs
2. Article 6
3. Security
4. Spam
5. Routing
6. Binding nature of ITU-T Recommendations and references to Recommendations of ITU vs. ITU-T
7. Use of the terms OA or ROA

These issues were difficult for the following reasons: (1) as noted earlier, any reference to Internet was considered anathema by the US and some other countries, and the proposed definitions of ICTs clearly included Internet, even if that term was not explicitly mentioned; (2) as noted earlier, any changes to charging and accounting were sensitive, in particular in light of proposals related to ETNO's call for restrictions on net neutrality regulations (see p. 31); (3) and (4) as noted earlier, the US and some other countries argued that any provisions regarding security or spam could result in restrictions on freedom of speech; (5) some of the routing proposals could be used to impose restrictions to commercial agreements and/or to facilitate surveillance; (6) binding incorporation of entire Recommendations could lead to divergent interpretations of the treaty; (7) some countries took the view that "recognized operating agencies" (ROAs) no longer existed, so the treaty should apply to "operating agencies" (OAs), while other countries took the view that this would be an unacceptable expansion of the scope of the treaty (see p. 64 for a more detailed discussion of this particular issue).

The following issues were identified as being less difficult:

8. Quality of service found in articles 3
9. Art. 3.2 on provision of facilities
10. Art. 3.5 on misuse
11. Art. 3.6 on calling line identification (CLI)
12. Art. 4.1 and 4.2
13. Art. 5.1
14. Art. 5.2
15. Art. 5.3
16. Free notification of emergency numbers
17. Art. 9

These issues were less difficult for the following reasons: (8) there was general agreement not to impose any quality of service requirements, but to retain a reference to quality of service, thus the issue was one of drafting, not principle; (9) this was also a matter of drafting; (10) and (11) there was general agreement that provisions on misuse and calling line identification could be included provided they were drafted so as to exclude clearly any Internet-related names, numbers, and addresses; (12), (13), (14), and (15) there was general agreement to maintain the existing text

---

However, Member States are free to impose rules within their own delegations, and to restrict speaking rights or attendance at selected meetings.

[13] Listed in the order in which they were presented at the meeting.

with some drafting changes to adapt it to the current environment; (16) there was general agreement that a provision could be added; (17) there was general agreement to retain the existing provision with some editorial changes.

Following discussions, a way forward was identified. Given the informal nature of the meeting, this way forward was not formally agreed, but it was generally accepted as a way to progress the work. The main points of dissension that remained were the use of the terms OA/ROA, the proposed Internet provisions, the proposed routing provisions, and the proposed security and spam articles.

The participants in this informal meeting were invited to consult with other participants in the conference and to return for an additional informal consultation. This was done primarily in regional coordination meetings but also in meeting of national delegations and in bilateral or multi-lateral meetings.

The Chairman held the additional informal consultation on the morning of 11 December. Most participants expressed support for use of the term "authorized operating agency" instead of OA/ROA, recognizing that this would align the ITRs with the change made in 1998 to the ITU Constitution (see p. 73). Little progress was made regarding the other issues.

The final informal consultation was held by the Secretary-General on 11 December, following the Chairman's consultation. This consultation was limited to four representatives from each of the six regional groups.[14] At this meeting, it was indicated that the proponents of treaty provisions regarding the Internet would be willing to withdraw those proposals if a resolution regarding the Internet could be approved. The Secretary-General was asked to draft such a resolution, and he did so, and presented it to the meeting. The text presented to the meeting was identical to the text that was subsequently approved as Resolution 3. There were no substantive comments made at the meeting regarding that draft resolution, but many delegates did state that they would reserve their formal decision until they saw the full compromise text that the Chairman was expected to propose for consideration by the conference. All but one region expressed support for the Chairman's proposal to use the term "authorized operating agency" instead of OA or ROA. No progress was made regarding other issues, but the various regional positions were clearly identified and so it became possible to envisage a compromise proposal that could get wide (albeit not unanimous) support.

The management team (Chairman, Secretary-General and senior members of the Secretariat) then proceeded to prepare the compromise text which excluded the more controversial proposals.

Analysis of the Compromise Text

It is instructive at this stage to list the various compromises made by what were essentially two sides. The tables below show the proposals made by one or the other side that were or were not included in the compromise text proposed by the Chairman. The tables show only proposals for actual new or revised text, not proposals

[14] Africa, Americas, Arab States, Asia-Pacific, Europe, and Regional Commonwealth in the field of Communications (Russian Federation and other countries previously associated with the Soviet Union). Some countries are in more than one regional group.

that called for no text to be added or modified. The tables show only the more significant and controversial proposals, not minor proposals.

The non-signatories opposed all the proposals shown on the left-hand column of the table below.

Proposals not included in the Chairman's compromise text

Proposals made by some of the 89 signatories	Proposals made by some of the 55 non-signatories
Extension of scope to Operating Agencies (OAs)	Restriction of scope to Recognized Operating Agencies (ROAs)
Extension to ICT	Purely liberalized approach to broadband deployment[19]
Various new definitions[15]	
References to Recommendations of the ITU instead of ITU-T Recommendations[16]	
Making some ITU Recommendations mandatory	
Routing transparency	
Use of the terms "naming, addressing and identification"[17]	
Provisions on data protection, privacy, cybersecurity, cybercrime	
Provisions regarding Internet	
Cost-oriented charges [18]	
General price transparency	
Fair compensation for traffic carried/terminated	

[15] These were numerous, and in some cases they were not referenced in substantive articles, so we do not list them in detail.

[16] There are ITU-R Recommendations, and also some ITU-D Recommendations.

[17] Many OECD countries took the position that use of such terms necessarily implied a reference to the Internet, and this despite the fact that such terms were defined and used in ITU well before the development of the Internet. Needless to say, this position was not well appreciated by the developing countries.

[18] This issue, and the ones listed below, were included in the first version of the Chairman's draft, but in square brackets, because discussions on those issues were still taking place in a sub-working group. Pursuant to the results of the discussion in the sub-working group, they were removed from the draft presented for formal approval.

[19] This proposal was actually contained in a proposed revised Resolution, which later became a proposed new Resolution. However, the operative part of the Resolution could have been proposed as treaty text.

Restrictions on taxation Restrictions on network neutrality Provisions regarding fraud[20] Alternative dispute resolution for international connectivity matters including Internet[21]	

See under Resolution 5 in Chapter 7 for a discussion of the provisions listed above that are related to financial matters.

The provisions regarding Internet were contained in contributions from the Russian Federation[22] and, subsequently, from a group of Member States.[23] The contributions in question were never added to the agenda of any WCIT session and were therefore not discussed by WCIT. This deliberate decision by the Chairman created some confusion and uncertainty, but it was accepted by the proponents of the proposals so long as a resolution regarding the Internet was approved, so the Chairman proposed what became WCIT Resolution 3 as part of the compromise package (see below for the outcome of that proposal).

There were various versions of proposed treaty text for Internet. The last proposal[24] (which, again, was never introduced or discussed) was:

a) Internet governance shall be effected through the development and application by governments, the private sector and civil society of shared

[20] Defined as use of any telecommunications facilities, resources or services with the intention of avoiding payment, without correct payment, with no payment at all, by making someone else pay, or by using a wrongful or criminal deception in order to obtain a financial or personal gain from the use of those facilities, resources or services. For more details, see the discussion under Resolution 5 in Chapter 7.

[21] It must be stressed that there were no proposals to create any new dispute resolution body, nor to give any new powers to ITU to resolve disputes; the proposals were in the nature of exhortations to make use of well-known dispute resolution methods such as international arbitration. See also the discussion under Resolution 5 in Chapter 7.

[22] See WCIT document 27 revision 1.

[23] See WCIT document 47, submitted by Algeria, Saudi Arabia, Bahrain, China, United Arab Emirates, Russian Federation, Iraq, Sudan. The intent to present this document was first mentioned on Friday 7 December, when it was stated that it was a compromise proposal. Non-authentic versions of the document quickly circulated and it became apparent to all delegates that the document did not contain a compromise but rather a compilation of the more extreme proposals. On the basis of private communications, it appears that the intent of this document was to express frustration with the progress of the work and to indicate that there might be significant support for some of the more extreme proposals. However, in the author's opinion, this proposal actually hardened positions, see the discussion in the Postscript.

[24] See WCIT document 47.

principles, norms, rules, decision-making procedures and programmes that shape the evolution and use of the Internet[25].

b) Member States shall have equal rights to manage the Internet, including in regard to the allotment, assignment and reclamation of Internet numbering, naming, addressing and identification resources and to support for the operation and development of basic Internet infrastructure.

c) Member States shall have the sovereign right to establish and implement public policy, including international policy, on matters of Internet governance, and to regulate the national Internet segment, as well as the activities within their territory of operating agencies providing Internet access or carrying Internet traffic.

d) Member States should endeavour to establish policies aimed at meeting public requirements with respect to Internet access[26] and use, and at assisting, including through international cooperation, administrations and operating agencies in supporting the operation and development of the Internet. Member States should ensure that administrations and operating agencies cooperate in ensuring the integrity, reliable operation and security of the national Internet segment[27], direct relations for the carrying of Internet traffic[28] and the basic Internet infrastructure[29].

These proposals are either recitals of what had been previously agreed in forums such as the World Summit on the Information Society (WSIS)[30], or, in the author's view, assertions of applicable national law[31]. And they refer to a relatively narrow definition of "Internet", comprising only the network itself and not the services that

---

[25] Defined as "*Internet*: An international conglomeration of interconnected telecommunication networks which provides for the interaction of connected information systems and their users, by carrying their traffic using a single system of numbering, naming, addressing, identification, protocols and procedures that is defined by Internet Standards."

[26] Defined as "*Internet Access*: The ability to interact through the exchange of Internet traffic with any information systems connected to the telecommunication networks that constitute the Internet".

[27] Defined as "*National Internet Segment*: Telecommunication networks or parts thereof which are located within the territory of the respective State and used to carry Internet traffic and/or provide Internet access."

[28] Defined as "*Internet Traffic*: Traffic generated by interacting information systems connected to the telecommunication networks that constitute the Internet."

[29] Defined as "*Basic Internet Infrastructure*: Telecommunication facilities and information systems which are vitally important for ensuring integrity, reliable operation and security of the Internet."

[30] See in particular paragraphs 29 ff. of the Tunis Agenda.

[31] National laws have routinely been applied to the Internet, see for example Gringras, Clive, 1997. *The Laws of the Internet,* Butterworths; Goldsmith and Wu (2006); Reed, Chris, 2012. *Making Laws for Cyberspace,* Oxford University Press; Reidenberg, Joel, 2005. "Technology and Internet Jurisdiction", 153 *University of Pennsylvania Law Review*, p. 1951; Brownsword, Roger, 2012. "The shaping of our on-line worlds: getting the regulatory environment right", *International Journal of Law and Information Technology*, vol. 20, p. 272. See also Hill (2014).

are offered on top of the network. However, needless to say, they provoked great consternation at WCIT, because most participants were of the view that Internet matters should not be discussed explicitly at WCIT, and this because it was understood that it would be very controversial to include explicitly in a treaty what had been agreed in a non-treaty context, or what was a de facto situation not explicitly covered by an existing treaty.

And indeed, as stated previously, these proposals were not discussed at WCIT. But the Chairman's proposal to deal with the Internet issues in the form of a Resolution proved to be unacceptable to a number of Member States (most developed countries and some developing countries) and that Resolution was adopted in an unusual manner: after a long and inconclusive discussion, the Chairman asked for a "temperature of the room" then, noting a strong majority in favor of the Resolution, he ruled that the Resolution was approved. This ruling was not formally challenged, so it stood. Formally, it was not a vote, but in practice it felt like a vote to many delegates. The ITU has a tradition of agreeing by consensus, but the term "consensus" is not defined in ITU. The practice in ITU is the same as that of other UN agencies: consensus is achieved when there is no formal opposition to a decision and no call for a vote. But in ITU it is common to continue discussions until no (or very little) opposition is expressed, and not to force an expression of formal opposition or a call for a vote. That is, it is unusual in ITU to cut off discussions and count on there being no formal opposition to a decision.[32]

The discussion and decision regarding this Resolution took place after midnight on Wednesday 12 December, that is, in the early hours of 13 December, which was in effect the last day during which the conference could work on the text of the provisions. The management team, and the delegates, were concerned that progress needed to be made and that no more time should be spent to discuss an issue on which there were clearly fundamentally differing views. Nevertheless, the action by the Chairman was unexpected because, for the previous 7 working days, he had patiently accepted continuing discussions of various issues for which there were fundamentally different views. In the author's opinion, this unexpected and unusual action increased the already high tensions and made it more difficult to find an agreement on other issues, see the discussion in the Postscript.

The proposed resolution[33] regarding broadband access was initially well accepted, but criticized subsequently. A final discussion of matters related to financial issues took place early in the morning on 13 December and the management team had planned to reopen discussions on this proposed resolution. But by then the atmosphere of the conference had become very tense, and the proponent of the resolution (the USA) withdrew it and requested that the Chairman of the meeting not discuss the matter. (We note in passing that an essentially identical text was subsequently approved as Opinion 2 of the 2013 World Telecommunication Policy Forum.)

---

[32] That practice is set forth, for example, in a letter of 17 June 2002 from Hans Correll, UN Under-Secretary for Legal Affairs and UN Legal Counsel to Mr Harndallaz Zedan, Executive Secretary of the Convention on Biological Diversity.

[33] WCIT document 9 add. 2.

The initial proposals regarding routing transparency were subject to ambiguous interpretations. After considerable discussion, the sub-working group dealing with that issue proposed the following for consideration by the conference[34]: "Member States may seek information on the international route of their traffic, where [technically, financially and legally] feasible. Member States shall cooperate - consistent with their national laws [and respective international obligations] - to provide this information to the Member State concerned." However, there was strong opposition to the very principle of such a provision, so it was not included in the Chairman's proposal to the conference.

Most of the non-signatories[35] opposed all the proposals shown on the left-hand column of the table below that are not included in the right-hand column. Several non-signatories opposed some of the proposals shown in the right-hand column.

Proposals included in the Chairman's compromise text

Proposals made by some of the 89 signatories	Proposals made by some of the 55 non-signatories
Respect of human rights	Respect of human rights
Transparency of mobile roaming prices and other provisions on roaming	Transparency of mobile roaming prices and other provisions on roaming
Proper use of international telecommunication numbering resources	Proper use of international telecommunication numbering resources
Charging and accounting provisions	Charging and accounting provisions[36]
Provision of calling line identification	
Enabling implementation of regional telecommunication traffic exchange points	
Provision of information on emergency call numbers	
Security and robustness of networks	
Combating spam	
Energy efficiency/e-waste	
Accessibility	

34 See WCIT DT 46 Rev.1.

35 Representative of a few of the non-signatory countries had supported various provisions during the discussions, but, after consulting with their capital, stated that they could not sign the treaty, pending further study. Such changes in positions were no doubt the result of lobbying from the United States.

36 The nature of the proposals regarding charging and accounting made by the two sides was not identical, see the discussion in Chapter 6 under Article 8.

For two key issues, the Chairman proposed a compromise that was not directly derived from any proposals submitted to the conference.

The first such issue was the question of the entities to which the treaty applies. The 1988 ITRs use the term "administrations and recognized private operating agencies". It was generally agreed that, since the term "administration" refers to the agency of a Member State that represents that state at the ITU, there was no need to use this term in the treaty text (except in Appendix 2). However, there was sharp disagreement regarding the term "recognized private operating agency", with some Member States preferring to use the term "recognized operating agency" (ROA) and others the term "operating agency" (OA). One Member State[37] suggested using ROA or OA selectively according to the nature of the substantive provisions of the treaty. There was also an informal suggestion to avoid using either term in the treaty, by reformulating all the provisions to avoid use of either term; however this option was not seriously explored.

Extensive discussions were held regarding this sensitive and important issue and it was pointed out that, because of a change to the ITU Constitution agreed in 1998, the ITRs had to be applied to "authorized operating agencies".[38] However, the US did not agree with this approach and proposed other alternatives, in particular involving use of the term "public correspondence". But that term is defined[39] as "any telecommunication which the offices and stations must, by reason of their being at the disposal of the public, accept for transmission". Adoption of this approach would have restricted the treaty to entities that mostly no longer exist (those that must provide service under national law) and, more importantly, would have contradicted no. 38 (Article 6) of the ITU Constitution which provides that Member States are bound to take the necessary steps to impose the observance of the provisions of the ITRs upon operating agencies authorized by them to establish and operate telecommunications and which engage in international services. In accordance with no. 32 (Article 4) of the ITU Constitution, in the case of inconsistency between a provision of the Constitution and a provision of the ITRs, the Constitution shall prevail.

Thus a large majority of the Member States accepted the Chairman's proposal regarding this issue, which, again, merely aligned the 2012 ITRs with the 1998 Constitution.

The second key issue was the question of whether or not to include articles regarding security and spam. There was strong support for their inclusion, but also strong opposition. The main argument against inclusion was that these articles related to the content of communications, whereas content is generally considered to be outside the scope of the ITU[40] (see also the discussion regarding Prism on pages 21 and 42). So, as a compromise, the Chairman proposed to include a provision in the purpose and scope that would explicitly exclude content. The Chairman's initial proposal was to add "to the exclusion of their content" to 1.1(a), so that it would

---

[37] Brazil, see WCIT document 18.

[38] See WCIT DT 30 and its revisions and also p. 73.

[39] No. 1004 of the ITU Constitution.

[40] But there are exceptions: the ITU does discuss measures to protect children online, and some of those measures are related to content.

have read: "These Regulations establish general principles which relate to the provision and operation of international telecommunication services offered to the public as well as to the underlying international telecommunication transport means used to provide such services, to the exclusion of their content." This proposal was accepted in principle, but it was felt that a better formulation could be found. Various Member States conducted consultations and it was subsequently agreed to add the following to 1.1(a): "These Regulations do not address the content-related aspects of telecommunications."

The agreed provision is broader than the original one, because it refers to "content-related" and not just content.

However, despite this provision, some Member States continue to consider that the security and spam articles are related to content and thus cannot be accepted (but, in the author's view, such criticism is unfounded, see p. 75).

On a different issue, a number of Member States (developing countries) did not accept the fact that the Chairman's proposal did not include any text related to non-discriminatory access to telecommunications networks. Cuba had originally proposed a treaty provision to that effect[41], but it proved controversial and no compromise could be found, nor was it agreed to adopt a Resolution instead of treaty text[42] (and this despite the fact that a related Resolution had been adopted by WTSA-12 just prior to WCIT: Resolution 69).

Despite repeated attempts by the Chairman and the Secretary-General to avoid inclusion of such a provision in the ITRs, the Conference finally decided, by a majority vote (which is unusual for the ITU) to adopt what is now the third paragraph of the Preamble. That provision has been severely criticized, but the criticism is unfounded, see p. 72. Be that as it may, it was the inclusion of that provision which prompted the European Union countries to decide not to sign the treaty[43].

Impact of the Media Campaign

To conclude the analysis of the compromise text, we provide an account of the discussions concerning the provision on respect of human rights. As noted above (see p. 40), there had been a media campaign suggesting that the ITRs could be used to impose censorship or restrict freedom of expression, and this despite the fact that such matters are exhaustively dealt with in the ITU Constitution and so WCIT could neither restrict nor broaden freedom of expression.

In reaction to this media campaign, Tunisia (supported by many other states, both developing and developed) proposed[44] to add a provision to recognize explicitly the

---

[41] See WCIT document 26. The proposed treaty text was: "Member States shall refrain from taking unilateral and/or discriminatory actions that could impede another Member State's access to public Internet sites."

[42] See WCIT DT/53.

[43] See Council of the European Union (2013).

[44] See WCIT document 25.

human rights provided for in Article 19 of the Universal Declaration of Human Rights and in Article 19 of the UN Covenant on Civil and Political Rights.[45]

During the first discussion of this topic many countries (both developing and developed) stated that they did not oppose the intent of the proposal, but felt that it was not necessary to add any text to the ITRs because the matter was already covered by the ITU Constitution and the cited UN instruments. As a consequence, it was agreed not to add any text to the ITRs and to issue a press release[46] confirming that the outcome of WCIT could not in any way restrict human rights or freedom of expression.

However, some countries (both developing and developed) felt that some text should be added to the treaty and they subsequently proposed[47] text for inclusion in the Preamble. So the matter was reopened and, following discussion, the new proposal was accepted, despite continued statements to the effect that the new text was not needed.

In the author's opinion, the discussions on the human rights issue were an unnecessary distraction, which used up time that could better have been used to discuss other issues, and which contributed to create tension and lack of trust. Since the ITRs can neither restrict nor broaden freedom of speech, from the legal point of view there was no reason to discuss this topic at WCIT. Of course not all discussions are purely legal and, from a symbolic point of view, the discussion could have been useful. However, as noted above, the discussion was largely triggered by the pre-WCIT media campaign and this must be considered in light of the revelations regarding US surveillance programs (see p. 21 and 42) parts of which, according to some, are not consistent with human rights,[48] and in light of the very differing national views regarding acceptable freedom of speech (see p. 81). Thus there was a certain amount of hypocrisy in the discussions, which made them difficult and no doubt affected the conference as a whole.

---

[45] The rights as formulated in those instruments are substantially identical to those provided in the ITU Constitution.

[46] ITU, 2012f. "World Conference on International Telecommunications affirms right to freedom of information online", *Press Release*, 4 December 2012.

[47] See WCIT document 44.

[48] A US judge held that "one aspect of the proposed collection [of information] – the 'upstream collection' of Internet transactions containing multiple communications – is, in some respects, deficient on statutory and constitutional grounds", see United States Foreign Intelligence Surveillance Court, Bates, John D., 2011. *Redacted*, , 3 October 2011. And several Latin American countries criticized the US surveillance at a UN Security Council meeting, see Shea, Carla, 2013."Latin America Condemns US Espionage at United Nations Security Council", *Global Research,* 17 August 2013; and United Nations, "Cooperation between United Nations, Regional, Subregional Organizations 'mainstay' of International Relations, Security Council Hears Throughout Day-Long Debate", *Press Release* regarding 6 August 2013 meeting.

Was WCIT-12 a Success or a Failure?

Various commentators have taken the view that WCIT was a failure[49], even though this is not the official view of the ITU itself. Indeed, it is hard to see how or why the ITU, as an institution, could consider a conference to be a failure when that conference did approve, in accordance with the ITU's procedures, a treaty, and when that treaty was signed on the last day of the conference by a majority of the states present and having authority to sign. In this context, it should be stressed that most treaties are not signed immediately after they are negotiated, so having 89 signatories on the day after a treaty is approved can be considered a success when compared to other treaty negotiations.

However, the ITU has a long tradition of consensus[50], and it had been expected that consensus would also be reached at this conference, so that the resulting treaty could be signed by a vast majority of the ITU Member States.

The conference failed to reach consensus for a number of reasons, including fundamentally different views about certain issues, but also because of external pressures engendered by a media campaign which, in the author's view (as noted above), can only be characterized as misinformation, in the sense that it stressed a supposed threat to free speech, whereas in reality the conference had no power or ability to change the free speech provisions that govern telecommunications since the founding of the ITU.[51]

Those provisions, found in the ITU Constitution[52], stipulate that Member States reserve the right to cut off, in accordance with their national law, any private telecommunications which may appear dangerous to the security of the State or contrary to its laws, to public order or to decency.

In summary it can be said that WCIT-12 was a failure in the sense that:

- It did not achieve its desired goal, which was full consensus.
- It resulted in a split[53] amongst the membership, resulting in a vote, which is unusual in ITU.
- Media coverage was partly inaccurate, influenced by a misinformation campaign.

---

[49] See for example Downes, Larry, "Requiem for failed UN Telecom Treaty: No One Mourns the WCIT" *Forbes*, 17 December 2012; and van Gelder, Stéphane "Is WCIT Failure the Start of a Digital Cold War?" *CircleID*, 14 December 2012.

[50] In ITU practice, consensus does not necessarily mean unanimity. Rather, it refers to the absence of formal objection. That is, if the Chairman of a meeting announces that something is approved, and if nobody formally objects to that announcement, then the matter is considered as having been approved by consensus.

[51] Pursuant to Article 4 of the ITU Constitution, in the case of inconsistency between a provision of the Constitution and a provision of the ITRs, the Constitution shall prevail.

[52] Article 34. It should be noted that this provision is essentially identical to the more general formulation found in Article 19 of the UN Covenant on Civil and Political Rights.

[53] See p. 54.

WCIT-12 was a success in the sense that:

- There was active participation from all parts of the world.
- There was broad agreement: 90% of the treaty is not controversial, 10% was agreed by 62% of Member States present and accredited to sign.[54]
- Key issues were identified and discussed.
- It was agreed to continue discussions with a view to reaching consensus.

[54] As stated above, of the Member States present and accredited to sign, 89 signed and 55 did not. As we will see in more detail later, only certain specific provisions of the treaty were controversial. Those provisions are contained in 6 paragraphs out of a total of 77 paragraphs that comprise the main text of the treaty.

CHAPTER 5

Overall Analysis of the 2012 treaty

As many commentators have pointed out, the agreements reached in ITU historically reflected a balance between competing interests and a combination of mandatory requirements and escape clauses. This was due to the general recognition that some basic rules have to be followed in order to enable international telecommunications to work, offset by the strong desire of many countries to assert their sovereign rights to conduct their telecommunications business as they please and in furtherance of their national interests.[1]

It was intended that the 2012 ITRs would have the same characteristics, and indeed the compromise proposal put forward by the Chairman, and approved by the conference, was considered by most participants to reflect an acceptable compromise.

However, it was not considered to be an acceptable compromise by some countries, in particular the United States, which was supported by other countries. As noted above, on the last day of the conference, 89 Member States signed the treaty, while 55 did not (see p. 54).[2]

Content of the 2012 ITRs

Much of the 1988 ITRs were retained with some editorial revisions to bring them up to date. In particular, the article on charging and accounting was significantly streamlined and brought into alignment with modern practices. In addition, new provisions were added to prevent misuse of telephone numbers, to ensure transmission of calling line identification, to ensure transparency of international roaming prices, to improve network security, to combat spam, to improve energy-efficiency and reduce e-waste, and to facilitate use of telecommunications by people with disabilities. The list below shows the content (not the titles) of the articles of the 2012 ITRs; the underlined items indicate provisions that were added in 2012.

Preamble (human rights, right to access)

[1] See for example Codding and Rutkowski (1982), p. 221; and Mestmaecker (1987), p. 14.

[2] Much of this chapter was originally published in Hill (2013); the material is included here with the kind permission of Oxford University Press.

Article 1: Purpose and scope (not content-related, Authorized Operating Agencies)

Article 2: Definitions

Article 3: Right to communicate at good technical quality; countries to coordinate their infrastructure (misuse, Calling Line Identification, traffic exchange points)

Article 4: International telecom services to be made available to the public (roaming transparency, quality and competition)**Article 5:** Priority to be given to emergency communications (emergency number notification)

Article 5A: Network security

Article 5B: Combating spam

Article 6: Charging and accounting (commercial agreements, encourage investments, competitive wholesale pricing)

Article 7: Suspension of services

Article 8: Dissemination of information (Member States to communicate information to ITU)

Article 8A: Energy efficiency, E-waste

Article 8B: Accessibility

Article 9: Special arrangements

Article 10: Entry into force; reservations

Appendix 1: Accounting rate system

Appendix 2: Maritime telecommunications

Some provisions of the old Appendix 3 on service telecommunications were moved to Article 6

As we will see in more detail below, only certain specific provisions of the treaty were controversial. Those provisions are contained in 6 paragraphs out of a total of 77 paragraphs that comprise the main text of the treaty. One Resolution adopted by WCIT was also controversial. If that is included, then the controversial text comprises less than 2 pages out of the total 24 pages approved at the conference.[3]

That is, over 90% of the treaty is not controversial. However, there has been sharp criticism of the controversial portions of the treaty, resulting in a refusal to sign the treaty, even though a more usual approach would have been to sign the treaty while expressing reservations[4] with respect to the few provisions that have been criticized.

Criticism of the 2012 ITRs

It has been said that the WCIT outcomes establish a new international regulatory regime for the Internet and give new powers to the ITU. This new regime threatens the current multi-stakeholder model for Internet governance which has proven its worth, and it threatens economic growth and freedom of speech around the world.[5]

---

[3] See *Final Acts: Word Conference on International Telecommunications (Dubai, 2012).*

[4] See articles 19 ff. of the *Vienna Convention on the Law of Treaties.*

[5] See European Commission, 2012. "No change to telecoms and internet governance – EU Member States amongst dozens not signing proposed new International

In particular a provision in the Preamble of the ITRs creates new rights for states (which threaten established individual rights); new articles on security and spam invite governments to take content-based action which could result in regulation of speech on the Internet; a new Resolution represents a direct extension of ITU's role and scope into the Internet and shifts the emphasis from community and consensus to centralization through government action.[6]

Analysis of the Criticism

The criticism of the 2012 ITRs appears to be based on a superficial and out-of-context reading of the provisions in question. When analysed[7] correctly from the legal point of view[8], it can be seen that the new provision in the Preamble does not conflict with existing rights of individuals or of states; that the new provisions on security and spam cannot be understood to relate to content; and that the new Resolution does not in any way expand ITU's role and scope, while it does recognize the multi-stakeholder model agreed at WSIS.

Thus it is incorrect to conclude that the WCIT outcomes establish a new international regulatory regime for the Internet and give new powers to the ITU. Nor do they threaten the current multi-stakeholder model for Internet governance or free speech.

We will now analyse each of the criticized provisions, stressing in particular the ordinary meaning to be given to the terms of the treaty in their context and in the light of its object and purpose.

Preamble

The criticized provision in the Preamble states: "These Regulations recognize the right of access of Member States to international telecommunication services."

It has been stated[9] that this is an unprecedented new clause which is inconsistent with established principles of international law. It is a dilution of human rights as

Telecommunications Regulations (ITR) Treaty, remain 100% committed to open internet", memo 12/992 of 14 December 2012; the various witness statements made at: US Energy and Commerce Committee, 2013. US House of Representatives, *Hearing: Fighting for Internet Freedom, Dubai and Beyond*, 5 February 2013; and New, William, 2013e. "European Commission VP Kroes Urges Open Internet, Prods Copyright Owners" *Intellectual Property Watch*, 21 March 2013. Similar arguments were given by the US at the Conference as reasons for not signing the treaty, see Popescu, Adam, 2012. "5 Reasons Why the US Rejected the ITU Treaty", *readwrite.com*, 14 December 2012.

[6] ibid.

[7] The analysis is provided as an aid to all who wish to understand the ITRs, with the understanding that states retain the sovereign right to interpret the treaty. Consequently, states retain full responsibility for any use that they might make of the present analysis and for any acts of omission or commission arising out of their use (or not) of the analysis.

[8] See article 31 of the *Vienna Convention on the Law of Treaties*.

[9] See the sources cited above.

applied to the individual and creates new rights for governments to avoid international sanctions.

However, the ITRs must be understood in light of the ITU Constitution. Thus the cited clause of the Preamble recognizes a general right, but any Member State can, pursuant to Article 35 of the Constitution, cut off communications with any other Member State, for any reason whatsoever, provided it informs the Secretary-General.[10]

So the Preamble of the ITRs does not create any additional rights or obligations, it merely recognizes the rights and obligations that already existed under the Constitution.

Further, the language used in the Preamble of the ITRs refers to "Member States" not to "governments". That is, the provision recognizes the right of the Member State as a whole, including its citizens, and not just the right of the government of the Member State.

In addition, under the customary rules for interpreting international treaties, a preamble constitutes a legal and moral basis for interpreting the text of a treaty but does not normally contain rules of law.[11] That is, the preamble presents the scope of the treaty, its objectives and the general principles that inspired it, which serve to clarify the will of the parties to the treaty. A preamble normally does not contain binding provisions, but rather serves to assist in the interpretation of the treaty.

Thus, in principle, a clause in the preamble should not be considered as an operative provision.

Also, it is not clear why this provision should be considered "unprecedented". There are many treaty provisions that recognize rights and obligations of Member States, which rights and obligations affect their citizens. For example the cited Article 35 recognizes the right of a Member State to suspend communications with another Member State. Implicitly, it recognizes that, absent suspension, all Member States have the right to communicate with each other. And article 42 of the ITU Constitution recognizes the right of Member States to establish special arrangements.

Use of the term "authorized operating agency"

The criticized provision reads: 'These Regulations also contain provisions applicable to those operating agencies, authorized or recognized by a Member State, to establish, operate and engage in international telecommunications services to the public, hereinafter referred as "authorized operating agencies"'.

---

[10] The exact text is "Each Member State reserves the right to suspend the international telecommunication service, either generally or only for certain relations and/or for certain kinds of correspondence, outgoing, incoming or in transit, provided that it immediately notifies such action to each of the other Member States through the Secretary-General."

[11] See paragraph 2 of article 31 of the *Vienna Convention on the Law of Treaties*; *South West Africa (2nd Phase)*, 1966. *ICJ Rep.* p. 34, paragraph 50; and *Argentina v Chile*, 1977. *Reports Of International Arbitral Awards*, Vol. XXI pp.53-264, p. 89, paragraph 19.

The 1988 ITRs referred to "private recognized operating agencies", so it has been said[12] that the new provision extends the scope, which would now include many new entities such as Internet Service Providers (ISPs).

However, since 1998, by virtue of no. 38 (Article 6) of the ITU Constitution, the ITRs apply to "operating agencies authorized by [Member States] to establish and operate telecommunications and which engage in international services". The text of the 2012 ITRs is a mere alignment of the ITRs with the Constitution and does not change the scope of the ITRs regarding the entities to which they apply.

It must be noted that nobody has ever complained about the situation that prevailed under the old ITRs, so there is no reason to think that the new ITRs (which apply to exactly the same entities) could create problems.

In particular, it cannot be said that the new ITRs apply to private networks merely because of the adoption of the new provision regarding "authorized operating agencies" (AOA).

Indeed, Article 1 of the ITRs states that "These Regulations establish general principles which relate to the provision and operation of international telecommunication services offered to the public ...".

So the treaty only deals with services offered to the public.

So, even if an entity offering a private service is an AOA according to a national interpretation of no. 38 of the ITU Constitution, the ITRs would not apply to its activities.

That is, only the public offerings of an AOA are subject to the ITRs, and the word "public" was included in the criticized provision in order to make this clear.

Further, many ISPs would presumably not be considered to be within the scope of the ITRs because they do not operate an installation intended for an *international* telecommunication service[13] and thus would presumably not be considered to be an operating agency[14]. For sure a local ISP allows its customers to connect internationally, but it does that by itself interconnecting to an entity that operates installations intended for *international* telecommunications; thus it is the upstream entity that is an operating agency, not the local ISP. In other words, many local ISPs do not offer a telecommunication capability between telecommunication offices that are in or belong to different countries: they offer a telecommunication capability between the user and itself, but both of those are in the same country.

It must be stressed that, to the extent that the ITRs apply to some AOAs and to some ISPs, this was the case since 1998. As stated above, nobody has ever complained about the situation that prevailed under the old ITRs, so there is no reason to think that the new ITRs (which apply to exactly the same entities) could create problems.

---

[12] See the sources cited above.

[13] The term "international telecommunication service" is defined in the ITU Constitution as "the offering of a telecommunication capability between telecommunication offices or stations of any nature that are in or belong to different countries".

[14] The term "operating agency", is defined in the ITU Constitution as "Any individual, company, corporation or governmental agency which operates a telecommunication installation *intended for an international telecommunication service* or capable of causing harmful interference with such a service." (emphasis added).

Scope of the ITRs

There is no other change to Article 1 (which defines the Purpose and Scope of the treaty) that could be seen to broaden the scope of the ITRs. On the contrary, a provision has been added at the end of 1.1(a) to clarify that the ITRs must be understood as not applying to content; that new provision, if anything, restricts their scope. That provision states: "These Regulations do not address the content-related aspects of telecommunications."

The new provisions regarding misuse of numbering resources, transmission of calling line identification, creation of an enabling environment for the implementation of regional telecommunication traffic exchange points, security, spam, accessibility, and energy efficiency and e-waste cannot be viewed as expanding the scope of the treaty. Indeed, the term scope, in this context, refers to the area covered by the treaty.[15] That area is defined in Article 1 as "general principles which relate to the provision and operation of international telecommunication services offered to the public as well as to the underlying international telecommunication transport means used to provide such services", "facilitating global interconnection and interoperability of telecommunication facilities", and "promoting the harmonious development and efficient operation of technical facilities, as well as the efficiency, usefulness and availability to the public of international telecommunication services". This scope was not changed in the new ITRs and it clearly covers the new provisions.

Indeed, in its formal position taken prior to WCIT[16], the European Union supported proposals to maintain the current scope of the ITRs[17], but also supported measures to promote greater international cooperation in relation to the security of networks used for international telecommunications traffic[18].

That is, the formal European position was that a new provision on security could be added to the ITRs, while maintaining the scope unchanged. And this is exactly what was done in Dubai.

Regional telecommunication traffic exchange points

Provision 3.7 states: "Member States should create an enabling environment for the implementation of regional telecommunication traffic exchange points, with a view to improving quality, increasing the connectivity and resilience of networks, fostering competition and reducing the costs of international telecommunication interconnections."

---

[15] For ITU instruments, the authoritative version is the French version (see no. 32 of the ITU Constitution). The French version uses the term "portée" for "scope", thus clearly indicating that scope does refer to the extent of the matters covered by the treaty.

[16] European Commission, 2012a. "Proposal for a Council Decision Establishing the EU Position for the review of the International Telecommunications Regulations to be taken at the World Conference on International Telecommunications or its preparatory instances" (COM(2012) 430; 2012/0207 (NLE); of 2 August2012).

[17] ibid, (d) of Annex.

[18] ibid. (f) of Annex.

It has been stated[19] that this will elicit discussion on the location of the regional telecommunications exchange point, at regional level, since each country cannot have one.

However, it is important to note that the provision does not contain binding language: it says "should create".

Further, many countries have already taken actions, so the article would presumably have no impact on them.

There is nothing in the article regarding national traffic exchange points, so it cannot be said that the provision somehow restricts national initiatives or actions regarding exchange points. Obviously discussions between countries in a region have to take place if a regional exchange point is to be created, but that is a fact of life, not a consequence of the ITRs.

More fundamentally, there is general agreement that implementation of national and regional Internet exchange points should be encouraged, because it generally leads to improved Internet access at lower costs.[20]

Thus it is hard to understand why this provision should be criticized.

Security and robustness of networks; and Unsolicited bulk electronic communications

These two new articles[21] state:

> '**5A**: Member States shall individually and collectively endeavour to ensure the security and robustness of international telecommunication networks in order to achieve effective use thereof and avoidance of technical harm thereto, as well as the harmonious development of international telecommunication services offered to the public.'
>
> And
>
> '**5B**: Member States should endeavour to take necessary measures to prevent the propagation of unsolicited bulk electronic communications and minimize its impact on international telecommunication services.
>
> Member States are encouraged to cooperate in that sense.'

It has been said[22] that the security provision is not useful and may place restrictions or limitations on the Internet and the content it carries.

And it has been stated that the provision on unsolicited bulk electronic communications (spam) regulates Internet issues and invites governments to take content-based action and moves the treaty into the realm of regulating speech on the Internet.

---

19 See the sources cited above.

20 See for example Opinion 1 of the 2013 World Telecommunications Policy Forum, which can be found in the Chairman's Report <http://www.itu.int/md/S13-WTPF13-C-0016/en>.

21 Provisionally numbered 5A and 5B in the cited Final Acts. They are Articles 6 and 7 in the final version of the treaty.

22 See the sources cited above.

But the provision on spam does not contain binding language. Note “should endeavor” and “are encouraged”. So it is not clear how the article could “regulate” anything.

Further, many countries already have practices in place regarding security and spam, so the articles would presumably have no impact on them. And many have recognized that “you cannot be open online, nor free, if you are constantly at risk of hacking, spying, or identity theft”[23], meaning of course that security on the Internet must be improved.

Further, it must be stressed that any state is free to do whatever it wants today, within the limits of its human rights obligations and any security-related treaties to which it may have agreed to be bound.[24] More importantly, the ITRs are subordinate to the ITU Constitution, which recognizes human rights (and is consistent with the relevant UN instruments on human rights), so nothing in the ITRs can limit the human rights obligations of states. To make this clear, a provision was added to the Preamble of the ITRs which says “Member States affirm their commitment to implement these Regulations in a manner that respects and upholds their human rights obligations.”

Further, the following was added to Article 1 Purpose and Scope: “These Regulations do not address the content-related aspects of telecommunications.” In this context, the term content must be understood in accordance with its ordinary meaning[25], which is “that which is contained in a receptacle”, that is the actual content of a telecommunication.

Since both new articles must be interpreted in light of Article 1, which defines the scope of the treaty, and since, pursuant to that article, the ITRs do not address content, the articles on security and spam cannot be seen to be addressing content.

Indeed, Article 1 makes it clear that content is not a matter within the scope of the ITRs. This is consistent with the general consensus that content is not within the scope of the ITU. So content has to be dealt with either at the national level or by some body other than ITU or by some treaty other than the ITRs.

Thus, Article 5A is about security measures that do not depend on content. There are many such measures, and some are described in Recommendations ITU-T E.408 and X.805.

And Article 5B is about measures to counter spam that do not depend on content. There are many such measures (such as address-filtering[26] and identifying unusual traffic volumes generated by end-users[27]), and some are described in Recommenda-

---

[23] European Commissioner Kroes, cited in New (2013e).

[24] The author is not aware of any treaties regarding spam, so presumably there are no international limitations to national sovereignty with respect to countering spam, apart from the cited human rights provisions.

[25] Paragraph 1 of article 31 of the *Vienna Convention on the Law of Treaties*.

[26] This can take the form of blocking messages coming from certain IP addresses. The lists of addresses to block are published by various private organizations, see Mueller (2010), p. 166.

[27] A good description of this particular technique was given by Art Brooks, General Manager of the Internet Service Providers Association of South Africa, at the 8 July 2013 ITU Workshop on Countering and Combating spam <http://www.itu.int/

tions ITU-T X.1231 and X.1240; others are described by an industry group that combats spam[28].

Further, article 5A encourages countries to work collectively, and this could be understood to include cooperation to adopt appropriate security measures, and to cooperate when doing so. Indeed, WTSA Resolution 50 on cybersecurity, which was agreed by consensus, states[29] "that there is a need for national, regional and international strategies and initiatives to be harmonized to the extent possible, in order to avoid duplication and to optimize the use of resources"; and it invites Member States "to cooperate and participate actively in the implementation of this resolution and the associated actions." (See pages 21 and 42 above for a discussion regarding cooperation in light of the 2013 revelations regarding the US Prism surveillance program).

Similarly, article 5B encourages countries to cooperate, and this could be understood to include cooperation to adopt appropriate spam legislation, and to cooperate when doing so. Indeed WTSA Resolution 52 on countering and combating spam, which was agreed by consensus, invites Member States "to take appropriate steps to ensure that appropriate and effective measures are taken within their national and legal frameworks to combat spam and its propagation". And the Internet Society recognizes that strong international cooperation is required to combat spam.[30]

Subsequent to WCIT, the Results of the Seoul Conference on Cyberspace 2013[31] recalls that States have repeatedly affirmed the need for cooperative action against threats resulting from the malicious use of ICTs; and calls for consideration of cooperative actions.

Many countries have security initiatives and spam legislation. Presumably it would be desirable for countries to cooperate to adopt best practices in these areas.[32] That is, security initiatives and spam legislation that clearly do not impinge on human rights, that respect due process, and that do not excessively restrict commercial speech.

So it would appear that the treaty-level calls for collective security efforts and for cooperation to counter spam are rather positive, because they should make it less likely that some country would (perhaps unwittingly) adopt inappropriate measures.

That is, the call for collective action and cooperation appears to make it more likely that security measures and initiatives to combat spam would follow the best-practices models that are generally agreed.

---

en/ITU-T/Workshops-and-Seminars/spam/201307/Pages/default.aspx> accessed 15 July 2013.

[28] O'Reirdan, Michael, 2013. "Top 'ten' things to do about spam for an ISP", M3AAWG presentation to the Internet Society workshop Combating Spam for Policy Makers, 9 September 2013.

[29] In its *noting* b).

[30] See Internet Society, 2013a. *Spam*.

[31] See in particular 4 of the Seoul Framework, 2013,which is one of the Results of the Seoul Conference on Cyberspace 2013.

[32] In this context, see the testimony presented to the US Congress by cybersecurity experts, summarized in Olsen, Chris, 2013. "EWI Expert Testifies on the Hill", EastWest Institute, 24 July 2013.

Those who argue, in the alternative, that there are no possible non-content-related measures regarding security and spam are in effect arguing that the two articles are inoperative, because Article 1 (Purpose and Scope) excludes content-related aspects and prevails over articles 5A and 5B. The usual approach to such a situation would be to sign the treaty with a reservation of the form "we will not apply article 5B because we believe that it is inconsistent with the Purpose and Scope".

In any case, by virtue of the "no content" provision of Article 1, no country could invoke the ITRs as justification for imposing content-filtering. That is, since content is outside the scope of the ITRs, so is content-filtering.

Of course a country might impose content-filtering, but it could not invoke the ITRs as a legal basis for doing so. That is, the "necessary measures" referred to in article 5B cannot be understood to include content-filtering.

Paradoxically, those who refuse to implement article 5B on the grounds that it is related to content are in effect arguing against limitations on measures to counter spam. Indeed at present there aren't (to the author's knowledge) any international treaties that limit what states can do regarding spam, apart from obligations relating to human rights. If it is understood that article 5B does not relate to content, then that article puts an obligation on states not to deal with the content-related aspects of spam. That is a significant restriction. Those who state that article 5B applies to content are in effect denying the restriction and opting for the status quo, where there are no restrictions (apart from human rights) regarding how to deal with spam. And they are in effect creating a situation where there is no basis in international law (apart from human rights) to complain regarding anti-spam measures.

Similar considerations apply regarding article 5A on security: refusal to accept this article is tantamount to refusing to accept restrictions on security measures (apart from those arising out of human rights obligations).[33]

However, see page 81 for a discussion on differing views of freedom of speech and human rights. Those differing views did affect the discussions and decisions at WCIT.

Resolution 3: To foster an enabling environment for the greater growth of the Internet

The operative part of Resolution 3 invites ITU Member States to discuss Internet-related technical, development and public-policy issues within the mandate of ITU at various ITU forums; and to engage with all their stakeholders in this regard. And it instructs the Secretary-General of ITU to continue to take the necessary steps for ITU to play an active and constructive role in the development of broadband and the multi-stakeholder model of the Internet as expressed in §35 of the Tunis Agenda; and to support the participation of Member States and all other stakeholders, as appropriate, in the activities of ITU in this regard.

According to its critics[34], this resolution represents a direct extension of ITU's role and scope into the Internet; shifts the emphasis from community and consensus to

[33] One academic speculated that the strong US opposition to inclusion of any treaty text regarding security was indeed related to a refusal to accept any constraints in that area, see Mueller (2012). This seems prophetic in light of subsequent revelations regarding the Prism surveillance program, see pages 21 and 42.

centralization through government action; and its highly selective references to the WSIS outcome documents do not reflect previous international agreement on Internet policy and governance.

As a preliminary matter, it should be noted that no state formally objected[35] to this resolution, so it entered into force on 14 December 2012 and applies to all ITU Member States, regardless of whether or not they signed[36] the Final Acts.

Given that the cited Resolution explicitly restricts discussion to issues within the mandate of the ITU, and given that that mandate regarding Internet governance is established in various Plenipotentiary and Council Resolutions, it is incorrect to say that WCIT Resolution 3 expands ITU's role and scope.

The operative part of Resolution 3 invites Member States to engage with all stakeholders.

Thus, not only does it not shift the emphasis from the multi-stakeholder model towards top-down government action, on the contrary, it promotes multi-stakeholder consultations.

The operative part of Resolution 3 does not cite any WSIS outcome documents. Selective citations elsewhere in the Resolution cannot be understood as implying that other portions of the WSIS outcomes do not apply, in particular because WCIT has no power to modify or override, through a Resolution, the agreed WSIS outcomes.

Summary

It appears that criticism of the ITRs may not be based solely on the legal analysis, but also on political and economic considerations.[37] Indeed, as stated earlier, objection to selected provisions of a treaty is not usually considered a sufficient reason to refuse to sign the treaty because objections to specific articles can be expressed in reservations.

As we have seen above, there were important economic and political issues underlying the discussions at WCIT, and the refusal to sign may be more related to a desire to make a statement regarding those issues than to the actual consequences of signing the treaty. In particular, those issues include the extent to which national restrictions on freedom of speech should or should not be allowed to restrict com-

---

[34] See the sources cited above.

[35] Sweden and Qatar did make declarations criticizing this resolution, but those declarations did not contain a formal objection of the form "we will not apply this Resolution".

[36] The signature formality applies only to the treaty text properly speaking. No formal signature is required for the non-treaty text.

[37] Indeed it has been said that a desire by the US to maintain a certain hegemony regarding Internet matters affected the conference, see for example Touray, Karim, S., 2013. "Much Ado About WCIT-12 and Multi-Stakeholderism", *CircleID,* 22 January 2013. And it has been said that the fact that the ITU is insufficiently open and transparent affected the conference, see for example Malcolm, Jeremy, 2012. "WCIT: Freemasons, Internet memes and salt", *Digital News Asia,* 28 December 2012.

munications on the Internet, and discussions regarding the current funding and pricing model for the Internet.[38]

These debates are related to the differences of views between developing countries and developed countries that characterize discussions in many international forums. From that point of view, the refusal of most developed countries to sign the treaty can be seen as a denial of democracy at the international level, if one accepts the "one-country, one-vote" model prevalent in the United Nations. But of course many democratic countries are not comfortable with that model because they believe that many other countries are not democratic, so "one country, one-vote" does not result in truly democratic decisions.[39]

Regarding the economic issues, it is not disputed that the cost of establishing telecommunications in rural areas was traditionally higher than the cost in urban areas, and many countries compensate for this at the national level through "universal service funds".[40] It has been argued that such cost differentials might decrease with the increasing deployment of Internet.[41] Be that as it may, Internet is relatively less prevalent in developing countries, and costs of connecting to Internet are relatively higher.[42] Thus the question arises: should developed countries in some way subsidize telecommunications connections for developing countries? Such subsidies were prevalent in the international telephone system prior to 1988 but were largely discontinued following the adoption of the 1988 ITRs and subsequent agreements in the World Trade Organization (WTO).[43]

Not surprisingly, many developing countries are of the view that the current financial arrangements for Internet traffic are not satisfactory and they seek ways to have access to Internet at lower costs. While there is general agreement that ways

---

[38] See for example Schiller, Dan, 2013. "Masters of the Internet", *Le Monde Diplomatique*, February 2013; Gurstein, Michael, 2012. "(Whose) Hands off (What) Internet: Reflections on WCIT 2012" *Gurstein's Community Informatics*, 9 December 2012; Bucak, Selin, 2012. "NANOG Rhetoric and WCIT-12 Reality", *The Global Journal*, 2 December 2012; Westby, Jody, 2012. "Google's Media Campaign Against the UN Slapped Down", *Forbes,* 4 December 2012; Nothias, Jean-Christophe, 2012. "The Battle for the Future of the Internet?", *Huffington Post,* 2 December 2012; Singh, Parminder Jeet, 2012. "Hyping one threat to hide another", *The Hindu,* 28 November 2012; Geist, Michael, 2012. "UN Internet meeting about who pays, not who rules: Geist", *The Star,* 25 November 2012; and Nothias, Jean-Christophe, 2012a. "The Hypocrisy Threatening the Future of the Internet", *The Global Journal,* 22 November 2012; and the summary of ITU work on International Internet Connectivity: ITU (2013).

[39] In this context, see Saez, Catherine, 2013a. "US Defender Of Internet Freedom, Keen On Protecting IP Rights", *Intellectual Property Watch,* 8 March 2013.

[40] See for example Compaign, Benjamine M. (ed.), 2001. *The Digital Divide: Facing a Crisis or Creating a Myth?,* MIT Press.

[41] ibid.

[42] See for example ITU (2013) and ITU (2012e).

[43] Hills (2007), pp. 133-138 and p. 206; and Stern (1990). A detailed summary of the evolution of accounting rates and the relation to WTO instruments is provided in ITU (2007).

and means should be found to lower the costs of Internet access for developing countries, there is no agreement on how best to do that.[44]

One of the main objectives of WCIT-12 was to find an agreement regarding how best to facilitate the rollout of Internet to developing countries. To some extent this was done by modernizing the old article 6, but it was agreed that further discussions should take place.[45] For a more detailed discussion of this issue, see p. 137.

Such further discussions are more likely to be productive if there is a clear separation between the technical and economical issues that have been well handled by the ITU over the years[46], and the human rights and free speech issues that should be handled elsewhere and that should not be conflated with technical and economical issues.

Regarding the freedom of speech and human rights issues it must be noted that there are indeed very different views, with a sharp split between countries. The split is most apparent between Western democracies and authoritarian countries, but there are differences even amongst the Western democracies (for example, restrictions on political speech are common in continental Europe, but unconstitutional in the USA). Restrictions in non-democratic countries can be widespread: apparently Chinese authorities monitor and remove posts on social networks[47], and Iran is developing software to control and restrict access to social networks[48]. In general, one can say that Western democracies privilege the rights of individual, while other countries seek to balance those rights with collective rights[49], that is, with the rights of a group or of the state as an entity[50]. For example, the Russian Federation stated[51]: "However, freedom to express opinion together with anonymity should not become a synonym of impunity. Member States shall take necessary measures to ensure balance between freedom of expression to one citizens and non-infringement of rights and freedom to other citizens." And Iran stated[52]: "Internet has been used as a tool/means to disseminate false, untrue, misleading, inciting, provocative information, propaganda, cultural attack which have had adverse impact on culture,

---

[44] See for example ITU (2013) and ITU (2012e).

[45] See Resolution 5 of WCIT-12.

[46] See Booz, Allen, Hamilton, 2004. "The World's Most Enduring Institutions".

[47] Simonite, Tom, 2013. "Reading the Tea Leaves of Censorship", *MIT Technology Review*, vol. 116 no. 4, July/August 2013, p. 20.

[48] Musil, Steven, 2013. "Iran develops software to control social networks", *CNET,* 6 January 2013.

[49] For example, at WCIT China stated that said that human rights concerned the rights of individuals, but also collective rights; and that they pertain to individuals and Member States alike. See 1.32 and 1.64 of WCIT document 77.

[50] The concept of group rights in international law is controversial, see for example Bisaz, Corsin, 2012. *The Concept of Group Rights in International Law: Groups as Contested Right-Holders, Subjects and Legal Persons*, Martinus Nijhoff.

[51] In a contribution to the ITU's World Telecommunication Policy Forum (WTPF), see 2.3.1(n) of document WTPF-IEG/3/6 <http://www.itu.int/md/S13-WTPF13IEG3-C-0020/en> accessed 3 August 2013.

[52] In a contribution to the WTPF, see 2.3.1(d) of WTPF-IEG/3/3 <http://www.itu.int/md/S13-WTPF13IEG3-C-0005/en> accessed 3 August 2013.

dignity, customs, tradition, conviction belief, friendship, family life, honor of peoples in certain circumstances, and for certain countries as well as social instability, security, integrity, unity, solidarity, integrity, political stability and peace in certain other countries."

However, it should be noted that the concept of protecting citizens from certain types of information exists also in Western democracies.[53] Apart from the well-known case of European restrictions on hate speech, negation of genocide, and certain political parties, the UK Prime Minister recently called for restrictions on search-engine results in order to reduce access to child abuse images, and default filtering by ISPs to reduce child access to pornography.[54] And India has taken actions in some cases to block access to web sites that were felt to contain hate speech that was promoting violence.[55] China has referred to the US Prism surveillance program (see p. 21) in order to justify what it considers Internet security measures (but what others consider censorship).[56]

Be that as it may, there are clear differences in approaches to balancing the right of the state to protect itself and its citizens with the right of free speech and other human rights. The tension arising from those differences affected the discussions at WCIT, and also the decision regarding whether or not to sign the ITRs, because of the symbolic and political implications of signing, and this quite independently of the legal implications (which, as we have seen, are non-existent with respect to free speech and human rights).

As shown in Chapter 6 below, the 2012 ITRs are an evolution with respect to the 1988 ITRs because they were systematically updated to reflect the privatized and liberalized environment that now dominates the telecommunications sector. As explained above, the 2012 ITRs are not a revolution because they do not bring about any fundamental changes in the roles of governments with respect to telecommunications, including the Internet; and the new provisions of the ITRs address issues that had been identified some years ago and thoroughly discussed before being incorporated in the treaty.

Legal Status of the ITRs and Obligations of Member States

In accordance with article 10[57] of the treaty, it enters into force on 1 January 2015. However, in accordance with the Vienna Convention on the Law of Treaties and the

---

[53] See Deibert (2013), p. 19. And more generally Deibert, Roland J. et al. (eds), (2008). *Access Denied: The Practice and Policy of Global Internet Filtering*, MIT Press; and Deibert, Roland J. et al. (eds), (2010). *Access Controlled: The Shaping of Power, Rights, and Rule in Cyberspace*, MIT Press.

[54] Cameron, David, 2013. "The internet and pornography: Prime Minister calls for action", *speech*, 22 July 2013.

[55] Jakarta Globe, 2012. "India Defends Internet Censorship", *Jakarta Globe,* 24 August 2012.

[56] Buckley, Chris, 2013. "Chinese Defense Ministry Accuses U.S. of Hypocrisy on Spying", *New York Times*, 27 June 2013.

[57] This is the provisional number used during the conference. In the final version, this article is numbered 14.

ITU Constitution[58], it will only bind Member States who have notified the Secretary-General of their intent to be bound by the treaty[59]. That is, the Member States that signed the treaty in Dubai are not necessarily bound to it. Conversely, Member States who did not sign the treaty in Dubai may accede to it at any time.

In accordance with the Vienna Convention on the Law of Treaties[60], relations between a country that has agreed to be bound by the 2012 ITRs and a country that has not agreed to be bound by the 2012 ITRs are governed by the 1988 ITRs[61]. Unless a country that has agreed to be bound by the 2012 ITRs denounces the 1988 ITRs, in which case there would be no international treaty governing the relations between the concerned countries.

All of the WCIT Resolutions entered into force on 14 December 2012 and apply to all ITU Member States, regardless of whether they signed[62] the Final Acts or not.

The consequences of a split regime, with some countries adopting the new ITRs while other countries do not do so, are hard to predict. It is possible that non-signatories could implement the new provisions that are not controversial (such as roaming transparency). It is possible that a split regime would have no practical consequences: the US did not adhere to any of the predecessors of the ITRs until 1973, and this did not appear to create any problems; but the situation today is different from what it was prior to 1973.

A refusal by some countries to implement the new ITRs could deprive their citizens of certain benefits (such as transparency of roaming prices, prevention of numbering misuse, transmission of calling party identification, improved accessibility for people with disabilities, and best practices regarding energy efficiency and e-waste).

Further, non-uniform implementation could create difficulties for companies operating worldwide, if different regulatory regimes emerge.

In the limit, refusal to implement the new ITRs might result in the development on non-harmonized national practices which might well lead to an undesired fragmentation of the Internet.[63]

---

[58] Article 14 of the Vienna Convention in conjunction with Article 54 of the ITU Constitution.

[59] Or, having signed it, have failed to notify the Secretary-General, before 1 January 2018, that they do not agree to be bound. See Article 54 of the ITU Constitution.

[60] Specifically paragraph 4(b) of Article 30.

[61] Except for countries that never agreed to be bound by the 1988 ITRs, but there are very few such countries. Only three countries are not signatories of either version: Antigua & Barbuda, Nauru and Solomon Islands. See ITU, 2013a. *The treaty signing process explained.*

[62] The signature formality applies only to treaty text, not to Resolutions. No country expressed a reservation regarding any of the Resolutions. Sweden did provide a declaration criticizing Resolution 3 (the one concerning Internet) but the declaration does not contain language of the form "we will not apply this Resolution" so it is not a reservation properly speaking.

[63] In its formal declaration annexed to the ITRs, Sweden stated "Sweden also considers that the public Internet and other Internet Protocol-based networks and ser-

There are various scenarios regarding what could happen in the future:

- The split between signatories and non-signatories of the 2012 ITRs persists, possibly leading to problems of interconnectivity
- Most countries agree to be bound by the 2012 ITRs
- Most countries do not agree to be bound by the 2012 ITRs
- Most countries implement the 2012 ITRs in a non-controversial manner:
    - Recognize that Preamble does not prevent suspension of services or otherwise modify existing rights and obligations
    - Recognize that there is no extension of the covered entities or of the scope
    - Recognize that the security and spam provisions do not relate to content
    - Recognize that Resolution 3 does not change the mandate of the ITU

Implementation of the 2012 ITRs in a non-controversial manner might appear to be the solution that is most consistent with a legal analysis of the treaty.[64] See also the discussion in Chapter 8.

vices, whether governmental, public or private, are outside the scope of the International Telecommunication Regulations." One is tempted to think of the old adage "be careful what you wish for, since your wish may be granted". If there were no international treaty concerning the Internet and IP-based networks, then there would be no limits on national sovereignty and countries would be free to control the Internet as they see fit within their national borders. In this context, see L.S. (2012).

[64] In accordance with article 31 of the Vienna Convention on the Law of Treaties, the treaty should be interpreted in accordance with the ordinary meaning of its text in light of its objective and purpose, and the context for interpretation includes any agreements made between all the parties, including agreements subsequent to the conclusion of the treaty and practices in the application of the treaty. So, if all (or at least most) Member States agreed on the interpretation of the controversial provisions, then other Member States would likely follow that interpretation.

CHAPTER 6

Article-by-Article Commentary

The following analysis[1] is based on the provisions of the Vienna Convention on the Law of Treaties, in particular section 3 of Part III[2]. The basic premise is that one must seek to understand the common intent of the parties that negotiated the treaty, the fundamental principle being interpretation in good faith in accordance with the ordinary meaning to be given to the terms of the treaty in their context and in the light of its object and purpose. This principle must be applied parsimoniously, in the sense that a clear text can stand on its own and does not need to be interpreted.

As we will see below, there are many terms in the treaty that are not defined. Such terms should, in the first instance, be interpreted in accordance with their ordinary meaning; if the relevant words in their natural and ordinary meaning make sense in their context, that is an end of the matter.[3] An undefined term must be understood in a manner that is not unreasonable or absurd and that does not contradict the purpose of the treaty.

If, on the other hand, the words in their natural and ordinary meaning are ambiguous or lead to an unreasonable result, then, and then only, must one, by resort to other methods of interpretation, seek to ascertain what the parties really did mean when they used these words.[4]

The other means of interpretation are the text of the treaty as a whole, its preamble, its purpose and scope, and any other instruments related to the treaty. Further, the interpretation must be such as to give effect to the provision, rather than such as to deny any effect of the provision.

---

[1] The analysis is provided as an aid to all who wish to understand the ITRs, with the understanding that states retain the sovereign right to interpret the treaty. Consequently, states retain full responsibility for any use that they might make of the present analysis and for any acts of omission or commission arising out of their use (or not) of the analysis.

[2] An elegant summary of those principles is found in considering 3.3 of Judgment 2C_436/2011 of the Swiss Federal Tribunal (in French).

[3] See International Court of Justice, 1950. *Competence of the General Assembly for Admission of a State to the United Nations: Advisory Opinion*, 3 March 1950.

[4] Ibid.

Subsequent practice between the parties is also an element that can be considered, as is reference to the legislative history of the provision.

The interpretation of treaties is the sovereign right of states, but an interpretation by one state does not bind other states unless other states agree to that interpretation, either explicitly or implicitly through their conduct.

If a term is deliberately left undefined, after failing to agree on its definition, then each state can legitimately use its own definition for its own purposes, but that definition would not necessarily bind other states.

Each of the following sections starts by presenting a provision of the 2012 ITRs shown as a revision of the 1988 ITRs. Text that was deleted with respect to the 1988 version is shown as ~~struck through~~. Text that was added is shown as underlined. However, the systematic replacement of "administration or recognized private operating agency" by "authorized operating agency" is not shown as a revision, nor is the systematic replacement of "CCITT" with "ITU-T" nor the systematic replacement of "member" and "administration" by "Member State". And purely editorial changes in provision numbers within an article and purely editorial updates of the names of ITU organs (such as the replacement of "Administrative Council" with "Council") are also not shown as revision marks.

The article numbering is that of the final version of the treaty, not the provisional numbering found in the Final Acts of WCIT-12. Thus, for example, the article provisionally numbered 5A is shown below as article 6.

Preamble

> While the sovereign right of each State to regulate its telecommunications is fully recognized, the provisions of the present International Telecommunication Regulations (hereafter referred to as "Regulations") ~~supplement~~ complement the Constitution and the Convention of the International Telecommunication Union, with a view to attaining the purposes of the International Telecommunication Union in promoting the development of telecommunication services and their most efficient operation while harmonizing the development of facilities for worldwide telecommunications.
>
> Member States affirm their commitment to implement these Regulations in a manner that respects and upholds their human rights obligations.
>
> These Regulations recognize the right of access of Member States to international telecommunication services.

The change in the **first paragraph** from "supplement" to "complement" is purely editorial and was done to align the ITRs with the ITU Constitution, according to which the ITRs complement the Constitution and Convention.

The purpose of the preamble is to set the context for the substantive articles: the overall principle of national sovereignty is recognized, but it is also recognized that the purpose of the ITRs is to harmonize certain aspects of international telecommunications so as to favor its development. That is, the purpose of the ITRs is, as for all treaties, to impose certain restrictions on national sovereignty, and this so as to favor the smooth interconnection of telecommunications around the world. The restrictions on national sovereignty can take the form of an obligation to do something (for example, to promote the development of international telecommunications services, as called for in provision 4.1), or they can take the form of an obligation to refrain from doing something (for example to refrain from authorizing special arrangements that cause technical harm, as called for in provision 9.1.(b)).

The **second paragraph** was added in response to fears that the ITRs could result in censorship, in particular of the Internet. As recognized by the conference itself, this provision has no operative effect because the human rights obligations of Member States are exhaustively determined by the ITU Constitution. See p. 65 for a fuller discussion.

The **third paragraph** was added at the request of countries whose residents are blocked from accessing web sites in certain countries, see p. 65. This provision has been severely criticized on the grounds that it creates new rights for states, but this is not correct because the provision is subordinate to the ITU Constitution and, in fact, it has no operative effect: see p. 72 .

Article 1: Purpose and Scope of the Regulations

1.1 *a)* These Regulations establish general principles which relate to the provision and operation of international telecommunication services offered to the public as well as to the underlying international telecommunication transport means used to provide such services. These Regulations do not address the content-related aspects of telecommunications. ~~They also set rules applicable to administrations or recognized private operating agencies.~~

b) These Regulations also contain provisions applicable to those operating agencies, authorized or recognized by a Member State, to establish, operate and engage in international telecommunications services to the public, hereinafter referred as "authorized operating agencies". ~~These Regulations recognize in Article 9 the right of Members to allow special arrangements.~~

c) These Regulations recognize in Article 13 the right of Member States to allow special arrangements.

1.2 In these Regulations, "the public" is used in the sense of the population, including governmental and legal bodies.

1.3 These Regulations are established with a view to facilitating global interconnection and interoperability of telecommunication facilities and to promoting the harmonious development and efficient operation of technical facilities, as well as the efficiency, usefulness and availability to the public of international telecommunication services.

1.4 References to Recommendations of the ITU Telecommunication Standardization Sector (ITU-T) ~~and Instructions~~ in these Regulations are not to be taken as giving to those Recommendations ~~and Instructions~~ the same legal status as these Regulations.

1.5 Within the framework of these Regulations, the provision and operation of international telecommunication services in each relation is pursuant to mutual agreement between authorized operating agencies.

1.6 In implementing the principles of these Regulations, authorized operating agencies should comply with, to the greatest extent practicable, the relevant ITU-T Recommendations.

1.7 *a)* These Regulations recognize the right of any Member State, subject to national law and should it decide to do so, to require that ~~administrations and private~~ authorized operating agencies which operate in its territory and provide an international telecommunication service to the public be authorized by that Member State.

b) The Member State concerned shall, as appropriate, encourage the application of relevant ITU-T Recommendations by such service providers.

c) The Member States, where appropriate, shall cooperate in implementing these Regulations ~~(for interpretation, also see Resolution no 2)~~.

1.8 These Regulations shall apply, regardless of the means of transmission used, so far as the Radio Regulations do not provide otherwise.

Provision **1.1**(a) defines the scope of the ITRs. The term "international telecommunication service" is defined later in the ITRs, and that definition is identical to the one found in the ITU Constitution, namely *"The offering of a telecommunication capability between telecommunication offices or stations of any nature that are in or belong to different countries."* The term "telecommunication" is also defined in the ITRs and the definition is also identical to the one found in the ITU Constitution, namely *"Any transmission, emission or reception of signs, signals, writing, images and sounds or intelligence of any nature by wire, radio, optical or other electromagnetic systems."* Thus the scope of the ITRs covers any capability to transmit, emit, or receive information of any nature by any electronic or optical means, as well as the network underlying such capabilities.

This scope clearly includes IP-based networks, that is, networks that are based on the TCP/IP protocol. Whether or not it includes "the Internet" depends on how one defines that term. Some definitions are narrow and refer only to the network per se[5], while others are broad and include the services offered using IP-based networks[6]. Be that as it may, it is clear that the scope of the ITRs covers at least some portion of "the Internet". And indeed this is the formal position taken, by consensus, by the

---

[5] See p. 60.

[6] See footnote xv of Kahn, Robert E. and Cerf, Vinton G., 1999. "What Is The Internet (And What Makes It Work)", which cites the 1995 definition of the US Federal Networking Council; a general discussion of definitions of the term "Internet" is given in Hill (2014).

ITU Member States, because Plenipotentiary Resolutions 101 and 102 cover, respectively, certain aspects of IP-based networks and of the Internet. These resolutions were first adopted in 1998 and have been revised at each subsequent plenipotentiary conference.

The ITRs use the term "public" which is not defined elsewhere in the ITU instruments. It is defined in the ITRs themselves, see below under 1.2.

The scope of the 2012 ITRs is the same as the scope of the 1988 ITRs, if one accepts that the 1988 ITRs do not apply to "content". In order to make it clear that the ITRs do not apply to content, text was added to 1.1(a). During discussions of this issue, there was a comment to the effect that the term "content" was not defined, however there was no discussion of a possible definition and the intent of the text initially proposed by the Chairman (to add to 1.1(a) "to the exclusion of their content") was understood to use the term "content" in its ordinary meaning, namely "that which is contained in a receptacle", that is, the actual content of a telecommunication as opposed to the address or protocol elements of the telecommunication.

After discussion, the formulation was changed as shown above, and the final approved text uses the term "content-related aspects", which is a broader exclusion. For example, in the context of E-Mail, "content" might refer only to the body of a message, whereas "content-related" clearly refers both to the body and to the subject of a message.

The text deleted in 1.1(a) was replaced by the new text in 1.1(b).

As noted above, the text in 1.1(b) has been criticized, but in reality it is nothing more than an alignment of the ITRs with the 1992 version of the ITU Constitution. By virtue of no. 38 of the ITU Constitution, the ITRs apply to "authorized operating agencies", see p. 73. The term "operating agency" is not defined in the ITRs, but it is defined in no. 1007 of the ITU Constitution, and that definition applies to the ITRs by virtue of Article 5 of the ITU Constitution. An "operating agency" is *"Any individual, company, corporation or governmental agency which operates a telecommunication installation intended for an international telecommunication service or capable of causing harmful interference with such a service."* This is a broad definition, but it excludes entities that do not have an international capability, see also the discussion at p. 73 ff. An "authorized operating agency" is an "operating agency" that has been authorized by its national government, see the discussion under 1.7 below.

The text deleted in 1.1(b) was moved to 1.1(c). That provision is purely editorial since it merely points to article 13 (the former article 9) on special arrangements.

Provision **1.2** defines the term "public". The definition is very broad, since it includes physical as well as legal persons, and private-law as well as public-law entities. This definition interacts with 1.1(a), because 1.1(a) defines the scope as "international telecommunication services offered to the public". Thus, it is clear that a company's internal private network is not covered by the ITRs, nor is a state's internal private network. A fortiori, a private military network is not covered, because such a network, even if it is international, does not offer services to the public. However, a telecommunication capability between the legal entity of an international conglomerate in one country and a different legal entity of the same conglomerate in a different country would, under the literal meaning of "public" be included: that is, communications between ABC, Inc. in the USA and ABC, Ltd. in the UK would be included because the two entities are different legal bodies. This literal interpretation was surely not intended and it seems more appropriate[7] to recognize that the internal network of a private company is not covered by the ITRs, even if that network includes connections between separate legal entities, provided of course that those legal entities are all part of the same private company. See also p. 73 for a discussion of what sorts of entities are covered.

Provision **1.3** further elaborates on the purpose of the ITRs, which is to promote the further growth of telecommunications around the world. As noted in Chapter 1, that objective underpinned all the predecessors of the ITRs.

Provision **1.4** makes it clear that references to ITU-T Recommendations do not change their legal status, which is non-binding. That is, implementation of ITU-T Recommendations is done on a voluntary basis, even if they are referred to in the ITRs. Various proposals had been presented to WCIT to include at the beginning the text "Unless otherwise specified", and to refer to "Recommendations of the ITU" rather than to "ITU-T Recommendations", but it was pointed out that there were no proposals to WCIT to specify the mandatory application of any ITU-T Recommendations, nor to refer to any Recommendations other than those of the ITU-T, so it was agreed that these proposed changes were not needed.[8]

Indeed the proposals were a leftover from older proposals that provided for the mandatory application of certain Recommendations: the initial proposal related to the Recommendations regarding safety of life and emergency telecommunications (and there are some ITU-R Recommendations related to that), subsequent proposals also referred to areas such as accounting and quality of service; but none of those proposals were actually presented to WCIT.

The replacement of "CCITT" with "ITU-T" is a purely editorial alignment reflecting the fact that the former CCITT was renamed ITU-T. The reference to "instruction" was deleted because there are no longer any such documents.[9]

In the course of the discussion of this provision, it was agreed to note in the plenary[10] that the ITRs refer only to ITU-T Recommendations. If there are any ITU-R or ITU-D Recommendations that are relevant to an ITU-T Recommendation they should be referenced in the ITU-T Recommendation. The Directors of the three Bureaux should endeavour to ensure that such cross-referencing, on a non-mandatory basis, is made as appropriate.

Provision **1.5** establishes the general principle of mutual agreement between parties that wish to establish an international interconnection. As noted earlier, the term used in 1988 "administrations or recognized private operating agencies" was re-

---

[7] Indeed this is a situation where the literal interpretation leads to an unreasonable result, so the intent of the legislator should be considered when interpreting the provision.

[8] See WCIT DT/31.

[9] An "instruction" was "A collection of provisions drawn from one or more CCITT Recommendations dealing with practical operational procedures for the handling of telecommunication traffic (e.g., acceptance, transmission, accounting)."

[10] See 2.36 of WCIT document 71.

placed by "authorized operating agencies" because the ITRs apply to such agencies by virtue of the ITU Constitution. It should be noted that a government-owned or operated telecommunications provider is an "authorized operating agency" so there is no need to explicitly add the term "administration" before the term "authorized operating agency".

Provision **1.6** exhorts, but does not mandate, compliance with relevant ITU-T Recommendations to the greatest extent practicable, that is, whenever technically feasible, so as to implement the principles of the ITRs. This is a general provision, which is supplemented in various articles by using the expression "relevant ITU-T Recommendations". The general exhortation to comply with relevant ITU-T Recommendations applies to the principles of the ITRs, while the specific exhortations refer to specific provisions and thus apply to the specific issues covered by certain Recommendations.

The ITU has published an extensive list of relevant ITU-T Recommendations in TSB Circular 55 of 18 September 2013.[11] The subsequent sections of this chapter highlight certain specific Recommendations that would appear to be particularly relevant. Consistent with 1.4, the reference to "instructions" that was present in the 1988 version was deleted from the 2012 version.

Provision **1.7**(a) recognizes the right of Member States to authorize, that is, to license or otherwise regulate, telecommunications providers that offer an international service to the public. As noted above, the term "public" should be interpreted restrictively to exclude the internal networks of a private company.

The expression "subject to national law" must be understood to mean that the authorization regime must be established by law, and not by some lower-level instrument such as executive decree. But of course the law could set a general framework and provide that details could be specified in executive decrees or other lower-level instruments.

There is no requirement that the authorization be individual; that is, a type-licensing regime could be considered to be an authorization, and thus all entities operating under the type-license would be "authorized operating agencies". It is of course a matter of national law to determine what entities are considered to be "authorized operating agencies". In the limit, a state that has a fully liberalized regime, with no licensing requirements whatsoever, could hold that all operating agencies are "authorized operating agencies", because they have all been authorized by the law establishing the fully liberalized no-license regime.

During discussions at the conference, it was pointed out that this provision creates the possibility of a non-globally-uniform situation: an entity that is not an "authorized operating agency" in one country might well be such in a different country. This observation is valid, but non-uniform regimes are a fact of life in many domains, ranging from taxation to electrical power outlets and voltage levels. Of course it would be preferable to have a uniform regime, but it was not possible to reach an agreement to that effect at the conference.

The revision marks with respect to the 1988 version are shown here because the insertion of the term "authorized" is an editorial mistake. The text should be under-

[11] Available at <http://www.itu.int/md/T13-TSB-CIR-0055/en>.

stood as reading "to require that operating agencies … be authorized". Indeed, the intent of the provision is to specify that some operating agencies may be subject to authorization, that is, the set of "authorized operating agencies" is a subset of the set of "operating agencies" (see under 1.1(b) above for a discussion of the definition of the term "operating agency"). Obviously "authorized operating agencies" are authorized, and the provision as written is a tautology, which was not intended.

That is, the provision should be read as if the underlined term "authorized" were not present.

Provision 1.7(b) is similar to 1.6 in that it encourages the application of ITU-T Recommendations. However, at first glance, it is stricter because it does not specify "to the greatest extent practicable". The term "such service providers" must be understood to refer to the entities specified in 1.7(a), that is, authorized operating agencies. Thus authorized operating agencies are encouraged to comply with relevant ITU-T Recommendations as appropriate. The term "as appropriate" replaces here the term "to the greatest extent practicable". At first glance, one might think that there is some deliberate intent in using different terms, so they are not synonymous. But a reference to the 1988 text clarifies the situation. In the 1988 text, provision 1.6 referred to "administrations and recognized private operating agencies", whereas provision 1.7(b) referred to authorized operating agencies. That is, provision 1.7(b) referred to a different category of entities than 1.6, so the use of different terms was deliberate and "appropriate" and "to the greatest extent practicable" were not necessarily meant as synonyms in 1988.

But, in the 2012 version, the two provisions apply to exactly the same entities, so the two terms must be understood as being synonymous in this context. That is, provision 1.7(b) had the identical effects as provision 1.6.

Provision 1.7(c) establishes the principle of cooperation between Member States in the implementation of the ITRs. The term "where appropriate" must be understood restrictively, that is, cooperation should be at least attempted whenever at all possible. The reference to Resolution 2 was deleted because that Resolution was deleted. The new Resolution 2 is not at all related to the old Resolution 2. The old Resolution 2 resolved "that, upon request by a Member concerned about the limited effectiveness of its national law in relation to international telecommunication services offered to the public in its territory, the Members concerned shall, where appropriate, consult on a reciprocal basis, with a view to maintaining and extending international cooperation between Members of the Union, in the spirit of Article 4 of the above-mentioned Convention for the improvement and rational use of telecommunications, including the orderly use of the international telecommunication network."

Article 1 of the ITU Constitution contains a provision whose intent is similar (to maintain and extend international cooperation among all its Member States for the improvement and rational use of telecommunications of all kinds), so the deletion of the old Resolution 2 cannot be understood as being significant.

Provision **1.8** provides that the ITRs do not apply if the Radio Regulations so specify. This provision specifies a hierarchy between the two sets of regulations, which hierarchy is not specified in the ITU Constitution.[12] However, it does not establish a general precedence between the two regulations, rather, it specifies that the Radio Regulations may, through a specific provision, provide that they take priority over the ITRs. However, there are no such provisions in the Radio Regulations.[13]

There were many proposals to add specific new items to article 1 (for example security). However, it was recognized that the article is not meant to be an index or table of contents of the ITRs, so it was agreed to maintain it as a general specification of the purpose and scope of the treaty.

Article 2: Definitions

2.1 For the purpose of these Regulations, the following definitions shall apply. These terms and definitions do not, however, necessarily apply for other purposes.

2.2 *Telecommunication:* Any transmission, emission or reception of signs, signals, writing, images and sounds or intelligence of any nature by wire, radio, optical or other electromagnetic systems.

2.3 *International telecommunication service:* The offering of a telecommunication capability between telecommunication offices or stations of any nature that are in or belong to different countries.

2.4 *Government telecommunications:* Telecommunications originating with any: Head of State; Head of a government or members of a government; Commanders-in-Chief of military forces, land, sea or air; diplomatic or consular agents; the Secretary-General of the United Nations; Heads of the principal organs of the United Nations; the International Court of Justice, or replies to government telecommunications mentioned above.

~~2.5 *Privilege Telecommunication* [text omitted]~~

2.5 *Service telecommunication:* A telecommunication that relates to public international telecommunications and that is exchanged among the following:

- Member States;
- authorized operating agencies; and
- the Chairman of the Council, the Secretary-General, the Deputy Secretary-General, the Directors of the Bureaux, the members of the Radio Regulations Board, and other representatives or authorized officials of the Union, including those working on official matters outside the seat of the Union.

[12] See Article 4 of the ITU Constitution.

[13] Articles 56 and 58 of the Radio Regulations do refer to the ITRs, but they state that the provisions of the ITRs, respectively, should be taken into account; and shall apply.

2.6 *International route:* Technical facilities and installations located in different countries and used for telecommunication traffic between two international telecommunication terminal exchanges or offices.

2.7 *Relation:* Exchange of traffic between two terminal countries, always referring to a specific service, if there is between their authorized operating agencies:

a) a means for the exchange of traffic in that specific service:
– over direct circuits (direct relation), or
– via a point of transit in a third country (indirect relation), and

b) normally, the settlement of accounts.

2.8 *Accounting rate:* The rate agreed between authorized operating agencies, in a given relation that is used for the establishment of international accounts.

2.9 *Collection charge:* The charge established and collected by an authorized operating agency from its customers for the use of an international telecommunication service.

~~2.10 *Instructions:* A collection of provisions drawn from one or more CCITT Recommendations dealing with practical operational procedures for the handling of telecommunication traffic (e.g., acceptance, transmission, accounting).~~

The only substantive changes to the definitions were the deletion of "privilege telecommunication" and "instructions" which are no longer used in the ITRs. These terms referred to, respectively, a type of telecommunication and a type of document that are no longer in use. So these terms were deleted in order to align the ITRs with modern practices.

There were numerous proposals to add new definitions to the ITRs. None of those proposals was accepted. Thus all terms other than the ones defined above must be understood in their ordinary meaning in context and in the light of the object and purpose of the treaty, see the beginning of this chapter.

One proposal was to add a new term "telecommunications/ICTs"[14], the intent being to broaden the scope of the ITRs to "ICTs". The only difference between that definition and the definition of "telecommunications" was to add the term "including processing" after "transmission, emission, or reception". That proposal was not a new proposal, it has been put forward by Arab States at various previous ITU meetings, including plenipotentiary conferences. The proposal was not included in the compromise text proposed by the Chairman because it was controversial, but also because the prevailing view was that there was no reason to envisage this change: the scope of the ITRs, under the existing definition of "telecommunications" is sufficiently broad to cover all intended activities. Indeed, it is not contested that contemporary transmission, emission, and reception technologies require some sort of "processing", so there is no need to add that explicitly to the definition.

The terms defined in provisions 2.2, 2.3, and 2.4 are also defined in the ITU Constitution, in identical terms. The term defined in 2.5 is also defined in the ITU Convention;

[14] See WCIT document 7 rev. 1.

however, the two definitions of this tern are not identical, because the Convention refers to "recognized operating agencies" whereas the ITRs refer to "authorized operating agency". Since the Convention prevails in case of inconsistency,[15] only "recognized operating agencies" are included for what regards "service telecommunications".

Article 3: International Network

3.1 Member States shall endeavour to ensure that authorized operating agencies cooperate in the establishment, operation and maintenance of the international network to provide a satisfactory quality of service.

3.2 Member States shall endeavour to ensure the provision of ~~to provide~~ sufficient telecommunication facilities to meet the ~~requirements of and~~ demand for international telecommunication services.

3.3 Authorized operating agencies shall determine by mutual agreement which international routes are to be used. Pending agreement and provided that there is no direct route existing between the terminal authorized operating agencies concerned, the origin authorized operating agency has the choice to determine the routing of its outgoing telecommunication traffic, taking into account the interests of the relevant transit and destination authorized operating agencies.

3.4 Subject to national law, any user, by having access to the international network ~~established by an administration or recognized private operating agency~~, has the right to send traffic. A satisfactory quality of service should be maintained to the greatest extent practicable, corresponding to the relevant ITU-T Recommendations.

3.5 Member States shall endeavour to ensure that international telecommunication numbering resources specified in ITU-T Recommendations are used only by the assignees and only for the purposes for which they were assigned; and that unassigned resources are not used.

3.6 Member States shall endeavour to ensure that international calling line identification (CLI) information is provided taking into account the relevant ITU-T Recommendations.

3.7 Member States should create an enabling environment for the implementation of regional telecommunication traffic exchange points, with a view to improving quality, increasing the connectivity and resilience of networks, fostering competition and reducing the costs of international telecommunication interconnections.

In provision **3.1**, the replacement of "shall ensure" with "shall endeavour to ensure" is a recognition of the fact that in today's liberalized environment states cannot ensure that operators do the things mentioned in the provision. States can only take measures to encourage operators to do those things.

[15] Article 4 of the ITU Constitution.

There was a systematic divergence of views between two camps regarding the use of terms such as "shall" versus "should" in various provisions. As a compromise, it was agreed to use "shall encourage" whenever possible. This formulation makes it clear that the state cannot necessarily ensure that something is done, but it also makes it clear that the state must take some action to at least encourage that something is done. That is, states that agree to be bound by the ITRs agree to make an effort, that is, to take measures, to achieve the goals specified in the articles that use this term. The French text, which is the authentic version under the ITU Constitution[16], uses "s'efforcent" for "shall endeavor" which clearly indicates the "make an effort" element of the term.

The steps or measures that a state may take in order to fulfill its obligations to "make an effort" are varied: it could be a general competitive environment that favors the achievement of the objectives, or specific programs such as subsidies, tax incentives, direct government intervention, binding regulations, etc.

The expression "satisfactory quality of service" should be understood to mean "that the level of quality of service (QoS) will be above a minimum level in accordance with relevant Recommendations of the ITU".[17]

Provision **3.2** was similarly aligned with today's liberalized environment, by recognizing that states cannot provide facilities, they can only take measure to ensure the provision of facilities; and by recognizing that states no longer set the requirements for telecommunication services: those requirements are a result of market demands.

Provision **3.3** was left unchanged, except of course for the use of the term "authorized operating agency". But, since the 1988 ITRs apply, since 1998, to authorized operating agencies, in reality there is no change at all in this provision. There were many proposals to change this provision, but, after discussion, it was recognized that the provision reflects current commercial realities, so no change was needed.

Provision **3.4** establishes the right of any user to send traffic, within the limits specified by national law, which limits must of course not violate human rights obligations. Further, the quality of service should be satisfactory, in accordance with ITU-T Recommendations, to the greatest extent practicable, that is, within the limits of technical feasibility. The provision applies not only to authorized operating agencies, but also to any other operating agency that, in accordance with national law, provides international access.

The relevant ITU-T Recommendations are listed under provision 4.3 below. See also p. 91.

Provision **3.5** was added in order to address the increasing misuse of telephone numbers, in particular the use of a national number in a high-termination-rate country to provide call-in services (often erotic phone services) to users in a different country without actually terminating the call in the high-termination-rate country. This is often done without the knowledge of the high-termination-rate country. That is, a call made to a number in country Y from country X actually stays within

[16] See no. 173 (Article 29) of the ITU Constitution.
[17] See 1.48 of WCIT document 72.

country X while being billed to the customer as if it were terminated in country Y. Such practices are illegal, or at least contrary to national regulations, in many countries, but not in all countries. So it was felt necessary to include a treaty provision, whose effect is that countries that agree to be bound by the ITRs agree to take steps to curtail such practices.

There was much concern that this provision could be held to apply to IP addresses or Internet domain names. In order to clarify that this is not the case, the provision specifies that it only applies to resources specified, that is defined, in ITU-T Recommendations.

The provision does apply to the International Mobile Subscriber Identity (IMSI) specified in Recommendation ITU-T E.211. Thus, countries that allow extra-territorial use of Mobile Country Codes (MCCs), must, under the terms of this provision, notify such extra-territorial use as specified in Annex E of E.212.

Non-treaty texts relating to this issue are found in WTSA Resolution 61 and Recommendation ITU-T E.156, and in the ITU-T Recommendations referenced in E.156. Although non-treaty text is not binding, Member States must take measures to ensure that numbering resources are used only for the purposes for which they are assigned, and the cited non-treaty texts do specify various measures to that effect.

Provision **3.6** was added in order to address the fact that calling line identification is increasingly not being transmitted, and this not because of technical limitations or because the originating user request that the identification not be transmitted, but to get around national regulations or even to perpetrate fraud.[18] The term "calling line identification" is not defined in the ITRs, but, in context, it must be understood as the term defined in the relevant ITU-T Recommendations.[19]

Although spoofing[20] was not specifically discussed, the provision must be understood to address spoofing that is not done for legitimate reasons, including SMS spoofing.[21]

Non-treaty text on this issue can be found in WTSA Resolution 65 and Recommendation ITU-T E.157 and in the ITU-T Recommendations referenced in E.157. See also p. 91.

Provision **3.7** was added in recognition of the general understanding[22] that Internet exchange points improve quality and lower the cost of Internet connectivity. Given

[18] The term fraud is used here to refer to the use of any telecommunications facilities, resources or services with the intention of avoiding payment, without correct payment, with no payment at all, by making someone else pay, or by using a deception in order to obtain a financial or personal gain from the use of those facilities, resources or services.

[19] Definitions contained in ITU-T Recommendations can conveniently be found using the ITU's database at <http://www.itu.int/ITU-R/index.asp?redirect=true&category=information&rlink=terminology-database>.

[20] As a term of art in telecommunications, this refers to displaying an identification that is not that of the actual originator.

[21] See *SMS spoofing*, 2013. Wikipedia.

the sensitivity of the use of the term “Internet”, and a desire that the ITRs should remain technology-neutral, the more general term “traffic exchange point” was used; this recognizes that such regional exchange points are useful also for non-Internet traffic. This provision has been criticized, but the criticism is unfounded, see p. 75.

Article 4: International Telecommunication Services

4.1 Member States shall promote the development ~~the implementation~~ of international telecommunication services and shall foster their availability to the public ~~shall endeavour to make such services generally available to the public in their national network(s)~~.

4.2 Member States shall endeavour to ensure that authorized operating agencies cooperate within the framework of these Regulations to provide, by agreement, a wide range of international telecommunication services which should conform, to the greatest extent practicable, to the relevant ITU-T Recommendations.

4.3 Subject to national law, Member States shall endeavour to ensure that authorized operating agencies provide and maintain, to the greatest extent practicable, a satisfactory ~~minimum~~ quality of service corresponding to the relevant ITU-T Recommendations with respect to:

a) access to the international network by users using terminals which are permitted to be connected to the network and which do not cause harm to technical facilities and personnel;

b) international telecommunication facilities and services available to users ~~customers~~ for their dedicated use;

c) at least a form of telecommunication service which is reasonably accessible to the public, including those who may not be subscribers to a specific telecommunication service; and

d) a capability for interworking between different services, as appropriate, to facilitate international telecommunication services ~~communications~~.

4.4 Member States shall foster measures to ensure that authorized operating agencies provide free-of-charge, transparent, up-to-date and accurate information to end users on international telecommunication services, including international roaming prices and the associated relevant conditions, in a timely manner.

4.5 Member States shall foster measures to ensure that telecommunication services in international roaming of satisfactory quality are provided to visiting users.

[22] See for example Opinion 1 of the Fifth World Telecommunications Policy Forum, available in the Chairman’s Report <http://www.itu.int/md/S13-WTPF13-C-0016/en>.

4.6 Member States should foster cooperation among authorized operating agencies in order to avoid and mitigate inadvertent roaming charges in border zones.

4.7 Member States shall endeavour to promote competition in the provision of international roaming services and are encouraged to develop policies that foster competitive roaming prices for the benefit of end users.

Provision **4.1** was aligned (similarly to the provisions in article 3) with today's liberalized environment, by recognizing that most states no longer directly implement telecommunications services, but rather create an environment which enables (or even favors) the development of such services. In keeping with the purpose and scope of the ITRs, this provision relates only to services that are available to the public.

Similarly, in provision **4.2**, the expression "shall endeavor" has been used to indicate that states cannot necessarily ensure an outcome, they can only take steps to favor an outcome. See p. 95.

There are numerous ITU-T Recommendations that specify international telecommunication services, in particular in the F-series, but also in the E.1xx series. See also p. 91.

In provision **4.3**, the requirement to provide a minimum quality of service has been replaced with a requirement to provide a satisfactory quality of service, which is of course a more stringent requirement. However, the service need only be provided for the listed items, namely access to the international network, dedicated international telecommunication facilities and services, some form of service which can be used by those that do not subscribe to services (for example, public telephone booths, or Internet cafés, etc.), and some form of interworking.

In provision 4.3(d), the term "international communications" has been replaced by "international telecommunication services". At first glance, this might appear to be a narrowing of the scope of the provision. However, it must be recalled that the ITRs apply only to international telecommunication services (see Article 1 above), so in reality this change merely aligns the provision with the purpose and scope of the treaty. Similar considerations apply to the change in 4.3(c).

On the other hand, provision 4.2(b) has been broadened to apply to users who are not necessarily subscribers, thus aligning this provision with 4.2(c).

Provision 4.3 uses the expression "subject to national law". This must be understood to mean that the requirements on authorized operating agencies must be established by a law, rather than by some lower-level instrument such as an executive decree. But of course the law could set a general framework and provide that details could be specified in executive decrees or other lower-level instruments.

There are numerous ITU-T Recommendations regarding quality of service, in particular in the E.4xx, E.8xx, G.1xx, I.35x, J.14x, J.24x, J.34x, Y.15xx, and P-series. See also p. 91.

Provision **4.4** was added in response to numerous user complaints regarding "mobile bill-shock", that is, unexpectedly high costs for roaming services. Many proposals were submitted to WCIT calling for actions in this respect, not only to ensure transparency as called for in article 4.4, but also to control prices. The proposals regarding prices were varied, with some calling for cost-oriented prices[23], others calling for prices to be reasonable[24]. More ambitious proposals had been presented to CWG-WCIT12, such as capping roaming prices at the national price of either the home country or the visited country; however, those proposals were not submitted to WCIT. And no proposals regarding prices were included in the new ITRs. This can of course be attributed to the lobbying power of mobile operators, for whom roaming is very profitable. It is worth noting that the strongest opposition to caps on roaming prices came from those Western countries who claim to be paragons of democracy. Indeed, the democratic system can at times work in favor of industrial lobbies, because a democratic government is often obliged to conduct a public consultation on a given issue, and corporate lobbyists will be sure to show up at the consultation, thus possibly biasing its outcome. But other factors may be at work.[25]

It must be stressed that the agreed treaty text does not specify what mechanism should be used to provide the price information to end-users. One common method is to send an SMS that tells the user what the cost would be to place and to receive a call to his or her home country. Another common method is to provide the information in an easily accessible format on a web site. The terms "in a timely manner" hint at the use of the SMS technique, but it is a national matter to determine exactly which method should be favored.

Non-treaty text on this issue is found in Recommendation ITU-T D.98. See also p. 91.

It should be noted that Article 27 of a proposed European Regulation[26] includes very specific measures that would appear to implement provision 4.4 of the ITRs and also some of the provisions of D.98.

Reference should also be made to the background paper and discussions presented at a 2013 ITU Workshop.[27]

Provision **4.5** specifies that measures should be taken to ensure that roaming services are available, and that their quality is satisfactory. This provision does not explicitly reference ITU-T Recommendations, so it is a national matter to determine what constitutes a satisfactory service.

---

[23] See WCIT DT/20.

[24] See WCIT DT/22.

[25] In Switzerland, the parliament refused in March 2013 the government's request to take actions to lower mobile roaming prices. This may be due to the fact that the government owns a significant proportion of the dominant operator and receives its share of the operator's profits.

[26] European Commission, 2013. *Regulation of the European Parliament and of the Council laying down measures concerning the European single market for electronic communications and to achieve a Connected Continent,* 11 September 2013.

[27] ITU, 2013e. *High-Level Workshop on Regulatory and Economic Aspects of Roaming*, 23-24 September 2013. The background paper is titled "International mobile roaming services: Facilitating competition and protecting users".

Provision **4.6** was added in response to the problem encountered by many mobile phone users who live near a national border: at times the phone will roam onto the network of the neighboring country without the user realizing it, and the user will then pay much higher prices when he or she receives or makes a call. This phenomenon is referred to as "inadvertent roaming". Avoidance of inadvertent roaming can be achieved to some extent by proper configuration of the radio antennas near the border, but this does not always eliminate the issue altogether. A unified pricing plan for users who are connected to base stations near the border would avoid the problem (that is, there would be no roaming charges for users near the border). Mitigation can be achieved as outlined above, or by warning a user that his phone has roamed, so that the user is aware of the issue.

Provision **4.7** recognizes the need to promote competition for roaming services so as to favor a reduction in prices. However it does not specify any particular pro-competition measures. Some such measures are found in Recommendation ITU-T D.98, and further measures might be agreed in the future by ITU-T Study Group 3. See also p. 91.

Article 5: Safety of life and priority of telecommunications

5.1 Safety-of-life telecommunications, such as distress telecommunications, shall be entitled to transmission as of right and, ~~shall~~ where technically practicable, have absolute priority over all other telecommunications, in accordance with the relevant articles of the Constitution and the Convention and taking due account of the relevant ITU-T Recommendations.

5.2 Government telecommunications, including telecommunications relative to the application of certain provisions of the United Nations Charter, shall, where technically practicable, enjoy priority over telecommunications other than those referred to in No. 45 (5.1) above, in accordance with the relevant provisions of the Constitution and the Convention and taking due account of the relevant ITU-T Recommendations.

5.3 The provisions governing the priority enjoyed by any ~~all~~ other telecommunication service are contained in the relevant ITU-T Recommendations.

5.4 Member States should encourage authorized operating agencies to inform all users, including roaming users, in good time and free of charge, of the number to be used for calls to the emergency services.

Provision **5.1** specifies that certain types of telecommunications have absolute priority whenever this is technically feasible (the deletion of the word "shall" is purely editorial and does not change the meaning of the provision). The relevant articles of the Constitution and Convention are, at present, just Article 40 of the Constitution. That article is similar to provision 5.1, but, in addition, it specifies that epidemiological telecommunications of exceptional urgency of the World Health Organization must also be given absolute priority, and this provision must of course also be implemented.

Article 40 of the Constitution does not mention ITU-T Recommendations, so the ITRs are more specific in this respect, because they refer to means that should be taken into account in order to achieve the stated objective.

During the preparatory process, there had been proposals to align this and other articles with the corresponding text of the Constitution, and there were also proposal to add to the ITRs text from the Constitution that was felt to be directly relevant to the ITRs, but these proposals did not have sufficient support and so they were not submitted to WCIT.

The relevant ITU-T Recommendations include E.106 and E.107. See also p. 91.

Provision **5.2** specifies that government telecommunications must be given priority (after safety-of-life telecommunications) when technically feasible. The term "government telecommunications" is defined in the ITRs, see the section above on Article 2. The relevant articles of the Constitution and Convention are, at present, Article 41 of the Constitution and, possibly, 40 of the Convention. Article 40 of the Constitution specifies that government telecommunications shall enjoy priority only upon specific request by the originator; since the Constitution prevails in case of discrepancy[28], the provision in the ITRs must be understood to apply only upon request.

Article 40 of the Convention states that Government telegrams and service telegrams may be expressed in secret language in all relations. Thus, all parties to the ITRs must permit those government telecommunications that are sent as telegrams to be expressed in secret language. However, this does not apply to government telecommunications that are not telegrams: a party to the ITRs is free to refuse the use of secret language for non-telegram government telecommunications.

Recommendations ITU-T E.106 and E.107 are relevant in this context. See also p. 91.

Provision **5.3** specifies that the priority of any other telecommunication service is specified in the ITU-T Recommendations, which, however, are not binding, as clearly stated in Article 1. The addition of the term "service" is an editorial alignment in order to ensure consistency of terminology and does not change the meaning of the provision.

Recommendations ITU-T E.106 and E.107 are relevant in this context. See also p. 91.

Provision **5.4** was added to address the fact that emergency numbers vary widely around the world, so a roaming user may not know which number to call in case of emergency. Many mobile handsets recognize multiple emergency numbers (in particular 112 and 911) and send a Signaling System 7 (SS7) emergency call message, however not all the numbers used in all countries are recognized, and the ITR provision is technology-neutral.

Non-treaty text regarding this issue is found in WCIT Resolution 2 (see below) and in Recommendation ITU-T E.161.1 and the Recommendations it references. See also p. 91.

[28] Article 4 of the Constitution.

Article 6: Security and robustness of networks

6.1 Member States shall individually and collectively endeavour to ensure the security and robustness of international telecommunication networks in order to achieve effective use thereof and avoidance of technical harm thereto, as well as the harmonious development of international telecommunication services offered to the public.

This provision was added in recognition of the fact that the security is an essential requirement for reliable telecommunications. Even though Internet is not mentioned specifically in the article, it has to be understood that the security of Internet communications is intended to be improved, because it is widely agreed that such improvements are needed.[29] This has led to severe criticism of the article, but such criticism is not justified, see p. 75. See also the discussion with respect to the US Prism surveillance program on pages 21 and 42.

There was no discussion of what might be intended by the term "robustness", but it would appear that the common meaning "sturdy", "hardy" is appropriate in this context.[30]

There was also no discussion of the meaning of the term " security". The common meaning "freedom from risk or danger, safety" clearly is not appropriate in the context of the ITRs; indeed, the term is used in the ITRs as a term of art referring to telecommunications network. That term of art "security" is defined in numerous ITU-T Recommendations. While the definitions are not identical, they are essentially consistent. The shortest definition is the one found in Recommendation ITU-T Y.140.1, according to which security is "the protection of information availability, integrity and confidentiality". In this context, integrity must be understood to include authenticity.[31]

The wording "shall individually and collectively endeavour" means that states that agree to be bound by the ITRs must take individual and cooperative[32] measures that favor the security and robustness of telecommunications networks. However, such measures must not prevent the effective use of such networks, nor stymie the harmonious development of services. For example, a strict, pervasive prohibition of anonymous communications would not be consistent with this provision (any more than it would be consistent with human rights obligations). Subsequent to WCIT,

[29] See the non-operative part of WTSA Resolution 50 and Talbot, David, 2005. "The Internet is broken", *MIT Technology Review,* December 2005/January 2006, p. 62. For a prescient analysis of what did come to pass, see Baran, Paul, 1967. "The Future Computer Utility", *National Affairs*, vol. 8, p. 75.

[30] Indeed the term is defined in Recommendation ITU-R M.1224 as "the ability to withstand random errors, burst errors and high bit error ratios over the whole service area", which is consistent with "sturdy", "hardy".

[31] See the definition of "cybersecurity" found in Recommendation ITU-T X.1205.

[32] It is clear from the legislative history that the term "collectively" must be understood as "by cooperating", since only the term "cooperation" was used in the proposals submitted to WCIT (see WCIT TD 8 rev.1) and, during the discussions, there were no statement to the effect that "collectively" meant anything other than "by cooperating".

and in the context of the revelations regarding Prism (see pp. 21 and 42), a large number of civil society organizations published a list of principles[33] that purported to capture best practices regarding human rights. States may wish to consider those principles when implementing article 6 of the ITRs.

See article 13 for a discussion of the term "technical harm".

Article 7: Unsolicited bulk electronic communications

> 7.1 Member States should endeavour to take necessary measures to prevent the propagation of unsolicited bulk electronic communications and minimize its impact on international telecommunication services.
>
> 7.2 Member States are encouraged to cooperate in that sense.

This article was added in order to address the issues created by what is commonly called spam.[34] However, spam is directly related to the Internet so, in an effort to minimize objections, the term "unsolicited bulk electronic communications" was used instead. However, this did not prevent criticism, even if the criticism is unfounded, see p. 75.

The expression "unsolicited bulk electronic communications" was taken from Recommendation ITU-T X.1240, which states: *"The meaning of the word "spam" depends on each national perception of privacy and what constitutes spam from the national technological, economic, social and practical perspectives. In particular, its meaning evolves and broadens as technologies develop, providing novel opportunities for misuse of electronic communications. Although there is no globally agreed definition for spam, this term is commonly used to describe unsolicited electronic bulk communications over e-mail or mobile messaging for the purpose of marketing commercial products or services."*

Thus it is clear that there was no common understanding of the expression "bulk electronic communications" and the interpretation of the expression is a national matter. In particular, states may wish to consider additional elements that are often associated with spam, namely the fact that the message is not just unsolicited, but unwanted, and at times harmful. See in this context the definition of spam contained in Recommendation ITU-T X.1242 which is *"electronic information delivered from senders to recipients by terminals such as computers, mobile phones, telephones, etc., which is usually unsolicited, unwanted, and harmful for recipients."*

Article 8~~6~~: Charging and accounting

> **8.1 International telecommunication arrangements**
>
> 8.1.1 Subject to applicable national law, the terms and conditions for international telecommunication service arrangements may be established through commercial agreements or through accounting-rate principles established pursuant to national regulation.

---

[33] *Necessary and Proportionate* (2013).

[34] See the non-operative part of WTSA Resolution 52.

8.1.2 Member States shall endeavour to encourage investments in international telecommunication networks and promote competitive wholesale pricing for traffic carried on such telecommunication networks.

8.2 Accounting-rate principles

Terms and conditions

8.2.1 The following provisions may apply where the terms and conditions of international telecommunication service arrangements are established through accounting-rate principles, established pursuant to national regulation. These provisions do not apply to arrangements established through commercial agreements.

8.2.2 For each applicable service in a given relation, authorized operating agencies shall, by mutual agreement, establish and revise accounting rates to be applied between them, in accordance with the provisions of Appendix 1 and taking into account the relevant ITU-T Recommendations.

8.2.3 Unless otherwise agreed, parties engaged in the provision of international telecommunication services ~~administrations and recognized private operating agencies~~ shall follow the relevant provisions as set out in Appendices 1 and 2.

8.2.4 In the absence of special arrangements concluded between authorized operating agencies, the monetary unit to be used in the composition of accounting rates for international telecommunication services and in the establishment of international accounts shall be:

- either the monetary unit of the International Monetary Fund (IMF), currently the Special Drawing Right (SDR), as defined by that organization;
- ~~or the gold franc, equivalent to 1/3.061 SDR.~~
- or freely convertible currencies or other monetary unit agreed between the authorized operating agencies.

~~6.3.2 In accordance with relevant provisions of the International Telecommunication Convention, this provision shall not affect the possibility open to administrations or recognized private operating agencies of establishing bilateral arrangements for mutually acceptable coefficients between the monetary unit of the IMP and the gold franc.~~

Collection charges

8.2.5 The charges levied ~~by an administration or recognized private operating agency~~ on customers for a particular communication should in principle be the same in a given relation, regardless of the international route used for that communication ~~chosen by that administration or recognized private operating agency. Each administration or recognized private operating agency shall, subject to applicable national law, establish the charges to be collected from its customers. The level of charges is a national matter; however,~~ In establishing these charges, Member States ~~administrations and~~

~~recognized private operating agencies~~ should try to avoid dissymmetry between the charges applicable in each direction of the same relation.

8.3 Taxation

8.3.1 Where, in accordance with the national law of a country, a fiscal tax is levied on collection charges for international telecommunication services, this tax shall normally be collected only in respect of international services billed to customers in that country, unless other arrangements are made to meet special circumstances.

8.4 Service telecommunications

8.4.1 Authorized operating agencies may in principle forgo the inclusion of service telecommunications in international accounting, under the relevant provisions of the Constitution and the Convention and these Regulations, having due regard for the need for reciprocal arrangements. Authorized operating agencies may provide service telecommunications free of charge.

8.4.2 The general operational, charging and accounting principles applicable to service telecommunications should take account of the relevant ITU-T Recommendations.

~~6.5.1 Administrations and recognized private operating agnecies shall follow the relevant provisions as set out in Appendix 3.~~

Provision **8.1.1** was added in recognition of the fact that the old accounting rate system (see p. 9) is no longer much used in practice (see p. 10). There had been proposals to delete entirely all the provisions related to the accounting rate system, however, during discussions it was stated that that system is still used in some parts of the world, so it was agreed to retain the old provisions while recognizing that they were no longer the only method used for financial arrangements. The provision makes it clear that the accounting rate system can only be established by explicit national regulation: absent such regulation, the financial arrangements will be based on commercial negotiations between the concerned parties.

However, such commercial negotiations are subject to national law and thus must comply with, in particular, national competition law and international trade law (because international trade law, such as the WTO agreements, are transposed into national law).

At first glance, provision 8.1.1 is revolutionary, because it is the first provision in an ITU treaty that explicitly provides for an alternative to the billing and accounting principles that had been historically enshrined in the ITU treaties.[35] However, in reality, the provision is just an explicit recognition of what had been implicitly provided by Article 9 of the 1988 ITRs, as explained on p. 10. Thus the provision is by no means revolutionary and it merely represents one additional step in the evolution of charging and billing arrangements for telecommunications (see also Chapter 2).

[35] See Chapter 1 and Mestmaecker (1987), p. 379.

Provision **8.1.2** was added in recognition of the fact that, even in today's privatized and liberalized environment, states should take measures[36] to encourage investments in telecommunications (because such investments benefit the economy as a whole and thus generate positive externalities), but they should also take measures to promote competition at the wholesale level[37]. See also the discussion under Resolution 5 in Chapter 7.

Provision **8.2.1** was added as a logical consequence of 8.1.1, and merely reinforces that provision. It makes it clear that the provisions of the accounting rate system do not apply to arrangements made through commercial negotiations. In particular, the accounting rate system does not apply to Internet interconnections.

Provision **8.2.2** concerns accounting rates, which is a term defined in the ITRs, see Article 2 above. Accounting rates are in effect the wholesale prices agreed between entities that use the accounting rate system.

This provision is identical to the old provision 6.1.1. It states that, under the accounting rate system, the concerned operators agree on the accounting rates, in accordance with the provisions of Appendix 1, while taking into account the relevant ITU-T Recommendations. As we will see below, the provisions of Appendix 1 are quite detailed.

The relevant ITU-T Recommendations are those in the D-series, D.1 through D.299, and in particular D.150 and D.195. See also p. 91.

Provision **8.2.3** corresponds to the old provision 6.4.1, but it has been generalized to apply to any entity that is using the accounting rate system. The imposition (unless agreed otherwise) of Appendices 1 and 2 includes provisions other than the accounting rates mentioned in provision 8.2.2.

Provision **8.2.4** corresponds to the old provision 6.3.1, but the reference to the gold franc was deleted because it was obsolete. A provision allowing use, by mutual agreement, of any other monetary unit was added to this article. As a consequence, the old provision 6.3.2 was deleted.

Provision **8.2.5** concerns collection charges, which is a defined term, see Article 2 above. Collection charges are in effect the retail prices charged to end-users.

This provision corresponds to the old provisions 6.1.1 and 6.1.2, but was modernized to recognize that states no longer chose routes or set the level of charges. Member States should, however, try to avoid dissymmetry of charges, but, again, this only applies when the accounting rate system is used (so it does not apply to Internet interconnections).

---

[36] See p. 95 for a discussion of the intent of the expression "shall endeavour".

[37] Although there is no explicit reference to mobile roaming in this article of the treaty, it was understood that the main area in which it is thought that there is lack of competition at the wholesale level is indeed mobile roaming. See for example OECD, 2011. "International Mobile Data Roaming" DSTI/ICCP/CISP(2010)12.

Provision **8.3.1** corresponds to the old 6.1.3. This provision had been considered to be difficult to interpret in light of the changes that had taken place since 1988, and numerous proposals to replace it were presented during the preparatory process. In particular, there were proposals to restrict the types of taxes that could be levied, to avoid international double taxation, to exhort that the level of taxes be reasonable, and so forth. However, due to the fiscal difficulties experienced by many countries in the time period preceding the conference, most states indicated that they were not willing to accept any restrictions on their ability to tax (apart of course from existing international double taxation treaties). Thus, while some proposals to revise the article were submitted to WCIT, there was also a proposal to delete the article entirely, so as to give complete freedom to states regarding taxation. However, there was insufficient support for this proposal, so it was agreed to retain the existing text, which does not limit the types of taxes that can be levied (in particular, excise taxes such as a tax on international traffic are not prohibited[38]).

Similarly, it was agreed to retain a related provision found in Appendix 1, namely:

> 1.6 Where an authorized operating agency has a duty or fiscal tax levied on its accounting-rate shares or other remunerations, it shall not in turn impose any such duty or fiscal tax on other authorized operating agencies.

Since provision 1.6 of Appendix 1 (hereafter 1/1.6) and provision 8.3.1 are related, we will discuss them together, and provide an interpretation that is adapted to the current telecommunications environment.

As a preliminary matter, we note that provision 8.3.1 is not related to the accounting rate system, whereas 1/1.6 is related to the accounting rate system.

The term "accounting-rate share" of 1/1.6 is not defined in the ITRs. But, in accordance with Recommendation ITU-T D.150, an "accounting rate share" is the share of the accounting rate that is received or retained by a particular administration or recognized operating agency; indeed the term is defined in ITU-T Recommendation D.000 as *"The part of the accounting rate corresponding to the facilities made available in each country; this share is fixed by agreement among the Administrations"*. According to A.2.3 of Recommendation ITU-T D.140, fiscal taxes are cost elements to be taken into account when determining accounting rates and accounting rate shares for the international telephone service.

Thus the ITRs distinguish between two different types of taxes: (1) those on collection charges, that is, the charges levied on customers and (2) those on accounting rate shares, that is, the amounts received from or paid to foreign entities under the accounting rate system.

The general principles set forth in the ITRs are (1) that taxes should be levied on collection charges only to the extent that the collection charges relate to services billed to a customer in the country that levies the tax and (2) that taxes levied on amounts retained or received or paid in relation to agreed accounting rates should not be passed on to the concerned foreign entity. However, principle (2) applies only if the accounting rate system is used, not otherwise.

Regarding taxation, see also the G20 leaders' declaration referred to on p 31.

---

[38] Such taxes may or may not be a good idea, see the discussions that took place at the 2011 ITU workshop: ITU, 2011c. *Workshop on Taxation of Telecommunication Services and Related Products,* 1-2 September 2011.

Provision **8.4.1** corresponds to the old provisions 1.2 and 1.1 of the old Appendix 3. The remaining provisions of Appendix 3 were considered obsolete, so there is no longer any Appendix 3. The term "service communications" is not defined in the ITRs, nor is it defined in any ITU-T or ITU-R Recommendation. The term should be understood to refer to telecommunications that relate primarily to the network itself rather than to information sent by a user; such telecommunications are typically initiated by the network without the user being aware of them. For example, various Signaling System 7 messages[39] fall into this category, as do various network management messages[40].

Provision **8.4.2** corresponds to the old Article 3 of Appendix 3, but the old reference to "privilege telecommunications" has been deleted because it was considered to be obsolete. This provision states that, if service communications are billed, then the relevant ITU-T Recommendations should be taken into account.

The relevant ITU-T Recommendation is D.192. See also p. 91.

The old provision 6.5.1 was deleted because there is no longer an Appendix 3.

See p. 137 for a discussion of various proposals whose intent was to allow developing countries to obtain greater revenues from Internet traffic.

Immediately after the conference, the European Commission stated[41]: "In the opinion of EU participants, the final text risked ... having the potential to undermine future economic growth. The EU was concerned about this possible harm not only within the EU, but globally, including in developing countries." As noted above, the new article 8 reflects well the current economic realities of the telecommunication sector, so it is hard to understand why anybody would see a potential to undermine future economic growth. Be that as it may, an overwhelming majority of developing countries approved the treaty, so the European criticism is tantamount to implying either that developing countries are unable to understand what is in their interests, or that developing country governments do not act in the interests of their countries.[42]

Article 9~~7~~: Suspension of services

9.1 If a Member State exercises its right in accordance with the Constitution and the Convention to suspend international telecommunication services partially or totally, that Member State shall immediately notify the

[39] See in particular Recommendations ITU-T Q.711-Q.719.

[40] See for example Recommendations ITU-T E.400-E.489.

[41] European Commission (2012).

[42] In the author's experience, representatives of developing countries are very competent, and less influenced by industrial lobbies than the representatives of many developed countries. One may thus wonder which set of representatives more truly represents the interests of its citizens: as noted elsewhere, at WCIT-12, developing countries proposed measures to reduce mobile roaming prices, while developed countries opposed such measures.

> Secretary-General of the suspension and of the subsequent return to normal conditions by the most appropriate means of communication.
>
> 9.2 The Secretary-General shall immediately bring such information to the attention of all other Member States, using the most appropriate means of communication.

Provision **9.1** is essentially a restatement of Article 35 of the ITU Constitution. At present, there are no provisions in the ITU Convention related to this matter.

Provision **9.2** is one of two provisions in the ITRs that impose an obligation on the Secretary-General, rather than on Member States (the other provision being 10.1). Arguably, this provision is not necessary, since the Secretary-General's duty to provide information is specified in no. 18 (Article 1) of the Constitution and in nos. 98 and 99 (Article 5) of the Convention. However, the provision in the ITRs is more specific.

Article 10~~8~~: Dissemination of information

> 10.1 Using the most suitable and economical means, the Secretary-General shall disseminate information provided, of an administrative, operational, ~~tariff~~ or statistical nature, concerning international telecommunication ~~routes and~~ services. Such information shall be disseminated in accordance with the relevant provisions of the Constitution and the Convention and of this Article, on the basis of decisions taken by the Council or by competent ITU conferences, and taking account of conclusions or decisions of ITU assemblies. If so authorized by the Member State concerned, the information may be transmitted to the Secretary-General directly by an authorized operating agency, and shall then be disseminated by the Secretary-General. Member States should transmit such information to the Secretary-General in a timely manner, taking into account the relevant ITU-T Recommendations.

Provision **10.1** is one of two provisions in the ITRs that impose an obligation on the Secretary-General, rather than on Member States (the other provision being 9.2). Arguably, the old part of this provision is not necessary, since the Secretary-General's duty to provide information is specified in no. 18 (Article 1) of the Constitution and in nos. 98 and 99 (Article 5) of the Convention. However, the provision in the ITRs is more specific.

The US had suggested restricting the provision to "information of a statistical nature"[43], but this would have deprived the provision of all meaning, because much non-statistical information is provided to the ITU and is published by the ITU, such as E.164 numbering plans[44].

However, the newly added text contains two important new elements. Firstly, it recognizes that information is often provided directly to ITU by operators, without

---

[43] See WCIT document 9, add. 2.

[44] See ITU, 2013c. *Numbering Resources* and the ITU Operational Bulletin: ITU, 2013d. *Service Publications*.

passing through the Member State – provided of course that such direct transmission is permitted by the Member State.

Secondly, it encourages Member States to transmit information in a timely manner. The incitation should not be understood to refer only to the situation where an operator transmits information to the Member State which then transmits it to the ITU; rather it should be understood to mean that Member States should encourage operators to transmit the information in a timely manner, whether directly to the ITU, or to the Member State which will then transmit it to the ITU.

The references to "tariffs" and "routes" have been deleted in recognition of the fact that such information changes rapidly and that it would not be of much value to report it to the ITU for publication.

Many ITU-T Recommendations relate to information that should be provided to the ITU and published by the ITU. The compendium of such Recommendations is found on the ITU web site for international numbering resources.[45] See also p. 91.

Article 11: Energy efficiency/e-waste

> 11.1 Member States are encouraged to adopt energy-efficiency and e-waste best practices taking into account the relevant ITU-T Recommendations.

Provision **11.1** was added in recognition of the fact that telecommunications are a significant source of energy consumption and electronic waste products (for example, mobile phones often are discarded after 2-3 years), so Member States should adopt best practices to limit energy consumption and electronic waste.

Although one might suppose that such a provision should be non-controversial, this was not the case: significant discussion and negotiation were required before the consensus text was agreed. As for other provisions, the objections came from developed countries.

Non-treaty text related to these issues is found in WTSA Resolution 73 and in the ITU-T Recommendations in the L.1xxx series (that is, L.1000, L.1001, etc.). See also p. 91.

Article 12: Accessibility

> 12.1 Member States should promote access for persons with disabilities to international telecommunication services, taking into account the relevant ITU-T Recommendations.

Provision **12.1** was added in recognition of the fact that telecommunications can significantly improve the life of people with disabilities (the deaf, people who that cannot travel easily, the blind, etc), provided that attention is paid to making it possible for disabled people to use appropriate telecommunication services.

Although one might suppose that such a provision should be non-controversial, this was not the case: significant discussion and negotiation were required before the

[45] Under "Lists of Codes and Numbers" at ITU (2013c).

consensus text was agreed.[46] As for other provisions, the objections came from developed countries.

Non-treaty text related to these issues is found in WTSA Resolution 70 and in numerous ITU-T Recommendations, in particular E.121, E.123, E.135, E.138. E.139, V.18, V.151, V.254, T.140, T.134, H.323 Annex G, H.248.2, and F.790; but provisions regarding accessibility are found in many other ITU-T Recommendations. See also p. 91.

Article 13~~9~~: Special arrangements

13.1 *a)* Pursuant to Article 42 of the Constitution, special arrangements may be entered into on telecommunication matters which do not concern Member States in general. Subject to national laws, Member States may allow authorized operating agencies or other organizations or persons to enter into such special mutual arrangements with Member States and authorized operating agencies, or other organizations or persons that are so allowed in another country for the establishment, operation and use of special international telecommunication networks, systems and services, in order to meet specialized international telecommunication needs within and/or between the territories of the Member States concerned, and including, as necessary, the financial, technical or operating conditions to be observed .

b) Any such special arrangements shall endeavour to ~~should~~ avoid technical harm to the operation of the telecommunication facilities of third countries.

13.2 Member States should, where appropriate, encourage the parties to any special arrangements that are made pursuant to No. 73 (13.1) above to take into account relevant provisions of ITU-T Recommendations.

Provision **13.1**, the former 9.1, was one of the key provisions of the 1988 ITRs, because it facilitated liberalization and the growth of the Internet, see p. 7. Arguably this provision is no longer needed because of the new provision 8.1.1, which explicitly recognizes the commercial arrangements made possible by the 1988 provision. However, it was felt prudent to retain the 1988 text, so as to avoid any possible misinterpretations of what was intended, which was to continue to allow liberalized and privatized telecommunications to flourish. In particular, 13.1 allows special arrangements for entities that may not be "authorized operating agencies"[47], and thus it is broader than 8.1.1.

---

[46] It would be remiss to fail to mention the key role played at WCIT in this respect by Ms Andrea Saks who has worked tirelessly to achieve recognition of the needs of people with disabilities.

[47] As explained under provision 1.7 above, it is a national matter to determine what is an "authorized operating agency" and a state may "allow" special arrangements to be made by operating agencies that are not, according to it " authorized operating agencies".

The text of provision 13.1 is more specific than the text of Article 42 of the Constitution, and it is consistent with the text of the Constitution. Thus it suffices to refer to 13.1.

Provision 13.1(b) was strengthened by replacing "should avoid" with "shall endeavour to avoid". As already noted (see p. 95), this means that a state that has consented to be bound by the ITRs must take steps to avoid technical harm. As explained on p. 7, "technical harm" was originally intended to refer to what is now known as malware, that is, viruses, Trojan horses, worms, etc.[48] So provision 9.1(b) is, in effect, a stronger exhortation to take measures against certain kinds of security threats than the exhortation contained in article 6.

In this context, it is worth noting the evolving international law principle of prevention, according to which states are obliged to monitor, respond to, and prevent significant transboundary disruptions to, or interference with, the security and stability of international telecommunications networks.[49]

It must be stressed that only the specific kind of security threat mentioned above is within the scope of Article 13. Indeed, there were proposals to WCIT to include a general statement about security in this article[50], but those proposals were not accepted, so it is clear that "avoiding technical harm" cannot be understood to refer to security in general.

Provision 13.2 encourages commercial operators to take into account, where appropriate, the provisions of relevant ITU-T Recommendations, for example D-series Recommendations such as D.50, D.98, D.99, D.156, and D.271, amongst others (see also p. 91). However, there is no obligation to do so and many commercial arrangements[51] do not comply with the provisions of those ITU-T Recommendations.

During the preparatory process, several proposals were presented to include in this article avoidance of "financial harm". Although that term was not defined, it was understood that the intent of such proposals was to prevent the use of special arrangements to obtain international interconnections at costs lower than those foreseen by the accounting rate system (see p. 9). However, the special arrangements clause of the 1988 version of the ITRs had been instrumental in facilitating the demise of that system (see p. 10) so of course these proposals could not be accepted and indeed they were not explicitly presented to WCIT.[52] Thus, it must be understood that Article 13 does not in any way limit the financial terms of commercial agreements.

---

[48] Malware should not be considered to be "content" in the sense of 1.1(a) of the treaty.

[49] See Weber, Rolf H, 2011. "Politics Through Social Networks and Politics by Government Blocking: Do We Need New Rules?", *International Journal of Communications*, vol. 5, p. 1190.

[50] See WCIT DT 39.

[51] In particular, regarding Internet interconnections, peering (no-cost) arrangements are very common, see Weller Woodcock (2013).

[52] However, vestiges of these proposals were presented, such as "not bring harm" and "not breach the rights of third parties", see WCIT DT 39.

Article 14~~10~~: Final provisions

14.1 These Regulations, of which Appendices 1 and 2 form integral parts, shall enter into force on 1 January 2015, and shall be applied as of that date, consistent with all the provisions of Article 54 of the Constitution.

14.2 If a Member State makes reservations with regard to the application of one or more of the provisions of these Regulations, other Member States shall be free to disregard the said provision or provisions in their relations with the Member State which has made such reservations.

~~10.2 On the date specified in No. 61, the Telegraph Regulations (Geneva, 1973) and the Telephone Regulations (Geneva, 1973) shall be replaced by these International Telecommunication Regulations (Melbourne, 1988) pursuant to the International Telecommunication Convention.~~

~~10.4 Members of the Union shall inform the Secretary General of their approval of the International Telecommunication Regulations adopted by the Conference. The Secretary General shall inform Members promptly of the receipt of such notifications of approval.~~

Provision **14.1** incorporates, by reference to Article 42 of the Constitution, the text regarding approval and information of approval that was previously found in provision 10.4.

The old provisions 10.2 and 10.4 were deleted since they are no longer required.

Provision **14.2** is identical to the old provision 10.3. It establishes a special regime for reservations, declarations, counter-reservations, and counter-declarations that is different from the regime specified in the ITU Constitution and in the Vienna Convention on the Law of Treaties. The Radio Regulations follow the regime specified in the ITU Constitution.

There were proposals to omit the provision, and thus to align the ITRs with the other ITU instruments, but, after discussion, it was agreed to maintain the special regime.

In essence[53], by virtue of this provision, any reservation made by a Member State can be enforced vis-à-vis other Member States only insofar as the latter have expressly accepted the reservation. Thus, a Member State which has not objected to a reservation but has not explicitly accepted it cannot be held to be bound by it. This would not be the case without provision 14.2.

The legal reasoning is complex and is best illustrated by an example. Suppose that Member State X expresses the following reservation: "In the application of Article 13, we understand that 'technical harm' includes spam." Under the regime in force for the ITRs Member State Y, unless it has expressly accepted the reservation, is free to disregard Article 13 in its relation with Member State X. The fact that Member State Y has not formulated an objection to the reservation made by

[53] See CWG-WCIT/C 62 for more details.

Member State X cannot result in Member State Y being bound by that reservation. Thus in the ITRs there is a regime of implicit or tacit **rejection** of reservations.

The more common regime (that of the ITU Constitution and the Vienna Convention on the Law of Treaties) is that of implicit or tacit **acceptance** of reservations. That is, a Member State is considered as having accepted a reservation for which it has not formulated in due time an objection (which objection is referred to as a 'counter-reservation' in ITU).

Without provision 14.2, the situation with respect to the example given above would be the following: if Member State Y remains silent with respect to the reservation made by Member State X, then Member State Y must abide by the provisions of Article 13 **as intended by Member State X**, that is, with the understanding that "technical harm" includes spam.

Under that legal regime, if Member State Y wishes to be free to disregard Member State X's version of Article 13, then it has to state explicitly its counter-reservation, for example "we do not accept that 'technical harm' includes spam".

As we will see later in the section on reservations, the above considerations are primarily of theoretical interest.

Appendix 1: General provisions concerning accounting

1 Accounting rates

1.1 For each applicable service in a given relation, Member States shall endeavour to ensure that authorized operating agencies, ~~administrations and recognized private operating agencies shall~~ by mutual agreement, establish and revise accounting rates to be applied between them, taking into account ITU-T Recommendations and trends in the cost of providing the specific telecommunication service, and divide such rates into terminal shares payable to the authorized operating agencies of terminal countries and, where appropriate, into transit shares payable to the authorized operating agencies of transit countries.

1.2 Alternatively, in traffic relations where ITU-T cost studies can be used as a basis, the accounting rate may be determined in accordance with the following method:

a) authorized operating agencies shall establish and revise their terminal and transit shares taking into account ITU-T Recommendations;

b) the accounting rate shall be the sum of the terminal shares and any transit shares.

1.3 When one or more authorized operating agencies acquire, either by flat-rate remuneration or other arrangements, the right to utilize a part of the circuit and/or installations of another authorized operating agency, the former have the right to establish their share as mentioned in Nos. 1/2 (1.1) and 1/3 (1.2) above, for this part of the relation.

1.4 In cases where one or more international routes have been established by agreement between authorized operating agencies and where traffic is diverted unilaterally by the authorized operating agency of origin to an international route which has not been agreed with the authorized operating agency of destination, the terminal shares payable to the authorized operating agency of destination shall be the same as would have been due to it had the traffic been routed over the agreed primary route, and the transit costs are borne by the authorized operating agency of origin, unless the authorized operating agency of destination is prepared to agree to a different share.

1.5 In cases where traffic is routed via a transit point without authorization and/or agreement to the transit share, the transit authorized operating agency has the right to set the level of the transit share to be included in the international accounts.

1.6 Where an authorized operating agency has a duty or fiscal tax levied on its accounting-rate shares or other remunerations, it shall not in turn impose any such duty or fiscal tax on other authorized operating agencies.

2 Establishment of accounts

2.1 Unless otherwise agreed, the authorized operating agencies responsible for collecting the charges shall establish a monthly account showing all the amounts due, and send it to the authorized operating agencies concerned.

2.2 The accounts should be sent as promptly as possible, taking into account relevant ITU-T Recommendations, and, except in cases of *force majeure*, before the end of a period of 50 days following the month ~~of the third month following that to which they relate~~, unless otherwise mutually agreed.

2.3 In principle, an account shall be considered as accepted without the need for specific notification of acceptance to the authorized operating agency which sent it.

2.4 However, any authorized operating agency has the right to question the contents of an account within a period of two calendar months after the receipt of the account, but only to the extent necessary to bring any differences within mutually agreed limits.

2.5 In relations where there are no special agreements, a quarterly settlement statement showing the balances of the monthly accounts for the period to which it relates shall be prepared and issued as soon as possible by the creditor authorized operating agency, and shall be sent to the debtor authorized operating agency, which, after verification, shall return a copy endorsed with its acceptance.

2.6 In indirect relations where a transit authorized operating agency acts as an accounting intermediary between two terminal points, Member States shall endeavour to ensure that authorized operating agencies ~~it shall~~ include accounting data for transit traffic in the relevant outgoing traffic account to authorized operating agencies beyond it in the routing sequence as soon as possible after receiving the data from the originating authorized operating agency, in accordance with the relevant ITU-T Recommendations.

3 Settlement of balances of accounts

3.1 Choice of the currency of payment

3.1.1 The payment of balances of international telecommunication accounts shall be made in the currency selected by the creditor, after consultation with the debtor. In the event of disagreement, the choice of the creditor shall prevail in all cases, subject to the provisions in No. 1/20 (3.1.2) below. If the creditor does not specify a currency, the choice shall rest with the debtor.

3.1.2 If a creditor selects a currency with a value fixed unilaterally or a currency the equivalent value of which is to be determined by its relationship to a currency with a value also fixed unilaterally, the use of the selected currency must be acceptable to the debtor.

3.1.3 Provided the periods of payment are observed, authorized operating agencies have a right, by mutual agreement, to settle their balances of various kinds by offsetting:

a) credits and debits in their relations with other authorized operating agencies;

b) any other mutually agreed settlements, if appropriate.

This rule also applies in case payments are made through specialized payment agencies in accordance with arrangements with authorized operating agencies.

3.2 Determination of the amount of payment

3.2.1 The amount of the payment in the selected currency, as determined below, shall be equivalent in value to the balance of the account.

3.2.2 If the balance of the account is expressed in the monetary unit of the IMF, the amount of the selected currency shall be determined by the relationship in effect on the day before payment, or by the latest relationship published by the IMF, between the monetary unit of the IMF and the selected currency.

3.2.3 However, if the relationship of the monetary unit of the IMF to the selected currency has not been published, the amount of the balance of account shall, at a first stage, be converted into a currency for which a relationship has been published by the IMF, using the relationship in effect on the day before payment or the latest published relationship. The amount thus obtained shall, at a second stage, be converted into the equivalent value of the selected currency, using the closing rate in effect on the day prior to payment or the most recent rate quoted on the official or generally accepted foreign-exchange market of the main financial centre of the debtor country.

~~3.2.4 If the balance of the account is expressed in gold francs, the amount shall, in the absence of special arrangements, be converted into the monetary unit of the IMF in accordance with the provisions of section 6.3 of the Regulations. The amount of payment shall then be determined in compliance with the provisions of 3.2.2. above.~~

3.2.4 If, in accordance with a special arrangement, the balance of the account is not expressed in the monetary unit of the IMF, the payment shall also be the subject of this special arrangement and:

a) if the selected currency is the same as the currency of the balance of account, the amount of the selected currency shall be the amount of the balance of account;

b) if the selected currency for payment is different from the currency in which the balance is expressed, the amount shall be determined by converting the balance of account to its equivalent value in the selected currency in accordance with the provisions of No. 1/28 (3.2.3) above.

3.3 Payment of balances

3.3.1 Payment of balances of account shall be effected as promptly as possible, but in no case later than two calendar months after the day on which the settlement statement is dispatched by the creditor authorized operating agency. Beyond this period, the creditor authorized operating agency may, subject to prior notification in the form of a final demand for payment, and unless otherwise agreed, charge interest at a rate of up to 6 per cent per annum, reckoned from the day following the date of expiry of the said period.

3.3.2 The payment due on a settlement statement shall not be delayed pending settlement of a query on that account. Adjustments which are later agreed shall be included in a subsequent account.

3.3.3 On the date of payment, the debtor shall transmit the amount of the selected currency as computed above by a bank cheque, transfer or any other means acceptable to the debtor and the creditor. If the creditor expresses no preference, the choice shall fall to the debtor.

3.3.4 The payment charges imposed in the debtor country (taxes, clearing charges, commissions, etc.) shall be borne by the debtor. Any such charges imposed in the creditor country, including payment charges imposed by intermediate banks in third countries, shall be borne by the creditor.

3.4 Additional provisions

3.4.1 If, between the time the remittance (bank transfer, cheques, etc.) is effected and the time the creditor is in receipt of that remittance (account credited, cheque encashed, etc.), a variation occurs in the equivalent value of the selected currency calculated as indicated in No. 1/25 (3.2) above, and if the difference resulting from such variations exceeds 5 per cent of the amount due as calculated following such variations, the total difference shall be shared equally between debtor and creditor.

3.4.2 Should there be a radical change in the international monetary system which invalidates or makes inappropriate one or more of the foregoing paragraphs, authorized operating agencies are free to adopt, by mutual agreement, a different monetary basis and/or different procedures for the settlement of balances of accounts, pending a revision of the above provisions.

Appendix 1 constitutes an integral part of the treaty, that is, its provisions have the same status as the provisions in the main text. However, this appendix concerns the details of the accounting rate system (see p. 9). This is a specialized topic that does not warrant a detailed provision-by-provision discussion in the present book. Therefore, we will highlight here only some key points.

Provision 1.1 was adapted to the current environment, by recognizing that states no longer impose rates.

See the discussion under 8.3.1 above (p. 108) for a discussion of provision 1.6.

Provision 2.2 is extremely important in practice for the users of the accounting rate system because it specifies the default period of time for the sending of accounts. Ever since 1865, this period had been three months (see p. 3), however, since 1988, the time periods required to process accounting data have steadily decreased, in particular thanks to the use of powerful computer systems. However, debtors prefer to defer payment, so there was much resistance to reducing the period of time, see p. 24 (and see also the history of the revisions of Recommendation ITU-T D.195). Even though the US took the position that the accounting rate system is no longer used or needed (see p. 26), US operators were very active in the discussions of this provision at WCIT. While there were proposals to reduce the time period to 30 days, there was no agreement on this (with US operators opposing the proposal), and it was finally agreed to adopt the same time period that had been agreed in ITU-T Study Group 3, namely 50 days (specified in Recommendation ITU-T D.195). The added text "taking into account relevant ITU-T Recommendation" must be understood to refer to D.195 and the Recommendations it references, with the intent of favoring the use of shorter time periods if shorter periods are agreed in future revisions of D.195.

Provision 2.6 was adapted to the current environment, by recognizing that states no longer send accounts, and the added text "taking into account relevant ITU-T Recommendation" must be understood to refer to D.195 and the Recommendations it references, with the intent of favoring the use of shorter time periods if shorter periods are agreed in future revisions of D.195.

Provision 3.1.3 corresponds to the old provision 3.4.1, with the addition of text to make it clear that the provision applies even if payments are made through intermediaries.

The old provision 3.2.4 was deleted because use of the gold franc is considered obsolete and consequently the reference to the gold franc in the new 3.2.4 (old 3.2.5) was also deleted.

Appendix 2~~3~~: Additional provisions relating to maritime communications

1 General

1.1 The provisions contained in Article 8 and Appendix 1, taking into account the relevant ITU-T Recommendations, shall also apply to maritime telecommunications when establishing and settling accounts under this Appendix, insofar as the following provisions do not provide otherwise.

2 Accounting authority

2.1 Charges for maritime telecommunications in the maritime mobile service and the maritime mobile-satellite service shall, in principle, and subject to national law and practice, be collected from the maritime mobile station licensee:

a) by the administration that has issued the licence; or

b) by an authorized operating agency; or

c) by any other entity or entities designated for this purpose by the administration referred to in No. 2/5 (2.1.*a)*) above.

2.2 The administration or the authorized operating agency or the designated entity or entities listed in 2.1 above are referred to in this Appendix as the "accounting authority".

2.3 References to authorized operating agency contained in Article 8 and Appendix 1 shall be read as "accounting authority" when applying the provisions of Article 8 and Appendix 1 to maritime telecommunications.

2.4 Member States shall designate their accounting authority or authorities for the purposes of implementing this Appendix and notify their names, identification codes and addresses to the Secretary-General for inclusion in the List of Ship Stations and Maritime Mobile Service Identity Assignments. The number of such names and addresses shall be limited, taking into account the relevant ITU-T Recommendations.

3 Establishment of accounts

3.1 In principle, an account shall be considered as accepted without the need for specific notification of acceptance to the service provider ~~accounting authority~~ that sent it.

3.2 However, any accounting authority has the right to question the contents of an account for a period of six calendar months after dispatch of the account, even after the account has been paid.

4 Settlement of balances of account

4.1 All international maritime telecommunication accounts shall be paid by the accounting authority without delay and in any case within six calendar months after dispatch of the account, except where the settlement of accounts is undertaken in accordance with No. 2/17 (4.3) below.

> 4.2 If international maritime telecommunication accounts remain unpaid after six calendar months, the administration that has licensed the mobile station shall, on request, take ~~all possible~~ steps, within the limits of applicable national law, to ensure settlement of the accounts from the licensee.
>
> 4.3 If the period between the date of dispatch and receipt exceeds one month, the receiving accounting authority should at once notify the originating service provider ~~accounting authority~~ that queries and payments may be delayed. The delay shall, however, not exceed three calendar months in respect of payment, or five calendar months in respect of queries, both periods commencing from the date of receipt of the account.
>
> 4.4 The debtor accounting authority may refuse the settlement and adjustment of accounts presented more than twelve ~~eighteen~~ calendar months after the date of the traffic to which the accounts relate, unless provided otherwise under national law in which case the maximum deadline can be within eighteen calendar months.

Appendix 2 constitutes an integral part of the treaty, that is, its provisions have the same status as the provisions in the main text. It is a revision of the old Appendix 3 and it concerns the details of the accounting rate system for maritime communications. This is a specialized topic that does not warrant a detailed provision-by-provision discussion in the present book. Therefore, we will highlight here only some key points and note that Recommendations ITU-T D.90 and D.91 relate to this topic as do Recommendations ITU-R M.585 and M.493 (in which the term "Mobile Maritime Service Identity" is defined).

Before turning to the key points, we note that the provisions of this appendix were originally contained in the Radio Regulations, but were moved to the ITRs in 1988 pursuant to a proposal from European countries, who felt that it was best to have all accounting-related provisions in one treaty. During the preparatory process for WCIT-12, European countries initially proposed to delete these provisions entirely, but then accepted that it was necessary to retain them. Some European countries (in particular Sweden) proposed to move the provisions back to the Radio Regulations, presumably so as to facilitate a possible future abrogation of the ITRs in their entirety, but this proposal did not get sufficient support, so, at the conference, Europe supported the retention of this appendix.

The term "administration" is used in this Appendix, because that term refers to the government agency that is actually responsible for the activities referred to in this Appendix.[54]

References in provisions and 3.1 and 4.3 to "service provider" are references to authorities other than "accounting authorities" which may be authorized by an

[54] See no. 1002 of the ITU Constitution, which states: "*Administration*: Any governmental department or service responsible for discharging the obligations undertaken in the Constitution of the International Telecommunication Union, in the Convention of the International Telecommunication Union and in the Administrative Regulations."

administration pursuant to provisions 2.1(c) and 2.4 and which may providing accounting services on behalf of an accounting authority.

In provision 4.2, the deletion of the text "all possible" means that the administration need only take reasonable steps, rather than all possible steps.

In provision 4.4, it was decided to shorten the period to 12 months, in recognition of modern practices, but it was pointed out that some countries still specify, at the national level, the old 18-month period, so the text was adjusted to allow for this, with the implicit understanding that states should align their national laws to the new 12-month period.

Declarations and Reservations

As a preliminary comment, we note that the reservation regime for the ITRs is special: it is explained under Article 13 above.

In keeping with ITU practices, there were numerous declarations and reservations, but most of them are general declarations (such as reserving the right to take measures if other states fail to comply with the ITRs) that have no particular operational effect with respect to specific treaty provisions. Thus we will comment here only those parts of declarations and reservations that appear to be of particular interest.

Ghana stated that it dissociates itself from any action which in any way results in the deregulation of telecommunications.

It is not clear which, if any, of the provisions of the ITRs would be targeted by this declaration, but it is an interesting declaration of principle, which stands in sharp contrast to the positions taken by developed countries.

Niger stated that it reserves the right to reject any provision of these regulations which, if applied, particularly in connection with the special arrangements, could be in any way detrimental to the operation of telecommunication facilities and services or to the exercise of its sovereign right to regulate telecommunications within its territory.

This allows Niger to impose restrictions on special arrangements, and, understood in context, is also a statement of principle that stands in contrast to the positions taken by developed countries.

Malaysia stated that it disassociates with any reference to universal human rights in these Regulations on the basis that it is not appropriate to be included in a technical document of a regulatory nature as well as being a subsidiary document to the Constitution of the ITU which does not expressly contain any reference to the same, and if at all, the reference to human rights should only appear in the said Constitution; this reservation, however, does not relate to the right of access of Member States to international telecommunication services.

Thus Malaysia accepts the third paragraph of the Preamble, but will not be bound by the second paragraph. As noted in the analysis of the Preamble, this reservation has no practical consequences, because the second paragraph of the Preamble does nothing more than refer to existing binding instruments.

Sweden criticized Resolution 3 and stated that it considers that the public Internet and other Internet Protocol-based networks and services, whether governmental, public or private, are outside the scope of the International Telecommunication Regulations.

As already stated, this reminds one of the old adage "be careful what you wish for, because your wish may be granted." If there were no international treaty concerning the Internet and IP-based networks, then there would be no limits on national sovereignty and countries would be free to control the Internet as they see fit within their national borders.[55]

The **Russian Federation** stated that it proceeds from the assumption that views the Internet as a new global telecommunication infrastructure, and also as a part of the national telecommunication infrastructure of each Member State, and, accordingly, at ensuring that Internet numbering, naming, addressing and identification resources are considered a critical transnational resource. It further stated that it reserves the right to (1) establish and implement public policy, including international policy, on matters of Internet governance, and ensure security of the national Internet segment, as well as regulate within their territory the activities of operating agencies providing Internet access or carrying Internet traffic; (2) establish policies aimed at meeting public requirements with respect to Internet access and use; (3) take necessary regulatory measures to ensure security and confidence in provision international telecommunications services, provide implementation of these measures by operating agencies; (4) take any action it may deem necessary to protect its sovereign rights and interests in the sphere of telecommunications should violation of the Regulations or reservations, or actions taken by other Member States jeopardize its telecommunication services.

This is essentially a restatement of the Russian Federation's submission to WCIT that was not discussed by the conference, see p. 60.

Qatar stated that it does accept any obligation in respect of the application of any provision of these ITRs to service other than public correspondence services. Further, it criticized Resolution 3.

Qatar thus adopted the restrictive US proposal[56] regarding the entities to which the ITRs apply, but this conflicts with the ITU Constitution[57] and thus the reservation will presumably not be accepted by other Member States.

The **Republic of Korea** stated that it fully recognizes the need for respecting and securing human rights of Korean citizens; however, it is considered to be right to include this in the Preamble of the ITU Constitution, not in the Preamble of the International Telecommunication Regulations, in the respect of legal framework ITU legal instrument.

This is a criticism of paragraph 2 of the Preamble, on the grounds that that paragraph is not necessary.

---

[55] In this context, see L.S. (2012).

[56] See p. 64.

[57] See p. 73.

Diverging Interpretation and Resolution of Disputes

The interpretation of treaties is the sovereign right of states. If there is a disagreement in interpretation, then that would be handled in the first instance by discussions between the concerned states, either at the government-government level, or at the government-ambassador level. If the disagreement persists, the next step is usually an exchange of notes (written complaint).

If the disagreement still persists, the states can agree to refer the matter to a judicial process, such as the arbitration scheme provided in the ITU Constitution[58] (but which has never been used in practice), or an ad hoc arbitration process, or the International Court of Justice, etc.

Alternatively, one of the states can decide to take retaliatory measures, such as "if you continue to do X, then I will do Y". Retaliatory measures are fairly common regarding trade disputes, but, at least to date, unusual (or even unheard of) regarding telecommunications disputes.

---

[58] Article 56 of the Constitution establishes the principle, Article 41 of the Convention specifies the detailed procedure.

CHAPTER 7

Resolutions

All of the 1988 resolutions, recommendations, and the one opinion were suppressed and five new resolutions were adopted. All the new resolutions entered into force on 14 December 2012 and they apply to all Member States, because no Member State expressed a formal reservation[1] and because the signature formality only applies to the treaty text, not to the resolutions. That is, the WCIT-12 Resolutions apply to all Member States, not just to those who signed the 2012 ITRs.

Resolutions are not treaties and therefore they do not bind Member States as do treaties. Resolutions could, in principle, bind Member States if a treaty provision specifies that a resolution is binding, or if a resolution concerns procedural matters internal to the ITU (for example, deadlines for document submission). However, none of the WCIT-12 resolutions contain such provisions and all clearly indicate that they are not binding on Member States because they use the expression "invites Member States".

Instructions in resolutions to the Secretary-General and other organs of the Secretariat do bind those organs and the WCIT-12 resolutions do contain such instructions.

Hierarchically, WCIT-12 resolutions are subordinate to Plenipotentiary Resolutions, because WCIT is subordinate to the Plenipotentiary Conference. But WCIT-12 resolutions are at the same hierarchical level as the resolutions of other conferences and assemblies, such as WTSA.

This point is relevant with respect to Resolution 3, which is subordinate to Plenipotentiary Resolutions 101, 102, and 133, which deal with Internet-related issues.

Resolution 1: Special measures for landlocked developing countries and small island developing states for access to international optical fibre networks

The World Conference on International Telecommunications (Dubai, 2012),

[1] As stated earlier and below, Sweden and Qatar, in their declarations, criticized Resolution 3 but did not formally declare that they would not apply it.

considering

a) Resolution 65/172 of 20 December 2010 of the United Nations General Assembly, on specific actions related to the particular needs and problems of landlocked developing countries (LLDCs);

b) Resolution 30 (Rev. Guadalajara, 2010) of the Plenipotentiary Conference, on special measures for the least developed countries (LDCs), small island developing states (SIDS), LLDCs and countries with economies in transition;

c) the Millennium Declaration and the 2005 World Summit Outcome;

d) the outcome of the Geneva (2003) and Tunis (2005) phases of the World Summit on the Information Society (WSIS);

e) the Almaty Declaration and Almaty Programme of Action addressing the special needs of LLDCs within a new global framework for transit transport cooperation for landlocked and transit developing countries,

recalling

a) the New Partnership for Africa's Development (NEPAD), which is an initiative intended to boost economic cooperation and development at regional level, given that many landlocked and transit developing countries are in Africa;

b) the Declarations of the ministers of communications of the Union of South American Nations (UNASUR) and the Roadmap for South American connectivity for integration of the Telecommunications Working Group of the South American Infrastructure and Planning Council (COSIPLAN);

c) Mandate No. 7 arising from the sixth Summit of the Americas, held in Cartagena, Colombia, on 14-15 April, 2012, in which the Heads of State and Government of the Americas resolved *"To foster increased connection of telecommunication networks in general, including fibre-optic and broadband, among the region's countries, as well as international connections, to improve connectivity, increase the dynamism of communications between the nations of the Americas, as well as reduce international data transmission costs, and, thus, promote access, connectivity, and convergent services to all social sectors in the Americas"*,

reaffirming

a) the right of access of landlocked countries to the sea and freedom of transit through the territory of transit countries by all means of transport, in accordance with applicable rules of international law;

b) that transit countries, in the exercise of their full sovereignty over their territory, have the right to take all measures necessary to ensure that the rights and facilities provided for landlocked countries in no way infringe upon their legitimate interests,

recognizing

a) the importance of telecommunications and new information and communication technologies (ICT) to the development of LLDCs and SIDS;

b) that current difficulties of LLDCs and SIDS continue to adversely affect their development,

noting

that access to international optical fibre networks for LLDCs and the laying of optical fibre across transit countries are not specified in the infrastructure development and maintenance priorities in the Almaty Programme of Action,

conscious

a) that fibre-optic cable is a profitable telecommunication transport medium;

b) that access by LLDCs and SIDS to international fibre-optic networks will promote their integral development and the potential for them to create their own information society;

c) that the planning and laying of international optical fibre call for close cooperation between LLDCs and transit countries;

d) that, for the basic investment in laying fibre-optic cable, capital investments are required,

resolves to instruct the Director of the Telecommunication Development Bureau

1 to study the special situation of telecommunication/ICT services in LLDCs and SIDS, taking into account the importance of access to international fibre-optic networks at reasonable cost;

2 to report to the ITU Council on measures taken with respect to the assistance provided to LLDCs and SIDS under *resolves to instruct* 1 above;

3 to assist LLDCs and SIDS to develop their required plans containing practical guidelines and criteria to govern and promote sustainable regional, subregional, multilateral and bilateral projects affording them greater access to international fibre-optic networks,

instructs the Secretary-General

to bring this resolution to the attention of the Secretary-General of the United Nations, with a view to bringing it to the attention of the United Nations High Representative for LDCs, LLDCs and SIDS,

invites the Council

to take appropriate measures to ensure that ITU continues to collaborate actively in the development of telecommunication/ICT services in LLDCs and SIDS,

invites Member States

1 to cooperate with LLDCs and SIDS in promoting regional, subregional, multilateral and bilateral projects and programmes for telecommunication infrastructure integration that afford LLDCs and SIDS greater access to international fibre-optic networks;

2 to assist LLDCs and SIDS and transit countries in executing telecommunication infrastructure integration projects and programmes,

encourages landlocked developing countries and small island developing states

to continue to accord high priority to telecommunication/ICT activities, by putting in place technical cooperation activities in order to promote integral socioeconomic development,

invites Member States, Sector Members, Associates and Academia

to continue to support ITU Telecommunication Development Sector studies of the situation of telecommunication/ICT services in LDCs, LLDCs, SIDS and countries with economies in transition so identified by the United Nations and requiring special measures for telecommunication/ICT development.

This resolution is self-explanatory.

Resolution 2: Globally harmonized national number for access to emergency services

The World Conference on International Telecommunications (Dubai, 2012),

considering

that it is important for travellers to be aware of a single well-known number to access local emergency services,

noting

that Recommendation ITU-T E.161.1, on guidelines to select emergency number for public telecommunication networks, specified two globally harmonized emergency numbers,

resolves to instruct the Director of the Telecommunication Standardization Bureau

to take the necessary action in order that Study Group 2 of the ITU Telecommunication Standardization Sector (ITU-T) continue exploring the option of introducing a single globally harmonized national number for access to emergency services in the future,

invites Member States

to introduce, in addition to their existing national emergency numbers, a globally harmonized national number for access to emergency services, taking into consideration the relevant ITU-T Recommendations.

The laudable intent of this resolution is to encourage the harmonization of emergency numbers, which vary widely across the globe. To achieve that purpose, the resolution foresees two actions: on the one hand, the Director of TSB should assist ITU-T Study Group 2 to explore options to introduce a single harmonized number; on the other hand, Member States are invited to implement the provisions of Recommendation E.161.1 (that is the only relevant ITU-T Recommendation).

The exhortation to Member States is useful, see also the discussion of provision 5.4 in Chapter 6. On the other hand, the exhortation to ITU-T Study Group 2 is not likely to have much practical effect, because the Study Group has already studied the matter in some detail and concluded by adopting Recommendation E.161.1, which does indeed call for the implementation of one (or both) of the numbers 911 and 112 in addition to existing national numbers. (Those two numbers were selected because they were already in use in many countries: 911 in countries using the North American Numbering Plan; and 112 in European countries).

Resolution 3: To foster an enabling environment for the greater growth of the Internet

The World Conference on International Telecommunications (Dubai, 2012),

recognizing

a) the outcome documents of the Geneva (2003) and Tunis (2005) phases of the World Summit on the Information Society (WSIS);

b) that the Internet is a central element of the infrastructure of the information society, which has evolved from a research and academic facility into a global facility available to the public;

c) the importance of broadband capacity to facilitate the delivery of a broader range of services and applications, promote investment and provide Internet access at affordable prices to both existing and new users;

d) the valuable contribution of all stakeholder groups in their respective roles, as recognized in § 35 of the Tunis Agenda for the Information Society, to the evolution, functioning and development of the Internet;

e) that, as stated in the WSIS outcomes, all governments should have an equal role and responsibility for international Internet governance and for ensuring the stability, security and continuity of the existing Internet and its future development and of the future internet, and that the need for development of public policy by governments in consultation with all stakeholders is also recognized;

f) Resolutions 101, 102 and 133 (Rev. Guadalajara, 2010) of the Plenipotentiary Conference,

resolves to invite Member States

1 to elaborate on their respective positions on international Internet-related technical, development and public-policy issues within the mandate of ITU at various ITU forums including, *inter alia*, the World Telecommunication/ICT Policy Forum, the Broadband Commission for Digital Development and ITU study groups;

2 to engage with all their stakeholders in this regard,

instructs the Secretary-General

1 to continue to take the necessary steps for ITU to play an active and constructive role in the development of broadband and the multistakeholder model of the Internet as expressed in § 35 of the Tunis Agenda;

2 to support the participation of Member States and all other stakeholders, as applicable, in the activities of ITU in this regard.

As noted above, this resolution has been criticized, but the criticism is unfounded, see p. 78. In reality, the resolution does not change ITU's mandate regarding Internet matters, nor could it, given that those matters are dealt with by Plenipotentiary Resolutions. Resolutions 101, 102, and 133 resolve:

> to explore ways and means for greater collaboration and coordination between ITU and relevant organizations* involved in the development of IP-based networks and the future internet, through cooperation agreements, as appropriate, in order to increase the role of ITU in Internet governance so as to ensure maximum benefits to the global community;
> *Including, but not limited to, the Internet Corporation for Assigned Names and Numbers (ICANN), the regional Internet registries (RIRs), the Internet Engineering Task Force (IETF), the Internet Society (ISOC) and the World Wide Web Consortium (W3C), on the basis of reciprocity.

And ITU Council Resolution 1305, which was engendered by the cited Plenipotentiary resolutions, and adopted by consensus, invites Members States to recognize the scope of work of ITU on international Internet-related public policy matters, represented by the list:

1. Multilingualization of the Internet Including Internationalized (multilingual) Domain Names
2. International Internet Connectivity
3. International public policy issues pertaining to the Internet and the management of Internet resources, including domain names and addresses
4. The security, safety, continuity, sustainability, and robustness of the Internet

5. Combating Cybercrime
6. Dealing effectively with spam
7. Issues pertaining to the use and misuse of the Internet
8. Availability, affordability, reliability, and quality of service, especially in the developing world
9. Contributing to capacity building for Internet governance in developing countries
10. Developmental aspects of the Internet
11. Respect for privacy and the protection of personal information and data
12. Protecting children and young people from abuse and exploitation

In its declarations, Sweden stated that it notes that WCIT-12 Resolution 3 does not address the full picture of the environment and situation of the Internet and Internet Governance; the resolution only quotes parts of the Tunis Agenda (2005) that contains a number of important aspects on Internet Governance. One of those aspects cannot be referenced to in isolation, as is the case in the clause "*recognizing e)*" of the resolution; in particular paragraph 55 of the Tunis Agenda states the following: "We recognize that the existing arrangements for Internet governance have worked to make the Internet the highly robust, dynamic and geographically diverse medium that it is today, with the private sector taking the lead in day-to-day operations, and with innovation and value creation at the edges." Sweden stated that it therefore considers that this resolution does not do justice to all stakeholders involved in Internet related matters, and that it does not recognize the fully working, self-developing, bottom-up multi-stakeholder formats that work and evolve today on the Internet.

Needless to say, Sweden's characterization of the Resolution, and its favorable view of the entities that current govern the Internet, are not shared by all Member States[2], but it is beyond the scope of the present book to analyze these issues in detail.

In its declarations, Qatar stated that it expresses its indisposition to Resolution 3 to foster an enabling environment for the greater growth of the Internet.

This should be understood as criticism of that Resolution, but not a formal reservation refusing its application.

Resolution 4: Periodic review of the International Telecommunication Regulations

The World Conference on International Telecommunications (Dubai, 2012),

[2] See for example the Secretary-General's Report to the 2013 World Telecommunication Policy Forum.

recalling

Resolution 171 (Guadalajara, 2010) of the Plenipotentiary Conference, on preparations for this conference on the International Telecommunication Regulations (ITRs),

considering

a) that the ITU Council Working Group to prepare the 2012 world conference on international telecommunications (WCIT-12) held extensive discussions on the ITRs;

b) that there have been wide consultations in all ITU regions, involving ITU Member States, ITU Sector Members, Associates and Academia and civil society groups, showing great interest in the revision of the ITRs;

c) that many input documents have been submitted by the ITU membership;

d) the outcome of this conference,

recognizing

a) Articles 13 and 25 of the ITU Constitution;

b) No. 48 (Article 3) of the ITU Convention;

c) that the ITRs are one of the pillars supporting ITU's mission;

d) that 24 years elapsed between the approval of the ITRs and their review at this conference;

e) that the ITRs consist of high-level guiding principles that should not require frequent amendment, but in the fast moving sector of telecommunications/ICTs may need to be periodically reviewed,

noting

a) that technological development and demand for services that require high bandwidth continue to increase;

b) that the ITRs:

i) establish general principles on the provision and operation of international telecommunications;

ii) facilitate global interconnection and interoperability;

iii) promote efficiency, usefulness and availability of international telecommunication services,

resolves

to invite the 2014 plenipotentiary conference to consider this resolution and to take necessary action, as appropriate, to convene periodically (for example every eight years) a world conference on international telecommunications to revise the ITRs, taking into account the financial implications for the Union, *instructs the Secretary-General*

1 to bring this resolution to the attention of the Plenipotentiary Conference;

2 to provide information to enable the Plenipotentiary Conference to consider the cost implications of convening WCIT,

invites Member States

to contribute to the work outlined in this resolution.

This resolution was proposed by developing countries who felt that the 24-year period that elapsed between the adoption of the ITRs and their revision was too long. Indeed, it may well have be the case that the revision of the ITRs would have been less difficult if it had taken place in 2002 rather than in 2012. Developed countries were not favorable to the idea of a more frequent revision of the ITRs, however they accepted that the matter would be discussed at the 2014 Plenipotentiary Conference, and this is what the operative part of the resolution calls for. The resolution does hint at an eight-year periodicity for the review of the ITRs (compared to the four-year period for the review of the Radio Regulations), but it remains to be seen whether this proposal will be accepted by the Plenipotentiary Conference.

Resolution 5: International telecommunication service traffic termination and exchange

The World Conference on International Telecommunications (Dubai, 2012),

considering

a) that the transition from dedicated phone and data networks to converged IP-based networks raises regulatory, technical and economic issues which need to be taken into consideration;

b) that many Member States have expressed a need for the initiation and implementation of commercial agreements between authorized operating agencies and service providers of international services, with the objective of empowering all the participants in the new value chain,

noting

a) that some Member States are observing a deterioration in the quality of international services and voice traffic;

b) that Study Group 3 of the ITU Telecommunication Standardization Sector (ITU-T) is mandated to study the development of Recommendations, resolutions and guidelines related to these issues;

c) that there is a need for broader understanding of alternative dispute resolution mechanisms arising out of commercial arrangements;

d) that some Member States have concerns for the prevention and mitigation of fraud in international telecommunications, *resolves to invite concerned Members States*

to collaborate so that:

i) each party in a negotiation or agreement related to or arising out of international connectivity matters can seek the support of relevant authorities of the other party's State in alternative dispute resolution;

ii) their regulatory frameworks promote the establishment of commercial agreements between authorized operating agencies and the providers of international services in alignment with principles of fair competition and innovation,

instructs the Director of the Telecommunication Standardization Bureau

to take necessary action in order that ITU-T Study Group 3 study recent developments and practices with regard to the termination and exchange of international telecommunication traffic under commercial agreements, so as to develop a Recommendation, if appropriate, and guidelines for concerned Member States, for the use of providers of international telecommunication services in regard to issues they consider relevant, such as:

i) conditions for the establishment of invoices

ii) conditions for sending invoices

iii) conditions for the payment of invoices

iv) conditions for dispute resolution

v) conditions on fraud prevention and mitigation

vi) conditions for charges for international telecommunication service traffic termination and exchange,

invites Member States

to provide contributions on international telecommunication service traffic termination and exchange to Study Group 3 for the furtherance of its work,

invites Sector Members

to provide information to Study Group 3 and share best practices in the area of international telecommunication services traffic termination and exchange, including in particular, invoicing.

As noted in Chapter 3, numerous proposals were made during the preparatory process regarding financial matters, and this because of a certain dissatisfaction with the evolution of the flow of funds in telecommunications since 1988 (see Chapter 2). Many of the proposals made during the preparatory process survived, albeit in a condensed form, and were presented for discussion at WCIT in the form of new elements to be added to article 6.[3] These proposals can be summarized as follows

[3] See WCIT DT 20 rev. 1.

(square brackets indicate that there were options, either to use one of the two alternatives shown in the brackets, or to accept or reject the text shown in the brackets):

a) Member States should foster continued investment in high-bandwidth infrastructures.

b) Member States should endeavour to take measures to ensure that an adequate return is provided on investments in network infrastructures in identified areas. If this cannot be achieved through market mechanisms, then other mechanisms may be used.

c) Members States may take necessary measures to optimize the utilization of the facilities of operating agencies in their territories and to ensure their sustainable development considering the public interest.

d) Member States shall [ensure | promote] transparency with respect to retail prices and quality of service.

e) Member States should promote cost-oriented [wholesale] pricing [to the extent that it fosters competition]. [Regulatory measures may be imposed by the Member States to the extent that this cannot be achieved through market mechanisms and to the extent that such measures do not hinder competition.]

f) Member States shall ensure that rates (in particular transit rates, termination rates, and roaming rates) are cost-oriented.

g) Member States shall collaborate in preventing and mitigating fraud[4] in international telecommunications.

h) The ITU Standardization Sector shall be responsible for disseminating the regulatory frameworks in place in administrations having an impact on matters related to fraud.

i) Subject to national law, Member States shall ensure that Operating Agencies collaborate in preventing and controlling fraud in international telecommunications by:

- Identifying and transmitting to the transit and destination Operating Agencies the pertinent information required for the purposes of payment for the routing of international traffic, in particular the originating Country Code, National Destination Code and the Calling Party Number.
- Following up requests of other Member States or their Operating Agencies to investigate calls that cannot be billed, and helping to resolve outstanding accounts.
- Following up requests of other Member States or their Operating Agencies to identify the source of calls originated from their territories exerting potential fraudulent activity.

j) Member States shall ensure that each party in a negotiation or agreement related to or arising out of international connectivity matters, including

[4] Various definitions of this term were proposed. They were all similar to the following: "*Fraud*: use of any telecommunications facilities, resources or services with the intention of avoiding payment, without correct payment, with no payment at all, by making someone else pay, or by using a wrongful or criminal deception in order to obtain a financial or personal gain from the use of those facilities, resources or services."

those for the Internet, will have access to alternative dispute resolution mechanisms and will have recourse to the relevant regulatory or competition authorities of the other party's State.

k) When evaluating significant market power and its abuse, national competition authorities should also take into account international market share and international market power.
l) Member States shall take measures to ensure that fair compensation is received for carried traffic (e.g. interconnection or termination). [Regulatory measures may be imposed by the Member States to the extent that this cannot be achieved through market mechanisms and to the extent that such measures do not hinder competition.]
m) Member states shall ensure that their regulatory frameworks drive the operating agencies to establish mutual commercial agreements with providers of international communication applications and services in alignment with principles of fair competition, innovation, adequate quality of service and security.
n) The Member States shall take measures to ensure that operating agencies have the right to charge providers of international communication applications and services appropriate access charges based on the agreed quality of service. [Regulatory measures may be imposed by the Member State in case that this cannot be achieved through commercial arrangements and to the extent that such measures do not hinder competition.]
o) Notwithstanding the provisions of Art. 1, § 1.4 and § 1.6, and to enshrine the purpose set out in the Preamble; in Art. 1, § 1.3; in Art. 3, § 3.3; and taking into account Art. 3, § 3.1, Member States shall, as appropriate, encourage administrations, recognized operating agencies, and private operating agencies which operate in their territory and provide international telecommunication services offered to the public, to apply the ITU-T Recommendations relating to charging and accounting and alternate calling procedures, including any Instructions forming part of, or derived from, said Recommendations.

Proposals (a) and (b) above and the wholesale price version of proposal (e) are reflected in provision 8.1.2. Proposal (f) is not reflected: there was no agreement to include a reference to cost-oriented rates in the treaty, even though Recommendation ITU-T D.150 does recommend application of the cost-orientation principle for accounting in international telephony and D.140 recommends that accounting rates for international telephone services should be cost-orientated. Needless to say, the opposition of the inclusion to cost-orientation in the treaty text was expressed by developed countries, who were presumably influenced by their operators and wished to avoid references to non-market mechanisms.

The intent of proposal (c) is reflected in the first paragraph of the Preamble: optimization of national facilities is a national matter.

Proposal (d) above is reflected in provisions 4.4 through 4.7, but only for roaming, not for other types of services.

Proposals (g), (h) and (i) were strongly opposed by developed countries, who felt that fraud was not a proper topic for the treaty. These proposals are not reflected in the treaty text. In this context it should be noted that similar opposition had been expressed during WTSA-12 (which took place immediately prior to WCIT-12) with respect to the inclusion of the term "fraud"[5] in some WTSA Resolutions, and this despite the fact that ITU-T Study Group 3 was studying the matter. That opposition created some tensions, which may have spilled over into WCIT.

However, it was agreed in (v) of the *instructs the Director of TSB* of Resolution 5 to further study the matter of fraud prevention and mitigation. As noted above, such studies are already taking place in ITU-T Study Group 3.

Proposals (j) and (k) were also strongly opposed by developed countries, who took the view that market mechanisms are at present functioning well. These proposals are not reflected in the treaty text.

However, it was agreed in (i) of the *resolves* that Member States are invited to collaborate with respect to portions of proposal (j) and it was agreed in (iv) of the *instructs the Director of TSB* of Resolution 5 to further study such matters and indeed such studies are already taking place in ITU-T Study Group 3.

Proposals (l), (m) and (n) were variations proposed by African and Arab countries of the ETNO proposal that had been submitted during the preparatory process, see p. 31. Although the language of these proposals is not identical to the language of the proposal submitted by ETNO during the preparatory process, their intent is the same: to find ways to obtain revenue from the so-called "over-the-top" (OTT) providers, such as Google, Facebook, etc. Needless to say, there was strong opposition by the US and its allies to the inclusion of such proposals and they are not reflected in the treaty text.

However, it was agreed in (vi) of the *instructs the Director of TSB* of Resolution 5 to study such matters further, but this will be the case only if members submit inputs on the topic to ITU-T Study Group 3.

More significantly, (ii) of the *resolves* is a vestige of the original African and African proposals, see below for a more detailed discussion of the legislative history of these proposals. And see the G20 decision referred to on p. 31.

Proposal (o) was a very old proposal, submitted during the early phases of the preparatory process, whose intent was to make certain ITU-T Recommendations mandatory. There was no significant support for this proposal and it is not reflected in the treaty text. Nor is it reflected in Resolution 5.

Issues (i), (ii) and (iii) of the cited *instructs* refer to a request from some African countries to develop material related to those issues. There was insufficient time to

[5] One argument given, in particular by the UK, was that "fraud" refers to a crime. Indeed the term "fraud" is used in the criminal law of some common law countries, but that term is not used globally, even if the behavior that is commonly referred to as fraud is a crime. Be that at it may, the intent was to use the term "fraud", and to define it, as a term of art in telecommunications, so in reality there was no conflict with criminal law.

consider actual proposals at the conference, so it was agreed to refer the matters to ITU-T Study Group 3.

It is important to note that the list of issues enumerated under *instructs the Director of TSB* refers to commercial arrangements, not to the accounting rate system, as stated in the chapeau of the cited *instructs*.

Thus Resolution 5 represents a compromise: it was agreed to study further certain issues that are not reflected in the approved treaty text. In order to understand fully the implications of this compromise, it is important to present another step of the legislative history of Resolution 5. The various proposals mentioned above were discussed, and were reduced to the following proposals[6]:

A) Member States should foster continued investment in high-bandwidth infrastructures.

B) Member States shall promote cost-oriented wholesale pricing.

C) Member States [should | shall endeavour to] ensure that [ROA | OA] collaborate in preventing and mitigating fraud in international telecommunications.

D) Member States shall ensure that each party in a negotiation or agreement related to or arising out of international connectivity matters can seek support of relevant authorities of other party's State in alternative dispute resolution.

E) Member States shall take measures to ensure that reasonable compensation is received for carried traffic (e.g. interconnection or termination).

F) Member states shall ensure that their regulatory frameworks promote the establishment of commercial agreements between operating agencies and the providers of international communication applications and services in alignment with principles of fair competition, innovation, adequate quality of service [and security].

G) The Member States shall take measures to ensure that Operating Agencies have the right to charge providers of international communication applications and services appropriate access charges based on the agreed quality of service.

Proposal (A) corresponds to (a) above and is reflected in 8.1.2. Proposal (B) corresponds to (e) and (f) and is reflected in 8.1.2. The proposal to include a an explicit reference to competition and market mechanisms was not included, but must be understood to be implied in 8.1.2.

Proposal (C) corresponds to (g), (h), and (i) and is reflected in (v) of of the *instructs the Director of TSB* of Resolution 5.

Proposal (D) corresponds to (j) and is reflected in (i) of the *resolves* of Resolution 5.

Proposal (E) corresponds to (l), proposal (F) corresponds to (m), and proposal (G) corresponds to (n). They are reflected in (vi) of the *instructs the Director of TSB* of Resolution 5 and in (ii) of the *resolves* of Resolution 5. During the final discussions in Plenary regarding (ii) of the *resolves*, it was suggested that the term "providers of

---

6 See WCIT DT 45 rev. 2. Not all the proposals contained in that document are presented here, and the order of the presentation has been changed.

international services" be replaced by "providers of international telecommunication services", but this proposal was not accepted.[7] Thus, it is clear that that element of the resolution refers to services provided on top of the telecommunication network, that is to the so-called "over the top" (OTT) services.

It is instructive to compare proposals (F) and (G) with a new proposed European Union Regulation[8]. Article 19 of that proposed Regulation states that, under certain conditions, any operator shall have the right to provide a European assured service quality (ASQ) connectivity product. That product is defined in (12) of Article 1 of the proposed Regulation as "a product that is made available at the internet protocol (IP) exchange, which enables customers to set up an IP communication link between a point of interconnection and one or several fixed network termination points, and enables defined levels of end to end network performance for the provision of specific services to end users on the basis of the delivery of a specified guaranteed quality of service, based on specified parameters". The language of proposals (F) and (G) are very different from the language of the proposed Regulation, nevertheless it should be recalled those proposals were related to the original ETNO proposal (see p. 31), which included the following proposed text for the ITRs: "Operating Agencies shall cooperate in the development of international IP interconnections providing both, best effort delivery and end to end quality of service delivery. Best effort delivery should continue to form the basis of international IP traffic exchange. Nothing shall preclude commercial agreements with differentiated quality of service delivery to develop."[9]

One might thus speculate regarding whether, after WCIT, the European Commission has changed its stance and no longer opposes the gist of the original ETNO proposal. In this context, see Whereas (49) and (50) of the proposed Regulation; (50) states "Providers of content, applications and services and providers of electronic communications to the public should therefore be free to conclude specialised services agreements on defined levels of quality of service as long as such agreements do not substantially impair the general quality of internet access services."

---

[7] See 1.15 to 1.18 of WCIT document 78.
[8] European Commission (2013).
[9] CWG-WCIT12/C – 109.

CHAPTER 8

Conclusions and Implications for National Legislators and Regulators

As indicated at the end of Chapter 5, it is the author's view that a persistent refusal by many countries to be bound by the 2012 ITRs might have undesirable consequences. One way to avoid this situation would be that more countries agree to be bound, while recognizing that the treaty must be implemented in a non-controversial manner, that is, so as to avoid the negative consequences that some fear may be engendered (see Chapter 5).

If this does not happen, then signatory states may choose to enter into additional arrangements that might be detrimental to the global interconnectivity of today's telecommunications systems, which include the Internet.[1] As a Canadian think-tank put the matter[2]:

> "the larger problem [of the split between signatories and non-signatories] in the long term is the overall degree of complexity introduced into the governance of international telecommunications, the potential for increased transaction costs and the eventual possibility of significant divergence between the two treaty regimes over time. Given the similarity between the two treaties [1988 versus 2012], as well as the long history of routine cooperation on international telecommunications and the resulting business relationships and accumulated social practice, there are reasons to believe that this complexity may be manageable, if suboptimal. This assessment may not apply, however, in the event that the parties to the new ITRs engage in subsequent negotiations, building on the accompanying resolutions to erect a parallel institution for Internet governance. In the event such a parallel institution duplicates the function of the Internet Assigned Numbers Authority or the IETF, the potential exists for serious harm to global interoperability.

---

[1] Taylor, Matthew, Hopkins, Nick and Kiss, Jemima, 2013. "NSA surveillance may cause breakup of internet, experts warn", *The Guardian*, 1 November 2013. The reference is to the Prism surveillance program, see p. 21 and p. 42.

[2] Raymond, M. and Smith, G., 2013. "Reimagining the Internet: The Need for a High-level Strategic Vision for Internet Governance," Centre for International Governance Innovation, Internet Governance Papers, Paper No. 1, July 2013.

> Further, since routing is currently done without regard for international borders, the existence of parallel Internet governance regimes that may evolve with very different privacy protections poses challenging questions about the sustainability and desirability of legacy routing practices."

As we have seen, the 2012 ITRs are an evolution of the 1988 ITRs: they reflect the changes that have taken place since 1988 in the telecommunications environment, in particular liberalization and privatization. Thus, the 2012 ITRs are mostly a reflection of the changes that have taken place in national legislation and regulation and they do not impose any radical changes: indeed, national laws and regulations already incorporate the provisions of the 1988 ITRs.

In this sense, it is not appropriate to speak of "success or failure" of WCIT: it is simply one step in the continuing evolution of the telecommunications environment. Some think it was a useful step, some think it was not a useful step. As indicated above, it is the author's view that WCIT was partly useful, even if it did not achieve its intended goal.

Some may take the view that there is no need for a treaty regarding international telecommunication matters: any matters requiring inter-governmental coordination can be handled by ITU Recommendations, or Resolutions, or bilateral or regional agreements. Indeed this is true for many matters, but it is the author's view that the divergence of views expressed at WCIT indicates that there is a need to agree some basic principles at a high level, and to enshrine them formally in a treaty. For example, lack of treaty-level agreement regarding cooperation with respect to network security issues in effect favors the current practices of unilateral surveillance such as the US Prism program (see p. 21 and p. 42), and in effect makes it more difficult to combat spam, to control international roaming prices, and to mitigate e-waste. And lack of treaty-level agreement may make it more difficult for smaller countries (and their operators) to negotiate equitable financial arrangements.

Indeed, in the author's view, WCIT was a lost opportunity to come to an agreement on a new international framework for telecommunications. As noted throughout this book, such a framework has always existed since the inception of electronic communications, and has helped to make telecommunications an essential component of modern economic and social activities. In this sense, WCIT was a repeat of WSIS[3]: an attempt to agree a framework, in particular regarding economic issues related to development, failed because of divergences regarding Internet governance. But other opportunities will surely arise in the future. Or perhaps the future will show that no international framework is needed. However, in this context it is worth considering the theory of cycles put forward by Wu[4]: telecommunication services have historically moved from open crude inventions to closed sophisticated products, leading at times to government interventions.

Although the new ITRs do not impose any radical changes to national laws or regulations, in some instances, national authorities may have to adapt regulations to comply with the revisions approved in 2012, and may have to adapt laws if the

[3] See Mueller (2010), pp. 57 ff.

[4] Wu, Tim, 2010. *The Master Switch: The Rise and Fall of Information Empires*, Knopf.

current laws do not give power to the executive branch to adapt the regulations. Further, developing countries may wish to consider how to contribute to further discussions of various issues, in particular the financial matters referred to in Resolution 5.

Indeed, as stated in a presentation[5] made at the 10-11 July 2013 Joint ATU-ITU Seminar on the outcomes of WTSA-12 and WCIT-12, the WCIT outputs address issues that are important for developing countries, in particular: loss of revenue, excessively high prices, lack of infrastructure, insufficient competition and transparency, lack of consensual mechanisms for dispute resolution and service provision, fraud, and low levels of access to infrastructure and services. Follow up actions including providing information on the new ITRs to all concerned at the national level, getting feedback from all concerned at the national level, and transposing the ITRs as appropriate and necessary into national laws and regulations. In summary, according to the cited presentation, WCIT-12 provided a good opportunity to discuss the key issues that affect the development of telecommunications in Africa and the good operation of international telecommunications; important decisions were taken and it is important that African states, whose commitment to such conferences is well known, get actively involved in the implementation of the WCIT outputs, so that telecommunications will continue to grow in Africa, and reach all geographic areas at prices that are affordable for all.

Thus we list here the various areas in which the revisions approved in 2012 might have an impact on national regulations.

Possible actions to consider

1. The 1988 ITRs applied to the same entities as the 2012 ITRs, namely "authorized operating agencies". States may wish to consider whether their national definition of such entities is sufficiently clear, see the discussion under 1.1(a), 1.2 and 1.7(a) in Chapter 6 .

2. States may wish to consider whether their legal and regulatory frameworks have been adapted to privatization and liberalization in a way that reflects the intent of provisions 3.1 and 3.2, see the discussion in Chapter 6.

3. States that do not currently prohibit misuse of numbering resources should do so pursuant to provision 3.5.

4. States that allow extra-territorial use of Mobile Country Codes (MCCs), should notify such extra-territorial use as specified in Annex E of E.212.

5. States should review their legal and regulatory frameworks to verify that they are consistent with the provision of calling line identification pursuant to provision 3.6, and whether they are sufficient to prevent illegitimate spoofing, including SMS spoofing.

---

[5] Adou Biendjui, Josephine, 2013. "Questions d'économie et de comptabilité liées aux résultat de la CMTI-12", ITU, July 2013.

6. States should review their legal and regulatory frameworks to verify that they are consistent with enabling the implementation of regional telecommunication traffic exchange points pursuant to provision 3.7.

7. States may wish to consider whether their legal and regulatory frameworks have been adapted to privatization and liberalization in a way that reflects the intent of provisions 4.1, 4.2, and 4.3, see the discussion in Chapter 6.

8. States that do not currently have measures regarding the provision of information on roaming prices should implement such measures pursuant to provision 4.4 (see the discussion in Chapter 6). They should consider measures related to quality of service of roaming pursuant to provision 4.5; and to promoting competition pursuant to provision 4.7. Further, they should consider contributing to further work on the matter, in particular in ITU-T Study Group 3.

9. States should foster cooperation to mitigate inadvertent roaming in border areas, see the discussion under provision 4.6 in Chapter 6.

10. States should encourage operators to inform users, including roaming users, of the emergency call number, see the discussion under provision 5.4 in Chapter 6. States should consider implementing Recommendation ITU-T E.161.1, and they may wish to contribute to the discussions in ITU-T Study Group 2 regarding harmonization of emergency numbers.

11. States should cooperate to ensure the security of international telecommunications networks, see the discussion under Article 6 in Chapter 6. In this context, states consider the principles[6] advocated by a large number of civil society organizations, and the Results[7] of the Seoul Conference on Cyberspace 2013.

12. States should cooperate to counter spam, see the discussion under Article 7 in Chapter 6. In particular, they should ensure their national laws adequately deal with spam, that end-users and service providers are made aware of appropriate methods to counter spam and that they have access to appropriate anti-spam software.

13. States may wish to consider whether their legal and regulatory frameworks encourage investments in international telecommunication networks and promote competitive wholesale pricing, see the discussion under provision 8.1.2 in Chapter 6.

14. States that use the accounting rate system should review their regulations to ensure that they are aligned with the revisions, in particular of Appendix 1.

15. States involved in maritime communications should review their regulations to ensure that they are aligned with the revisions of Appendix 2 (the former Appendix 3), see in particular the discussion under provision 4.4 of Appendix 2 in Chapter 6.

---

[6] *Necessary and Proportionate* (2013).
[7] In particular the Seoul Framework (2013).

16. States may wish to review their taxation policies to ensure that they are consistent with the ITRs, see the discussion under provision 8.3.1 in Chapter 6. And they may wish to refer to the G20 leaders' declaration referred to on p. 31.

17. States may wish to consider authorizing operators to submit information directly to the ITU pursuant to Article 10, and they should review their procedures to ensure that information is transmitted in a timely manner as called for in provision 10.1.

18. States that do not already have programs regarding energy-efficiency and e-waste management should consider establishing such programs pursuant to Article 11.

19. States that do not already promote access for persons with disabilities should consider establishing such programs pursuant to Article 12.

20. States that authorize special arrangements should take steps to avoid the propagation of malware, see the discussion under 13.1(b) in Chapter 6.

21. Landlocked states, small island nations, and their neighbors should consider the actions listed in Resolution 1.

22. States and all concerned entities should consider participating in the ongoing discussions on Internet-related matters as called for in Resolution 3.

23. States may wish to consider, as called for in Resolution 4, whether more frequent revision of the ITRs would be desirable.

24. States and operators, in particular developing countries, should consider contributing to the discussions of the financial matters referred to in Resolution 5.

25. The relevant authorities of states that do not already do so should consider whether they have standing to consider international connectivity disputes as outlined in *resolves* (i) of Resolution 5, see the discussion under Resolution 5 in Chapter 7.

26. States may wish to consider whether their legal and regulatory frameworks promote the establishment of commercial agreements as outlined in *resolves* (ii) of Resolution 5, see the discussion under Resolution 5 in Chapter 7.

WCIT Analysed According to Dispute Resolution Theory

The purpose of this chapter is not to criticize any of the parties involved in the conference. Its purpose is to look at what happened at the meta-level, from the point of view of the theory and practice of negotiation and dispute resolution, and this so as to indicate how future conferences on difficult topics might be managed so as to bridge differences and come to consensus.

There is a vast literature on the theory and practice of negotiation and dispute resolution.[1] The analysis below is based on a particularly well-known, clear, and concise framework for difficult negotiations.[2] That framework applied well to WCIT, even if WCIT was a multi-party negotiation, and even if the Chairman and Secretariat facilitated the negotiations, with the Chairman at times acting as a mediator. As in all facilitated negotiations (or mediations), the ultimate responsibility for the preparation of the negotiations, the negotiations themselves, and their outcome rests with the parties, not with the facilitators.

According to the cited framework (which consists of a set of steps and tips):

0: The first, and most important step, is to prepare, prepare, prepare. Of course this was understood by the participants and management team[3] at WCIT. However, for various reasons, it proved difficult to prepare adequately for the conference. In some cases there were serious differences of views within regions or countries, which made it difficult to agree a coherent and well thought-out regional

[1] The author is a certified mediator and has contributed to that literature.

[2] Ury, William, 1991. *Getting Past No: Negotiating in Difficult Situations,* Bantam.

[3] We will use the term "management team" to refer to the Secretariat, the Chairman, and the Chairmen of the various working parties and sub-working parties. During the conference, that team acted pretty much like a mediator, in accordance with ITU practices, even if the term "mediator" is not used within ITU for these activities.

or national negotiating strategy.[4] Because of those differences, there was considerable reluctance to use the preparatory process to agree on relatively non-controversial issues (such as numbering misuse), so even such issues had to be negotiated at the conference. It proved difficult to identify well in advance suitable chairmen for any position other than the Chairman of the conference so, as a consequence, the chairmen of the working groups and sub-working groups started to prepare only at the conference itself. And it proved difficult to assign sufficient secretariat staff full-time to the substantive issues until shortly before the conference.

Within the management team, there was insufficient understanding of the extent to which certain countries were willing to maintain what were obviously extreme positions: the ITU has a long tradition of coming to consensus, and experienced ITU participants simply did not believe that it would prove impossible to come to consensus. As a consequence, there wasn't adequate planning to deal with the scenario that emerged during the last days of the conference. In particular, repeated reassurances that consensus would be found and that voting would not take place turned out, in retrospect, to have been excessively optimistic. There was also the difficult issue of the perceived scope of the conference, with some taking the view that it could affect the flow of content on the Internet, and others saying that it had little or nothing to do with the Internet. In reality, the financial issues to be discussed were related to the Internet, as were issues such as security and spam. For the reasons mentioned above, this difference in views was not adequately addressed during the preparatory process, leading to participants talking, at times, at cross purposes during the conference.

1. Don't react: go to the balcony. This aphorism means that, when confronted with an opposing party who appears to be rigid and extreme, it is better not to react by also expressing rigid and extreme positions: it is better to step back and let things cool off before restarting the negotiations. Of course this was well understood by the participants and management team at WCIT, and indeed pausing negotiations on difficult topics (either for a short break, or for a day or two) is standard practice in ITU. For example, the discussions on a particularly difficult issue, the OA/ROA matter, were deliberately spread over time. However, there were strong differences of view on essentially all matters, so it proved impossible to postpone all discussions. That is, because of time constraints, it became necessary to discuss issues even when the opposing parties were clearly reacting to each others' extreme statements.

2. Don't argue: step to their side. This aphorism means that, when confronted with what appears to be an unreasonable demand from one party, one should not react to it by restating one's own extreme position. Rather, one should acknowledge the other parties' points, agree as far as possible, and restate calmly one's own requirements. It is important to overcome suspicion and lack of trust. Again, of course this was well understood by the participants and management team at WCIT, and is routinely practiced in ITU. But, again, given the strong differences in views,

[4] In technical terms, there was insufficient attention paid to the BATNAs: the Best Alternatives to Negotiated Agreements.

and time pressure, many sessions turned into sterile restatements of positions, rather than acknowledgements of understanding what the other party wanted. This of course resulted in an increase in suspicion and lack of trust. The leadership team repeatedly identified this process issue and strove to overcome it, but unfortunately it was not always possible to do so.

3. Don't reject: reframe. This aphorism means that, when confronted with an unacceptable request, it is better not to reject it outright, but rather to ask why the party is making that request and to find ways to reframe the issue so that both parties can benefit. Once again, this was well understood by the participants and management team at WCIT, and is routinely practiced in ITU. Indeed, many issues at WCIT were resolved by applying this technique: for example, the OA/ROA issue was resolved by accommodating the need to modernize the terminology with the need to avoid unduly expanding the entities covered by the treaty; sensitivity regarding censorship was accommodated by adding a "no content" provision to the Preamble; sensitivity regarding possible expansion of the numbering misuse provision to Internet names and addresses was accommodated by drafting the provision so that it could not be understood to imply that; etc. However, once again primarily because of the strong positions taken by the parties and because of time pressure, it proved impossible to use this technique to accommodate all the diverging interests.

4. Don't push: build them a golden bridge. This aphorism means that, when coming close to an agreement on a sensitive matter, it is better not to push hard for acceptance: instead one should find ways to draw the other party into the direction that one wishes. Once again, this was well understood by the participants and management team at WCIT, and is routinely practiced in ITU. However, time pressure and the divisions within countries and regions made it difficult to apply this technique successfully to the more sensitive issues. For example, the opponents of using any term other than ROA were not convinced that the solution adopted (AOA) was in fact nothing other than the status quo. And the opponents of an article on spam were not convinced that the "no-content" provision in the Preamble adequately met their concerns regarding possible censorship. Further, in retrospect, it would appear that more time should have been allowed for participants to negotiate Resolution 3, rather than imposing it after determining that there was majority support for it.

5. Don't escalate: use power to educate. This aphorism means that, if there is a refusal to compromise that results in a breakdown in negotiations, it is better not to escalate the issue through power tactics: it is better calmly to point out the consequences of not agreeing and to educate the other party on the benefits of compromising and the disadvantages of not compromising. Once again, this was well understood by the participants and management team at WCIT, and is routinely practiced in ITU. But, after the first week of the conference, the level of frustration was rather high, for the reasons explained above, so some participants started to escalate matters (in particular, a group of countries presented an extreme proposal). This did not cause the other parties to back down, on the contrary, it caused them to harden their positions (which is exactly what dispute resolution theory predicts). This in turn led to counter-hardening and finally resulted in difficult discussions regarding the third paragraph of the Preamble that led to the formal vote.

Indeed, in terms of tactics, it would appear that developing countries might have been better off if they had not pushed for the inclusion of the third paragraph of the Preamble, and if they had not supported the proposals from the Russian Federation and the proposals presented at the end of the first week by a group of countries. Neither the Russian nor the group-of-countries proposals were ever on the agenda, so they were not introduced or discussed; nevertheless their existence as formal proposals increased tensions and some countries stated, at least in private, that they would ask for those proposals to be introduced and discussed if progress was not made on other issues. This is a typical "power-negotiating" tactic and, predictably, resulted in a hardening of the positions of the other side, even if its intent was probably the opposite, namely to induce a softening in the positions of the other side by worsening their perceived worst-case outcome.

Conversely, regarding the tactics of the developed countries, it would appear in retrospect that they could have acknowledged more clearly that they understood the concerns of developing countries; that of course the conference could not result in restrictions on freedom of speech; and that certain Internet-related issues would be addressed, but not others. Further, the developed countries could have acknowledged more clearly, towards the end of the conference, the various "golden bridges" that had been offered to them and that are mentioned above. And some countries (in particular the US) had both publicly and privately stated what their bottom line was; this is unheard of in negotiations (especially treaty negotiations): parties usually have some room to negotiate away from their stated position. Because it is unheard of to state the bottom line at the beginning, most participants simply did not believe that the stated position was the bottom line and kept trying to negotiate concessions. This of course led to increasing the frustration and suspicion of all sides, and to frustration within the management team.

In terms of the future, the relevant maxim would appear to be 5 above: don't escalate, use power to educate. Both signatory and non-signatory nations should not try to force the other side to join them, rather they should discuss the objective advantages and disadvantages of a situation in which not all countries accede to the 2012 ITRs, and they should strive to find ways to accommodate their mutual concerns. Indeed, the discussions that took place at the fifth World Telecommunication Policy Forum were very much in that spirit[5], so an optimistic view of the future is not unrealistic.

[5] See for example Pruzin, Daniel, 2013. "U.S. Satisfied With Internet Forum: Has Concerns With Brazilian Proposal", *Bloomberg Daily Report for Executives,* 22 May 2013.

References

Note: well known treaties and individual ITU conference documents, Resolutions and Recommendations are not listed here. They are referenced as needed in footnotes in the main text.

.edu, 2013. Wikipedia <http://en.wikipedia.org/wiki/.edu> accessed 28 July 2013.

Ackerman, Elise, 2012. "The U.N. Fought the Internet The Internet – And The Internet Won; WCIT Summit in Dubai Ends", *Forbes,* 14 December 2012 <http://www.forbes.com/sites/eliseackerman/2012/12/14/the-u-n-fought-the-internet-and-the-internet-won-wcit-summit-in-dubai-ends/> accessed 12 October 2013.

Ackerman, Spencer and Lewis, Paul, 2013. "US senators rail against intelligence disclosures over NSA practices", *The Guardian,* 31 July 2013 <http://www.theguardian.com/world/2013/jul/31/us-senate-intelligence-officials-nsa> accessed 2 August 2013.

Adas, Michael, 2006. *Dominance by Design: Technological Imperatives and America's Civilizing Mission,* Harvard Belknap Press.

Adou Biendjui, Josephine, 2013. "Questions d'économie et de comptabilité liées aux résultat de la CMTI-12", ITU, July 2013 <http://www.itu.int/en/ITU-T/Workshops-and-Seminars/atu-itu/201307/Pages/default.aspx> accessed 28 July 2013.

Anti-Counterfeiting Trade Agreement, 2013. Wikipedia <http://en.wikipedia.org/wiki/Anti-Counterfeiting_Trade_Agreement#Secrecy_of_negotiations> accessed 14 October 2013.

Argentina v Chile, 1977. *Reports Of International Arbitral Awards*, Vol. XXI pp. 53-264 <http://untreaty.un.org/cod/riaa/cases/vol_XXI/53-264.pdf> accessed 15 March 2013.

AT Kearney, 2010. *A Viable Future Model for the Internet,* December 2010 <http://www.atkearney.com/index.php/Publications/a-viable-future-model-for-the-internet.html> accessed 16 July 2013.

Atkin, David, Lau, Tuen-Yu and Lin, Carolyn, 2008. "Still on hold? A retrospective analysis of competitive implications of the Telecommunication Act of 1996, on its 10th year anniversary", *Telecommunications Policy*, vol. 30 no. 2, pp. 80-95.

Barabas, Emily, and Bankston, Kevin, 2013. "It's Not Just About the US: How the NSA Threatens Human Rights Internationally", *Center for Democracy and Technology,* 12 June 2013 <https://www.cdt.org/blogs/1206it's-not-just-about-us-how-nsa-threatens-human-rights-internationally> accessed 15 June 2013.

Baran, Paul, 1967. "The Future Computer Utility", *National Affairs*, vol. 8, p. 75 <http://www.nationalaffairs.com/public_interest/detail/the-future-computer-utility> accessed 21 November 2013.

Bird, Robert C. and Cahoy, Daniel R., 2007. "The Emerging BRIC Economies: Lessons from Intellectual Property Negotiation and Enforcement", *Northwestern Journal of Technology and Intellectual Property*, vol. 5 no. 3, p. 1 <http://scholarlycommons.law.northwestern.edu/cgi/viewcontent.cgi?article=1131&context=njtip> accessed 28 July 2013.

Bisaz, Corsin, 2012. *The Concept of Group Rights in International Law: Groups as Contested Right-Holders, Subjects and Legal Persons*, Martinus Nijhoff.

Booz, Allen, Hamilton, 2004. "The World's Most Enduring Institutions" <http://www.boozallen.com/media/file/143411.pdf> accessed 11 March 2013.

Bosco, David, 2013. "Brazil Wants UN to Help Safeguard Internet", *Foreign Policy,* 8 July 2013 <http://bosco.foreignpolicy.com/posts/2013/07/08/brazil_wants_un_to_help_safeguard_internet> accessed 14 July 2013.

Bowden, Casper, 2013. "The US National Security Agency (NSA) surveillance programmes (PRISM) and Foreign Intelligence Surveillance Act (FISA) activities and their impact on EU citizens' fundamental rights", *Note for the European Parliament* <http://www.europarl.europa.eu/meetdocs/2009_2014/documents/libe/dv/briefingnote_/briefingnote_en.pdf> accessed 23 September 2013.

Brownsword, Roger, 2012. "The shaping of our on-line worlds: getting the regulatory environment right", *International Journal of Law and Information Technology*, vol. 20, p. 272.

Bucak, Selin, 2012. "NANOG Rhetoric and WCIT-12 Reality", *The Global Journal*, 2 December 2012 <http://theglobaljournal.net/article/view/930/> accessed 11 March 2013.

Buckley, Chris, 2013. "Chinese Defense Ministry Accuses U.S. of Hypocrisy on Spying", *New York Times*, 27 June 2013 <http://www.nytimes.com/2013/06/28/world/asia/chinese-defense-ministry-accuses-us-of-hypocrisy-on-spying.html?_r=0> accessed 1 November 2013.

Burstein, Dave, 2012. "ITU Secrecy Disappearing as U.S. ITAC Open to All", *Fast Net News,* 7 August 2012 <http://fastnetnews.com/policy/177-p/4826-itu-secrecy-disappearing-as-us-itac-open-to-all> accessed 6 October 2013.

Cameron, David, 2013. "The internet and pornography: Prime Minister calls for action", *speech*, 22 July 2013 <https://www.gov.uk/government/speeches/the-internet-and-pornography-prime-minister-calls-for-action> accessed 28 July 2013.

Center for Democracy and Technology, 2012. "Civil Society Must Have Voice as ITU Debates the Internet", *CDT Policy Post*, 6 March 2012 <https://www.cdt.org/policy/civil-society-must-have-voice-itu-debates-internet> accessed 29 September 2013.

Chomsky, Noam 2000. *Rogue States: The Rule of Force in World Affairs*, South End Press.

Civil society, 2013. Wikipedia <http://en.wikipedia.org/wiki/Civil_society> accessed 10 June 2013.

CNN staff, 2013. "Holder: leaks damaged U.S. Security", *CNN*, 14 June 2013 <http://edition.cnn.com/2013/06/14/world/europe/nsa-leaks/index.html?hpt=hp_t1> accessed 15 June 2013.

Codding, George A. Jr., and Rutkowski, Anthony M., 1982. *The International Telecommunication Union in a Changing World*, Artech House.

Compaign, Benjamine M. (ed.), 2001. *The Digital Divide: Facing a Crisis or Creating a Myth?,* MIT Press.

Conneally, Paul, 2012. "The Google Campaign - An ITU View", *ITUblog,* 23 November 2012 <http://itu4u.wordpress.com/2012/11/23/the-google-campaign-an-itu-view/> accessed 4 October 2013.

Convergence, 2013. Wikipedia <http://en.wikipedia.org/wiki/Convergence_(telecommunications)> accessed 6 October 2013.

Cooper, Mark and Kimmelman, Gene, 2001. "The Digital Divide confronts the Telecommunications Act of 1996: Economic Reality versus Public Policy", in Compaine, Benjamin M. (ed), 2001. *The Digital Divide: Facing a Crisis or Creating a Myth*, MIT Press.

Correa, Carlos M., 2013. "Investment Agreements: A New Threat to Health and TRIPS Flexibilities", *Southviews,* no. 64, 27 June 2013 <http://us5.campaign-archive2.com/?u=fa9cf38799136b5660f367ba6&id=4f3a0bcccf&e=68bd9f2db7> accessed 28 July 2013.

Council of the European Union, 2013. Document DS 1335/13, 24 February 2013, "Outcome of the World Conference on International Telecommunications (WCIT)", publicly available at <http://www.hill-a.ch/wcit>.

Couts, Andrew, 2012. "Interview: US Ambassador David Gross Explains UN 'Takeover' of the Internet", *Digital Trends,* 9 August 2012 <http://www.digitaltrends.com/web/fmr-us-ambassador-david-gross-explains-un-takeover-of-the-internet/> accessed 23 March 2013.

Cowhey, Peter and Aronson, P.J. 1991. "The ITU in Transition", *Telecommunications Policy*, vol. 15 no. 4, p. 301.

Crandall, Robert, 2005. *Competition and Chaos: US Telecommunications since the 1996 Telecom Act*, Brookings Institution Press.

Crawford, Susan, 2013. *Captive Audience: The Telecom Industry and Monopoly in the New Guilded Age,* Yale University Press. A summary is provided by Gustin, Sam, 2013. "Is Broadband Internet Access a Public Utility?" *Time,* 9 January 2013 <http://business.time.com/2013/01/09/is-broadband-internet-acces-a-public-utility/?goback=%2Egde_65453_member_204153607> accessed 28 July 2013.

Crispin, Olivier, 2013. "What Happened at WCIT in December 2012", 14 March 2013 <http://fr.slideshare.net/ocl999/what-happened-at-wcit-in-december-2012> accessed 31 March 2013.

da Costa Cabral, Manuel, 2012. "Revising the International Telecommunications Regulations", CEPT ComITU, 19 April 2012 <http://www.itu.int/dms_pub/itu-t/oth/06/5B/T065B0000160012PDFE.pdf> accessed 10 August 2013.

Deibert, Roland J. et al. (eds), (2008). *Access Denied: The Practice and Policy of Global Internet Filtering*, MIT Press.

Deibert, Roland J. et al. (eds), (2010). *Access Controlled: The Shaping of Power, Rights, and Rule in Cyberspace*, MIT Press.

Deibert, Ronald J., (2013). *Black Code: Inside the Battle for Cyberspace*, Signal (McCelland and Stewart).

Dionisio, Daniele, 2013. "WHO Performance Undermined By Inadequate EU Participation", *Intellectual Property Watch,* 23 October 2013 <http://www.ip-watch.org/2013/10/23/who-performance-undermined-by-inadequate-eu-collaboration/> accessed 25 October 2013.

Dourado, Eli, 2012. "Behind closed doors at the UN's attempted 'takeover of the Internet'", *Arstechnica,* 20 December 2012 <http://arstechnica.com/tech-policy/2012/12/behind-closed-doors-at-the-uns-attempted-takeover-of-the-internet/> accessed 5 August 2013.

Downes, Larry, "Requiem for failed UN Telecom Treaty: No One Mourns the WCIT" *Forbes*, 17 December 2012 <http://www.forbes.com/sites/larrydownes/2012/12/17/no-one-mourns-the-wcit/> accessed 11 March 2013.

Drake, William J., 1988. "Restructuring the International Telecommunication Regulations" *Telecommunications Policy*, September 1988, p. 217.

Eisenberg, Ted, et. al, 1989. "The Cornell Commission: On Morris and the Worm", *Communications of the ACM*, June 1989, vol. 32 no. 6, p. 706.

EPFL Congress on Privacy and Surveillance, Ecole Fédéral Polytechnique de Lausanne, 30 September 2013 <http://ic.epfl.ch/privacy-surveillance> accessed 4 October 2013.

Ergas, Henry, 1998. "International Trade in Telecommunications Services: An Economic Perspective", in Hufbauer, Gary Clyde and Wada, Erika (eds) *Unfinished*

Business: Telecommunications after the Uruguay Round, Institute for International Economics.

Ermert, Monika, 2013. "Controversial Debate on TTIP Mandate in EU Council of Ministers", *Intellectual Property Watch,* 14 June 2013 <http://www.ip-watch.org/2013/06/14/audiovisual-sector-out-of-eu-mandate-for-ttip/> accessed 1 November 2013.

Ermert, Monica, 2013b. "EU Hearing: War Against Whistleblowers, War Against Journalists, War Against Democracy", *Intellectual Property Watch*, 1 October 2013 <http://www.ip-watch.org/2013/10/01/hearing-war-against-whistleblowers-war-against-journalists-war-against-democracy/> accessed 4 October 2013.

Ermert, Monica, 2013c. "German Parliament Votes to Protect News Snippets from Republishing", *Intellectual Property Watch,* 22 March 2013 <http://www.ip-watch.org/2013/03/22/german-parliament-votes-to-protect-news-snippets-from-republishing/> accessed 15 April 2013.

Ermert, Monica, 2013d. "A New Model for Internet Governance Is In The Air", *Intellectual Property Watch,* 23 October 2013 <http://www.ip-watch.org/2013/10/23/a-new-model-for-internet-governance-is-in-the-air/> accessed 23 October 2013.

Ermert, Monica, 2013e. "At IGF, Glimpses of Future IP Governance Overshadowed By Mass Surveillance", *Intellectual Property Watch,* 28 October 2013 < http://www.ip-watch.org/2013/10/28/at-igf-glimpses-of-future-ip-governance-overshadowed-by-mass-surveillance/> accessed 30 October 2013.

Ermert, Monica, 2013f. "European Court Upholds Confidentiality in International Trade Talks", *Intellectual Property Watch,* 20 March 2013 <http://www.ip-watch.org/2013/03/20/european-court-upholds-confidentiality-in-international-treaty-talks/> accessed 22 March 2013.

European Commission, 2012. "No change to telecoms and internet governance – EU Member States amongst dozens not signing proposed new International Telecommunications Regulations (ITR) Treaty, remain 100% committed to open internet", memo 12/992 of 14 December 2012 <http://europa.eu/rapid/press-release_MEMO-12-991_en.htm> accessed 11 March 2013.

European Commission, 2012a. "Proposal for a Council Decision Establishing the EU Position for the review of the International Telecommunications Regulations to be taken at the World Conference on International Telecommunications or its preparatory instances" (COM(2012) 430; 2012/0207 (NLE); of 2 August2012) <http://eur-lex.europa.eu/LexUriServ/LexUriServ.do?uri=COM:2012:0430:FIN:EN:PDF> accessed 11 March 2013.

European Commission, 2013. *Regulation of the European Parliament and of the Council laying down measures concerning the European single market for electronic communications and to achieve a Connected Continent,* 11 September 2013 <https://ec.europa.eu/digital-agenda/en/news/regulation-european-parliament-and-

council-laying-down-measures-concerning-european-single> accessed 24 October 2013.

European Parliament, 2012. "Joint Motion for a Resolution" *B7-0498/2012, B7-0499/2012,* 20 November 2012 <http://www.europarl.europa.eu/sides/getDoc.do?pubRef=-//EP//NONSGML+MOTION+P7-RC-2012-0498+0+DOC+PDF+V0//EN> accessed 6 October 2013.

Fahmi, Alaa M., 2000. *Council Working Group on the ITRs: General Overview* <http://www.itu.int/ITU-T/itr/files/itr_overview.ppt> accessed 6 October 2013.

Falkvinge, Rick, 2012. "European Parliament Unanimously Passed Resolution Against ITU Asserting Control Over Internet", *Falkvinge & Co.,* 22 November 2012 <http://falkvinge.net/2012/11/22/european-parliament-unanimously-passed-resolution-against-itu-asserting-control-over-internet> accessed 6 October 2013.

Fernàndez González, Juan Alonso, 2011, "Economic sustainability of international telecommunication networks", *Info,* vol. 13 no. 11, p. 6.

Flynn, Sean, 2013. "WIPO Treaty For The Blind Shows That Transparency Can Work (And Is Necessary)", *Intellectual Property Watch,* 26 June 2013 <http://www.ip-watch.org/2013/06/26/wipo-treaty-for-the-blind-shows-that-transparency-can-work-and-is-necessary/> accessed 28 July 2013.

Franzen, Karl, 2012. "Fearing Web Restrictions, Google Launches Campaign Against U.N. Conference", *TPM,* 20 November 2012 <http://idealab.talkingpointsmemo.com/2012/11/google-free-open-campaign-against-un-conference.php> accessed 28 July 2013.

Freedom of information legislation, 2013. Wikipedia <http://en.wikipedia.org/wiki/Freedom_of_information_legislation> accessed 6 October 2013.

Fulton, Scott, 2012. "FCC Commissioner: Ending ICANN could lead to an 'Engineering Morass'", *ReadWrite Mobile*, 28 February 2012 <http://www.readwriteweb.com/mobile/2012/02/fcc-commissioner-ending-icann.php> accessed 15 June 2013.

G20, 2013. Wikipedia <http://en.wikipedia.org/wiki/G20> accessed 11 October 2013.

G20 Leaders, 2013. "Tax Annex to the St. Petersburg Declaration", *G20*, 6 September 2013 <http://www.g20.org/news/20130906/782776427.html> accessed 11 October 2013.

Gallagher, Ryan, 2013. "FBI Pursuing Real-Time Gmail Spying Powers as 'Top Priority' for 2013", *Slate,* 25 March 2013 <http://www.slate.com/blogs/future_tense/2013/03/26/andrew_weissmann_fbi_wants_real_time_gmail_dropbox_spying_power.html> accessed 31 July 2013.

Garbage in, garbage out, 2013. Wikipedia <http://en.wikipedia.org/wiki/Garbage_in,_garbage_out> accessed 29 July 2013.

Gattuso, James, 2005. “House Telecom Rewrite Needs a Rewrite”, *The Heritage Foundation,* 23 September 2005 <http://www.heritage.org/research/reports/2005/09/house-telecom-rewrite-needs-a-rewrite> accessed 12 October 2013.

Geist, Michael, 2012. “UN Internet meeting about who pays, not who rules: Geist”, *The Star,* 25 November 2012 <http://www.thestar.com/business/2012/11/25/un_internet_meeting_about_who_pays_not_who_rules_geist.html> accessed 11 March 2013.

Gellman, Barton and Nakashima, Ellen, 2013. “U.S. spy agencies mounted 231 offensive cyber-operations in 2011, documents show”, *Washington Post,* 31 August 2013 <http://www.washingtonpost.com/world/national-security/us-spy-agencies-mounted-231-offensive-cyber-operations-in-2011-documents-show/2013/08/30/d090a6ae-119e-11e3-b4cb-fd7ce041d814_story.html> accessed 3 September 2013.

Goldberg, Mark Leon, 2012. “Proof that the UN Does Not Want to Control Your Internet”, *UN Dispatch*, 6 June 2012 <http://www.undispatch.com/proof-that-the-un-does-not-want-to-control-your-internet> accessed 10 March 2013.

Goldsmith, Jack and Wu, Tim, 2006. *Who Controls the Internet: Illusions of a Borderless World*, Oxford University Press.

Greenwald, Glenn, 2013. “XKeyscore: NSA tool collects ‘nearly everything a user does on the internet’”, *The Guardian*, 31 July 2013 <http://www.theguardian.com/world/2013/jul/31/nsa-top-secret-program-online-data> accessed 1 August 2013.

Gringras, Clive, 1997. *The Laws of the Internet,* Butterworths.

Gross, David and Lucarelli, Ethan, 2012. “The 2012 World Conference On International Telecommunications: Another Brewing Storm Over Potential UN Regulation Of The Internet”, *WhosWhoLegal,* November 2011 <http://www.whoswholegal.com/news/features/article/29378/the-2012-world-conference-international-telecommunications-brewing-storm-potential-un-regulation-internet/> accessed 25 September 2013.

Gurstein, Michael, 2012. “(Whose) Hands off (What) Internet: Reflections on WCIT 2012” *Gurstein's Community Informatics*, 9 December 2012 <http://gurstein.wordpress.com/2012/12/09/whose-hand-off-what-internet-some-reflections-on-wcit-2012/> accessed 11 March 2013.

Gurstein, Michael, 2013. “‘Internet Freedom’ and post-Snowden Global Internet Governance”, *Gurstein's Community Informatics,* 24 September 2013 <http://gurstein.wordpress.com/2013/09/24/internet-freedom-and-post-snowden-global-internet-governance/> accessed 4 October 2013.

Gustin, Sam, 2013. “Is Broadband Internet Access a Public Utility?” *Time,* 9 January, 2013 <http://business.time.com/2013/01/09/is-broadband-internet-acces-a-public-utility/?goback=%2Egde_65453_member_204153607> accessed 28 July 2013.

Hamid, Triska, 2013. "The WCIT and the future of internet privacy", *The National,* 29 March 2013 <http://www.thenational.ae/business/industry-insights/telecoms/the-wcit-and-the-future-of-internet-privacy> accessed 31 July 2013.

Headrick, Daniel R., 1991. *The Invisible Weapon: Telecommunications and international Politics 1851-1945*, Oxford University Press.

Hill, Richard, 2012. "World Conference on International Telecommunications", ITU, 19 April 2012 <http://www.itu.int/dms_pub/itu-t/oth/06/5B/T065B0000160011PDFE.pdf> accessed 10 August 2013.

Hill, Richard, 2012a. "EU Parliament Resolution on WCIT Flawed", *ITUblog,* 26 November 2012 <http://itu4u.wordpress.com/2012/11/26/eu-parliament-resolution-on-wcit-flawed/> accessed 6 October 2013.

Hill, Richard, 2013. "WCIT: Failure or success, impasse or way forward?" *International Journal of Law and Information Technology*, vol. 21, no. 3, p. 313 <http://ijlit.oxfordjournals.org/content/21/3/313> accessed 4 November 2013.

Hill, Richard, 2013a. "Internet Governance: The Last Gasp of Colonialism or Imperialism by Other Means" in Rolf H. Weber, Roxana Radu, Jean-Marie Chenou (eds), *The evolution of global Internet policy: new principles and forms of governance in the making?*, Schulthess, Publikationen aus dem Zentrum für Informations- und Kommunikationsrecht der Universität Zuerich.

Hill, Richard, 2014. "The Internet, its governance, and the multi-stakeholder model", *Info*, vol. 16 no 1 (forthcoming).

Hills, Jill, 2007. *Telecommunications and Empire,* University of Illinois Press.

Hruska, Joseph, 2012. "FCC fires FUD at the idea of a UN-controlled internet", *ExtremeTech*, 23 February 2012 <http://www.extremetech.com/computing/119481-fcc-fires-fud-at-the-idea-of-a-un-controlled-internet> accessed 15 June 2013.

Hruska, Joel, 2013. "The NSA's Prism leak could fundamentally change or break the entire Internet", *Extreme Tech,* 10 June 2013 <http://www.extremetech.com/computing/157761-the-nsas-prism-leak-could-fundamentally-change-or-break-the-entire-internet> accessed 13 June 2013.

Hufbauer, Gary Clyde and Wada, Erika (eds), 1998. *Unfinished Business: Telecommunications after the Uruguay Round,* Institute for International Economics.

IAHC, 2013. Wikipedia <http://en.wikipedia.org/wiki/IAHC> accessed 5 June 2013.

Intellectual Property Watch, 2013. "New Trans-Pacific Partnership Caucus in US Congress", *Intellectual Property Watch,* 30 October 2013 <http://www.ip-watch.org/2013/10/30/new-trans-pacific-partnership-caucus-in-us-congress/> accessed 1 November 2013.

International Court of Justice, 1950. *Competence of the General Assembly for Admission of a State to the United Nations: Advisory Opinion*, 3 March 1950 <http://www.worldcourts.com/icj/eng/decisions/1950.03.03_admission_to_UN.htm > accessed 19 March 2013.

International Monetary Fund, 2013. *Factsheet* <http://www.imf.org/external/np/exr/facts/sdr.HTM> accessed 6 October 2013.

Internet Governance Forum, 2013. *Internet Governance Forum* <http://www.intgovforum.org/cms/>.

Internet Society et al., 2013. *Montevideo Statement on the Future of Internet Cooperation,* AFRINIC, ARIN, APNIC, IAB, ICANN, IETF, ISOC, LACNIC, RIPE NCC, W3C, 7 October 2013 <http://www.internetsociety.org/news/montevideo-statement-future-internet-cooperation> accessed 20 October 2013.

Internet Society, 2013. *Statement on the Importance of Open Global Dialogue Regarding Online Privacy,* ISOC, 12 June 2013 <http://www.internetsociety.org/news/internet-society-statement-importance-open-global-dialogue-regarding-online-privacy> accessed 15 June 2013.

Internet Society, 2013a. *Spam* <http://www.internetsociety.org/spam> accessed 28 July 2013.

ITU/TeleGeography Inc., 1999. *Direction of Traffic: Trading Telecom Minutes,* ITU, October 1999 <http://www.itu.int/ITU-D/ict/publications/dot/1999/index.html> accessed 6 October 2013.

ITU, 1996. *Direction of Traffic* <http://www.itu.int/osg/spu/intset/whatare/howwork.pdf> accessed 6 October 2013.

ITU, 1997. *World Telecommunication Development Report (1996/1997)* <http://www.itu.int/osg/spu/intset/whatare/wtdr/chap_6.pdf> accessed 6 October 2013.

ITU, 2005. *World Summit on the Information Society* <http://www.itu.int/wsis/index.html>.

ITU, 2005a. *Internet Governance* <http://www.itu.int/wsis/wgig/index.html>.

ITU, 2005b. *Training Workshop on Telecommunications Policy and Regulation for Competition,* 11-15 July 2005 <http://www.itu.int/ITU-D/treg/Events/Seminars/2005/Thailand/>.

ITU, 2007. *Accounting Rate Reform undertaken by ITU-T Study Group 3* <http://www.itu.int/ITU-T/studygroups/com03/accounting-rate/index.html> accessed 6 October 2013.

ITU, 2007a. *International Telecommunication Regulations* <http://www.itu.int/ITU-T/itr/> accessed 6 October 2013.

ITU, 2009. *WTPF 2009* <http://www.itu.int/osg/csd/wtpf/wtpf2009/> accessed 6 October 2013.

ITU, 2011. *History of the ITU-T surveys of accounting rates* <http://www.itu.int/en/ITU-T/studygroups/com03/Pages/hs-acctrate.aspx> accessed 6 October 2013.

ITU, 2011a. *Past work on ITRs* <http://www.itu.int/osg/spu/stratpol/ITRs/itrs_past.html> accessed 6 October 2013.

ITU, 2011b. *International Telecommunication Regulations* <http://www.itu.int/ITU-T/itr-eg/> accessed 6 October 2013.

ITU, 2011c. *Workshop on Taxation of Telecommunication Services and Related Products,* 1-2 September 2011 <http://www.itu.int/ITU-T/worksem/taxation/201109/index.html>.

ITU, 2012. *ITU World Telecommunication/ICT Indicators Database*, <http://www.itu.int/en/ITU-D/Statistics/Pages/publications/wtid.aspx> accessed 5 June 2012.

ITU, 2012a. *Regional Preparatory Meetings* <http://www.itu.int/en/ITU-T/wtsa-12/prepmeet/Pages/default.aspx> accessed 4 October 2013.

ITU, 2012b. *Landmark decision by ITU Council on proposal for public consultation and open access to key conference document* <http://www.itu.int/net/pressoffice/press_releases/2012/46.aspx>.

ITU, 2012c. *Draft of the future ITRs* <http://www.itu.int/en/wcit-12/Documents/draft-future-itrs-public.pdf> accessed 6 October 2013.

ITU, 2012d. *IPv6* <http://www.itu.int/en/ITU-T/others/ipv6/Pages/default.aspx> accessed 10 September 2013.

ITU, 2012e. *Workshop on "Apportionment of Revenues and International Internet Connectivity"*, 23-24 January 2012 <www.itu.int/ITU-T/worksem/apportionment/201201/index.html> accessed 2 November 2013.

ITU, 2012f. "World Conference on International Telecommunications affirms right to freedom of information online", *Press Release*, 4 December 2012 <http://www.itu.int/net/pressoffice/press_releases/2012/90.aspx> accessed 10 June 2013.

ITU, 2013. *International Internet Connectivity* <http://www.itu.int/ITU-T/studygroups/com03/iic/index.html> accessed 15 March 2013.

ITU, 2013a. *The treaty signing process explained* <http://www.itu.int/en/wcit-12/Pages/treaties-signing.aspx> accessed 6 October 2013.

ITU, 2013b. *Home Page* <http://www.itu.int> accessed 29 August 2013.

ITU, 2013c. *Numbering Resources* <http://www.itu.int/en/ITU-T/inr/Pages/default.aspx> accessed 15 March 2013.

ITU, 2013d. *Service Publications* <http://www.itu.int/pub/T-SP/e> accessed 15 March 2013.

ITU, 2013e. *High-Level Workshop on Regulatory and Economic Aspects of Roaming*, 23-24 September 2013 <http://www.itu.int/en/ITU-D/Regulatory-Market/Pages/Events2013/GE_Roaming/home.aspx> accessed 5 November 2013. The background paper is titled "International mobile roaming services: Facilitating competition and protecting users".

ITU Convention, 1865. ITU <http://www.itu.int/dms_pub/itu-s/oth/02/01/S02010000014002PDFF.pdf>.

ITU Convention, 1947. ITU <http://www.itu.int/dms_pub/itu-s/oth/02/01/S02010000194006PDFE.pdf>

ITU International Radiotelegraph Convention, 1908. ITU <http://www.itu.int/dms_pub/itu-s/oth/02/01/S02010000104003PDFF.pdf>.

ITU International Telegraph Conference, 1885. ITU <http://www.itu.int/en/history/Pages/TelegraphAndTelephoneConferences.aspx?conf=21&dms=S0201000006> accessed 2 November 2013.

ITU International Telegraph Conference, 1932. ITU <http://www.itu.int/en/history/Pages/PlenipotentiaryConferences.aspx?conf=5&dms=S0201000018> accessed 2 November 2013.

ITU membership list, 2013. ITU <http://www.itu.int/online/mm/scripts/mm.list?_search=ITUstates&_languageid=1>

ITU Telegraph Regulations, 1949. ITU <http://www.itu.int/dms_pub/itu-s/oth/02/01/S02010000164012PDFE.pdf>.

ITU World Administrative Telegraph and Telephone Conference, 1973. ITU <http://www.itu.int/en/history/Pages/TelegraphAndTelephoneConferences.aspx?conf=32&dms=S020100001E> accessed 2 November 2013.

ITU World Administrative Telegraph and Telephone Conference, 1988. ITU <http://www.itu.int/en/history/Pages/TelegraphAndTelephoneConferences.aspx?conf=33&dms=S0201000021> accessed 2 November 2013.

Jakarta Globe, 2012. "India Defends Internet Censorship", *Jakarta Globe,* 24 August 2012 <http://www.thejakartaglobe.com/archive/india-defends-internet-censorship/> accessed 28 July 2013.

Jones, Gavin, 2013. "Italy eyes 'Google tax' to help fix public finances", *Reuters*, 4 November 2013 < http://www.reuters.com/article/2013/11/04/us-italy-internet-tax-idUSBRE9A30RL20131104> accessed 5 November 2013.

Jungholt, Thorsten, 2013. "Deutscher Datenschutz soll Massstab fuer EU sein", *Die Welt,* 5 August 2013 <http://www.welt.de/politik/deutschland/article118689823/Deutscher-Datenschutz-soll-Massstab-fuer-EU-sein.html> accessed 5 August 2013.

Kahai, Simran K., Kahai, Paramjit S, and Leigh, Adrian, 2006. "Traditional and non-Traditional Determinants of Accounting Rates in International Telecommunications", *International Advances in Economic Research*, vol. 12 no. 4, p. 505.

Kahn, Robert E. and Cerf, Vinton G., 1999. "What Is The Internet (And What Makes It Work)" <http://www.cnri.reston.va.us/what_is_internet.html> accessed 10 August 2013.

Kaminski, Margot, 2013. "Capture, sunlight, and the TPP leak", *Concurring Opinions*, 14 November 2013 <http://www.concurringopinions.com/archives/2013/11/capture-sunlight-and-the-tpp-leak.html#> accessed 16 November 2013.

Kampfner, Jon, 2013. "Prism surveillance: spies thrive in the Internet's legal free-for-all", *The Guardian,* 12 June 2013 <http://www.guardian.co.uk/commentisfree/2013/jun/12/prism-surveillance-internet-william-hague> accessed 15 June 2013.

Karimi, Faith, 2013. "Facebook, Microsoft disclose information on user data request", *CNN,* 15 June 2013 <http://edition.cnn.com/2013/06/15/politics/data-tech-giants/index.html?hpt=hp_t1> accessed 15 June 2013.

Kays, Laurel, 2012. "WCIT-12: A Threat to the Free and Open Internet, *Digital Liberty*, 19 November 2012 <http://www.digitalliberty.net/wcit-threat-free-open-internet-a120> accessed 29 September 2013.

Kerr, Dara, 2012. "Amendments to UN treaty could censor the Internet", *CNET*, 24 June 2012 <http://news.cnet.com/8301-1023_3-57459564-93/amendments-to-u.n-treaty-could-censor-the-internet/> accessed 29 September 2013.

Kim, Jino W., 2005. "Economic Theory and Practices: Telecommunication Policy and Regulation for Competition", ITU <http://www.itu.int/ITU-D/treg/Events/Seminars/2005/Thailand/Reference%20Material/Background%20Paper%20-%20Economic%20Theory%20and%20Practices.pdf> accessed 23 August 2013.

Kiss, Jemima, 2013. "NSA furore has roots in US internet imperialism", *The Guardian*, 1 November 2013 <http://www.theguardian.com/technology/2013/nov/01/nsa-furore-roots-us-internet-imperialism> accessed 4 November 2013.

Klimburg, Alexander, 2013. "The Internet Yalta", Center for a New American Security, 5 February 2013 <http://www.cnas.org/files/documents/publications/CNAS_WCIT_commentary%20corrected%20(03.27.13).pdf> accessed 4 August 2013

Koot, Matthijs, 2013. "Dutch govt position concerning U.S. spying for economic purposes + answers to Parliamentary questions re: Snowden/Le Monde", *notebook,* 28 October 2013 <http://blog.cyberwar.nl/2013/10/dutch-govt-position-concerning-us.html?m=1> accessed 30 October 2013.

Krishnatrarok, 2012. "UN 'Internet takeover' about subsidizing phone companies", *DSLReports,* 21 June 2012 <http://www.dslreports.com/shownews/UN-Internet-Takeover-About-Subsidizing-Phone-Companies-120034> accessed 3 June 2013.

Kruger, Lennard G., 2013. *Internet Governance and the Domain Name System: Issues for Congress,* Congressional Research Service, 13 April 2013 <http://www.fas.org/sgp/crs/misc/R42351.pdf> accessed 6 October 2013.

L.S., 2012. "A digital cold war?", *The Economist,* 14 December 2012 <http://www.economist.com/blogs/babbage/2012/12/internet-regulation> accessed 28 July 2013.

Laidi, Zaki, 2012. "BRICS: Sovereignty power and weakness" *International Politics,* vol. 49, September 2012, pp. 614-632 (an earlier version is Laidi, Zaki, 2011."The BRICS Against the West", CERI Strategy Papers, No. 11, November 2011<http://spire.sciences-

po.fr/hdl:/2441/eu4vqp9ompqllr09i4icocu28/resources/n11-112011.pdf> accessed 28 July 2013).

Langdale, John V., 1989. "International telecommunications and trade in services", *Telecommunications Policy*, vol. 13 no. 3, pp. 223-232.

Malcolm, Jeremy, 2012. "WCIT: Freemasons, Internet memes and salt", *Digital News Asia,* 28 December 2012 <http://www.digitalnewsasia.com/insights/wcit-freemasons-internet-memes-and-salt> accessed 5 August 2013.

Masnik, Mike, 2013. "Yes, You Can Have An Open and Transparent Treaty Negotiation for Intellectual Property", *TechDirt,* 27 June 2013 <http://www.techdirt.com/articles/20130626/17445123631/yes-you-can-have-open-transparent-treaty-negotiation-intellectual-property.shtml> accessed 14 October 2013.

McCarthy, Kieren, 2012. "Verisign loses dot-com piggybank", *.nxt,* 30 November 2012 <http://news.dot-nxt.com/2012/12/06/verisign-loses-dot-com-piggyba> accessed 8 June 2013.

McClanahan, Paige, 2013. "Roberto Azevedo says that the WTO 'needs a fresh perspective from inside'", *The Guardian,* 3 May 2013 <http://www.guardian.co.uk/global-development/2013/may/03/roberto-azevedo-world-trade-organisation> accessed 28 July 2013.

McCoy, Alfred, 2013. "Surveillance Blowback: The Making of the US Surveillance State, 1898-2020", *Popular Resistance*, 15 July 2013 <http://www.popularresistance.org/surveillance-blowback-the-making-of-the-us-surveillance-state-1898-2020/> accessed 30 August 2013.

McCullagh, Declan and Downs, Larry, 2012. "U.N. could tax U.S.-based Web sites, leaked docs show", *CNET,* 7 June 2012 <http://news.cnet.com/8301-1009_3-57449375-83/u.n-could-tax-u.s.-based-web-sites-leaked-docs-show/?part=rss&subj=news&tag=2547-1_3-0-20> accessed 4 October 2013.

McCullagh, Declan, 2012a. "U.N. takeover of the Internet must be stopped, U.S. warns", *CNET,* 31 May 2012 <http://news.cnet.com/8301-1009_3-57444629-83/u.n-takeover-of-the-internet-must-be-stopped-u.s-warns/> accessed 3 March 2013.

McDowell, Robert, 2012. "The U.N. Threat to Internet Freedom", *The Wall Street Journal*, 21 February 2012 <http://online.wsj.com/article/SB10001424052970204792404577229074023195322.html?mod=WSJ_article_comments#articleTabs%3Darticle> accessed 15 June 2013.

McGregor, Richard 2007. "China blames WTO blockage on US and EU", *Financial Times,* 12 March 2007 <http://www.ft.com/cms/s/0/5cbb1056-d060-11db-836a-000b5df10621.html#axzz2aLE1XT39> accessed 28 July 2013.

McKinnon, Rebecca, 2012. *Consent of the Networked: The Worldwide Struggle for Internet Freedom*, Basic Books.

Mestmaecker Ernst-Joachim (ed.), 1987. *The Law and Economics of Transborder Telecommunications,* Nomos.

Morozov, Evgeny, 2013. "The Price of Hypocrisy", *Frankfuter Allgemeine,* 24 July 2013 <http://www.faz.net/aktuell/feuilleton/debatten/ueberwachung/information-consumerism-the-price-of-hypocrisy-12292374.html> accessed 31 July 2013.

Morris, Ian, 2011. *Why the West Rules – For Now,* Profile Books, paperback edition.

Mueller, Milton, 2002. *Ruling the Root: Internet Governance and the Taming of Cyberspace,* MIT Press.

Mueller, Milton, 2010. *Networks and States: The Global Politics of Internet Governance*, MIT Press.

Mueller, Milton, 2012. "Threat Analysis of the WCIT Part 4: the ITU and Cybersecurity", *Internet Governance Project*, 21 June 2012 <http://www.internetgovernance.org/2012/06/21/threat-analysis-of-the-wcit-4-cybersecurity/> accessed 15 March 2013.

Mueller, Milton, 2012a. "We Want TD64! ITU Transparency Begins at Home", *Internet Governance Project,* 5 June 2012 <http://www.internetgovernance.org/2012/06/05/we-want-td64-itu-transparency-begins-at-home/> accessed 10 March 2013.

Mueller, Milton, 2012b. "TD64 for Breakfast", *Internet Governance Project,* 6 June 2012 <http://www.internetgovernance.org/2012/06/06/td-64-for-breakfast/> accessed 10 March 2013.

Mueller, Milton, 2012c. "Threat Analysis of WCIT Part 2: Telecommunications versus Internet", *Internet Governance Project,* 7 June 2012 <http://www.internetgovernance.org/2012/06/07/threat-analysis-of-wcit-part-2-telecommunications-vs-internet/> accessed 10 March 2013.

Mueller, Milton, 2012d. "Threat Analysis of WCIT Part 3: Charging You, Charging Me", *Internet Governance Project,* 9 June 2012 <http://www.internetgovernance.org/2012/06/09/threat-analysis-of-wcit-part-3-charging-you-charging-me/> accessed 10 March 2013.

Mueller, Milton, 2013. "An Internet 'Free From Government Control': A Worthy Principle", *Internet Governance Project,* April 14, 2013 <http://www.internetgovernance.org/2013/04/14/an-internet-free-from-government-control-a-worthy-principle/> accessed 28 July 2013.

Muller, Jerry Z., 2002. *The Mind and the Market,* Alfred A. Knopf.

Multiple authors, 2012. "Letter to Secretary-General Dr Hamadoun Toure", Center for Democracy and Technology, 17 May 2012 <https://www.cdt.org/files/pdfs/Civil_Society_WCIT_Letter%20.pdf> accessed 10 March 2013.

Multiple authors, 2012a. "Letter to the ITU Secretary-General and to the Chairman of WCIT", Access Now, 9 December 2012 <https://www.accessnow.org/blog/2012/12/09/wcit-watch-civil-society-delivers-letter-to-itu-sg-and-conference-chair> accessed 14 October 2014.

Musil, Steven, 2013. "Iran develops software to control social networks", *CNET,* 6 January 2013 <http://news.cnet.com/8301-1023_3-57562295-93/iran-develops-software-to-control-access-to-social-networks/> accessed 15 June 2013.

Nachszunow, Gregory, 1989. *Development of Telecommunications and International Organizations*, Willy Nachszunow.

Naughton, John, 2013. "Edward Snowden's not the story. The fate of the Internet is", *The Guardian,* 28 July 2013 <http://www.theguardian.com/technology/2013/jul/28/edward-snowden-death-of-internet> accessed 31 July 2013.

Necessary and Proportionate, 2013. Necessary and Proportionate <https://en.necessaryandproportionate.org/text> accessed 1 August 2013.

Nesto, Matt, 2013. "Are You Ready for a Federal Online Shopping Tax?", *Yahoo! Finance*, 29 August 2013 <http://finance.yahoo.com/blogs/breakout/ready-federal-online-shopping-tax-154631835.html> accessed 14 October 2013.

Network Neutrality, 2013. Wikipedia <http://en.wikipedia.org/wiki/Network_neutrality> accessed 6 October 2013.

Network neutrality in the United States, 2013. Wikipedia <http://en.wikipedia.org/wiki/Network_neutrality_in_the_United_States> accessed 1 June 2013.

New, William, 2013. "WIPO Annual Assembly Breaks Down; Extraordinary Meeting Eyed for December", *Intellectual Property Watch*, 3 October 2013 <http://www.ip-watch.org/2013/10/03/wipo-annual-assembly-breaks-down-extraordinary-meeting-eyed-for-december/> accessed 4 October 2013.

New, William, 2013a. "USTR Froman: FTAs A Way To Get Higher IP Standards Into Global Trade 'Bloodstream'", *Intellectual Property Watch,* 31 October 2013 <http://www.ip-watch.org/2013/10/31/ustr-froman-ftas-a-way-to-get-higher-standards-on-ip-into-global-trade-bloodstream/> accessed 1 November 2013.

New, William, 2013b. "United States Chided as TRIPS Scofflaw at WTO", *Intellectual Property Watch*, 16 March 2013 <http://www.ip-watch.org/2013/03/26/united-states-chided-as-trips-scofflaw-at-wto/> accessed 29 March 2013.

New, William, 2013c. "USTR: IPRs Amongst 'Most Challenging' Issues as TPP Talks Accelerate", *Intellectual Property Watch*, 14 March 2013 <http://www.ip-watch.org/2013/03/14/ustr-iprs-among-most-challenging-issues-as-tpp-talks-accelerate/> accessed 15 March 2013.

New, William, 2013d. "WIPO Folklore Talks Stalling; Work Continues On New Draft Text", *Intellectual Property Watch*, 18 July 2013 <http://www.ip-watch.org/2013/07/18/wipo-folklore-talks-stalling-work-continues-on-new-draft-text/> accessed 28 July 2013.

New, William, 2013e. "European Commission VP Kroes Urges Open Internet, Prods Copyright Owners", *Intellectual Property Watch*, 21 March 2013, <http://www.ip-watch.org/2013/03/21/european-commission-vp-kroes-urges-open-internet-prods-copyright-owners/> accessed 22 March 2013.

New, William, 2013f. "Wikileaks's Release of TPP Chapter on IP Blows Open Secret Trade Negotiation", *Intellectual Property Watch*, 13 November 2013 <http://www.ip-watch.org/2013/11/13/wikileaks-release-of-tpp-chapter-on-ip-blows-open-secret-trade-negotiation/> accessed 14 November 2013.

news24, "Brazil to host internet governance summit", *news24* (10 October 2013) <http://www.news24.com/Technology/News/Brazil-to-host-internet-governance-summit-20131010> accessed 14 October 2013.

Non-governmental organization, 2013. Wikipedia <http://en.wikipedia.org/wiki/Non-governmental_organization> accessed 6 October 2013.

Nothias, Jean-Christophe, 2012. "The Battle for the Future of the Internet?", *Huffington Post,* 2 December 2012 <http://www.huffingtonpost.com/jeanchristophe-nothias/internet-governance_b_2227820.html> accessed 11 March 2013.

Nothias, Jean-Christophe, 2012a. "The Hypocrisy Threatening the Future of the Internet", *The Global Journal*, 22 November 2012 <http://theglobaljournal.net/article/view/904/> accessed 16 July 2013.

Nothias, Jean-Christophe, 2013, "And Now the Second Battle of the Internet", *Huffington Post Blog,* 13 June 2013 <http://www.huffingtonpost.com/jeanchristophe-nothias/internet-governance_b_3435812.html> accessed 15 June 2013.

O'Reirdan, Michael, 2013. "Top 'ten' things to do about spam for an ISP", M3AAWG presentation to the Internet Society workshop Combating Spam for Policy Makers, 9 September 2013 <http://www.internetsociety.org/sites/default/files/Top%20Ten%20things%20to%20do%20about%20spam.pdf>; the workshop is at <http://www.internetsociety.org/african-telecommunications-union-atu-combating-spam-policy-makers> accessed 18 September 2013.

OECD, 2011. "International Mobile Data Roaming" DSTI/ICCP/CISP(2010)12 <http://www.oecd.org/sti/broadband/48127892.pdf> accessed 6 October 2013.

OECD, 2011a. *Communications Outlook 2011* <http://www.oecd.org/sti/broadband/oecdcommunicationsoutlook2011.htm> accessed 5 June 2012.

Olsen, Chris, 2013. "EWI Expert Testifies on the Hill", EastWest Institute, 24 July 2013 <http://www.ewi.info/rauscher-testifies-congress> accessed 13 August 2013.

Open government, 2013. Wikipedia <http://en.wikipedia.org/wiki/Open_government> accessed 6 October 2013.

Ortoo, 2013. Wikipedia <http://en.wikipedia.org/wiki/Ortoo> accessed 5 June 2013.

Payne, Ed, 2013. "Morales challenges U.S. after Snowden rumor holds up plane in Europe", *CNN,* 4 July 2013 <http://edition.cnn.com/2013/07/04/world/americas/bolivia-morales-snowden/index.html?hpt=hp_t3> accessed 14 July 2013.

Petropoulos, Sotiris, 2013. "The emergence of the BRICS – implications for global governance", *Journal of International and Global Studies*, vol. 4 no. 2, May 2013, pp. 37-51 <http://www.lindenwood.edu/jigs/docs/volume4Issue2/essays/37-51.pdf> accessed 28 July 2013.

Pfanner, Eric, 2012. "U.S. Rejects Telecommunications Treaty." *New York Times,* 13 December 13 2012 <http://www.nytimes.com/2012/12/14/technology/14iht-treaty14.html> accessed 10 August 2013.

Pfanner, Eric, 2012a. "Debunking rumors of an Internet takeover", *New York Times,* 11 June 2012 <http://www.nytimes.com/2012/06/11/technology/debunking-rumors-of-an-internet-takeover.html?_r=0> accessed 3 November 2013.

Pipe, G., 1989. "WATTC Agrees on New Telecom Rules", *Telecommunications International*, vol. 23 no. 1, p. 19.

Popescu, Adam, 2012. "5 Reasons Why the US Rejected the ITU Treaty", *read-write.com*, 14 December 2012 <http://readwrite.com/2012/12/14/5-reasons-why-the-us-rejected-the-itu-treaty> accessed 30 October 2013.

Pruzin, Daniel, 2013. "U.S. Satisfied With Internet Forum: Has Concerns With Brazilian Proposal", *Bloomberg Daily Report for Executives,* 22 May 2013.

Purkayastha, Prabir, 2012. "Is ITU Really Threatening the Internet?", *Newsclick,* 8 November 2012 <http://newsclick.in/india/itu-really-threatening-internet> accessed 28 March 2013.

Purkayastha, Prabir and Bailey, Rishab, 2013. "How NSA is Hacking the Whole World", *Frontline,* 12 July 2013 <http://newsclick.in/international/how-nsa-hacking-whole-world> accessed 6 October 2013.

Rangnath, Rahhmi, 2012. "Public Knowledge Disappointed that ITU Documents Remain Closed to the Public", *Public Knowledge,* 12 July 2012 <http://publicknowledge.org/public-knowledge-disappointed-itu-documents-remain> accessed 6 October 2013.

Raymond, M. and Smith, G., 2013. "Reimagining the Internet: The Need for a High-level Strategic Vision for Internet Governance," Centre for International Governance Innovation, Internet Governance Papers, Paper No. 1, July 2013 <http://www.cigionline.org/sites/default/files/no1_4.pdf> accessed 10 August 2013.

Reed, Chris, 2012. *Making Laws for Cyberspace,* Oxford University Press.

Reidenberg, Joel, 2005. "Technology and Internet Jurisdiction", 153 *University of Pennsylvania Law Review*, p. 1951.

Reuters, 2013. "Online sales tax bill moving ahead in U.S. House", *Reuters,* 12 September 2013 <http://www.reuters.com/article/2013/09/12/us-usa-tax-online-idUSBRE98B17O20130912> accessed 11 October 2013.

Rizo, Chris, 2012. "Int'l proposals for U.N. Internet regulations draws bipartisan rebuke", *FierceOnlineVideo,* 20 June 2012 <http://www.fierceonlinevideo.com/story/plans-un-internet-regulations-draws-bipartisan-rebuke/2012-06-20> accessed 28 July 2013.

Robinson, Peter, 1991. “The international dimension of telecommunications policy issues”, *Telecommunications Policy*, vol. 15 no. 2, p. 97.

Roman Roads, 2013. Wikipedia <http://en.wikipedia.org/wiki/Roman_roads> accessed 5 June 2013.

Rousseff, Dilma, President of Brazil, 2013. “Statement at the Opening of the General Debate of the 68th Session of the United Nations General Assembly”, United Nations, 24 September 2013 <http://gadebate.un.org/sites/default/files/gastatements/68/BR_en.pdf> accessed 4 October 2013.

Rutkowski, Anthony M., 1986. “Regulation for Integrated Services Networks: WATTC-88”, *Intermedia*, vol. 14 no. 3, International Institute of Communication, pp. 10-19.

Rutkowski, Anthony M., 2011. “Public international law of the international telecommunication instruments: cyber security treaty provisions since 1850”, *Info*, vol. 13 no. 1, p.13 <http://www.emeraldinsight.com/journals.htm?articleid=1902130> accessed 3 June 2013.

Saez, Catherine 2013. “WIPO Committee To Decide Fate of Treaties To Protect TK, Generic Resources, Folklore” *Intellectual Property Watch,* 23 July 2013 <http://www.ip-watch.org/2013/07/23/wipo-committee-to-decide-fate-of-treaties-to-protect-tk-genetic-resources-folklore/> accessed 28 July 2013.

Saez, Catherine, 2013a. “US Defender Of Internet Freedom, Keen On Protecting IP Rights”, *Intellectual Property Watch*, 8 March 2013 <http://www.ip-watch.org/2013/03/08/us-as-defender-of-internet-freedom-keen-on-protecting-ip-rights> accessed 11 March 2013.

Savage, Charlie, Wyatt, Edward, and Baker, Peter, 2013. “U.S. Confirms that it Gathers Online Data Overseas”, *The New York Times,* 6 June 2013 <http://www.nytimes.com/2013/06/07/us/nsa-verizon-calls.html?_r=0> accessed 8 June 2013.

Schiller, Dan, 2013. “Masters of the Internet”, *Le Monde Diplomatique*, February 2013 <http://mondediplo.com/2013/02/15internet> accessed 11 March 2013.

Schiller, Dan, 2013a. “Whose Internet?”, *Le Monde Diplomatique.* October 2013 <http://mondediplo.com/2013/10/09surveillance> accessed 4 October 2013.

Schneier, Bruce, 2013. “Has U.S. Started an Internet War?”, *CCN,* 18 June 2013 <http://edition.cnn.com/2013/06/18/opinion/schneier-cyberwar-policy/index.html> accessed 19 June 2013.

Seoul Framework, 2013. In the Results of the Seoul Conference on Cyberspace 2013<http://www.seoulcyber2013.kr/en/media/View.do?media_id=2242> accessed 30 October 2013.

Shea, Carla, 2013.“Latin America Condemns US Espionage at United Nations Security Council”, *Global Research,* 17 August 2013 <http://www.globalresearch.ca/latin-america-condemns-us-espionage-at-united-nations-security-council/5346120> accessed 26 August 2013.

Simonite, Tom, 2013. "Reading the Tea Leaves of Censorship", *MIT Technology Review*, vol. 116 no. 4, July/August 2013, p. 20.

Singh, Parminder Jeet, 2012. "Hyping one threat to hide another", *The Hindu,* 28 November 2012 <http://www.thehindu.com/opinion/lead/hyping-one-threat-to-hide-another/article4140922.ece> accessed 11 March 2013.

SMS spoofing, 2013. Wikipedia <http://en.wikipedia.org/wiki/SMS_spoofing> accessed 6 October 2013.

*Sophie in 't Veld vs European Commission,*2013. European General Court T-301/10, 19 March 2013 <http://curia.europa.eu/juris/document/document.jsf?text=&docid=135225&doclang=EN&cid=173202> accessed 22 March 2013.

South West Africa (2nd Phase), 1966. *ICJ Rep.*

Stern, Peter A., 1990. *The International Telecommunications Settlement Process: What's Needed? Destroy and Replace It or Adjust It?*, IIC Telecommunications Forum, 25-25 October 1990 <http://www.itu.int/osg/spu/intset/indu/settle90.pdf> accessed 6 October 2013.

Talbot, David, 2005. "The Internet is broken", *MIT Technology Review,* December 2005/January 2006, p. 62 <http://www.technologyreview.com/news/405318/the-internet-is-broken/> accessed 15 March 2013.

Taylor, Matthew, Hopkins, Nick and Kiss, Jemima, 2013. "NSA surveillance may cause breakup of internet, experts warn", *The Guardian*, 1 November 2013 <http://www.theguardian.com/world/2013/nov/01/nsa-surveillance-cause-internet-breakup-edward-snowden> accessed 4 November 2013.

Touray, Karim, S., 2013. "Much Ado About WCIT-12 and Multi-Stakeholderism", *CircleID,* 22 January 2013 <http://www.circleid.com/posts/20130122_much_ado_about_wcit_12_and_multi_stakeholderism/> accessed 5 August 2013.

Uhlenbruck, Klaus et al., 2006. "The Impact of Corruption on Entry Strategy: Evidence from Telecommunication Projects in Emerging Economies", *Organization Science*, vol.17 no. 3, p. 402 <http://voxprofessor.net/eden/Publications/Uhlenbruck-et-al-OS-2006.pdf> accessed 2 November 2013.

United Nations, "Cooperation between United Nations, Regional, Subregional Organizations 'mainstay' of International Relations, Security Council Hears Throughout Day-Long Debate", *Press Release* regarding 6 August 2013 meeting <http://www.un.org/News/Press/docs//2013/sc11087.doc.htm> accessed 2 October 2013.

United States Foreign Intelligence Surveillance Court, Bates, John D., 2011. *Re-dacted*, 3 October 2011 <https://www.eff.org/sites/default/files/filenode/fisc_opinion_-_unconstitutional_surveillance_0.pdf> accessed 23 August 2013.

United States v. Scheinberg, 2013. Wikipedia <http://en.wikipedia.org/wiki/United_States_v._Scheinberg> accessed 8 June 2013.

Ury, William, 1991. *Getting Past No: Negotiating in Difficult Situations,* Bantam.

US Congress, 2012. *Congressional Record*, vol. 158, no.116 (Wednesday, August 1, 2012), House, pp. H5599-H5602 <http://www.gpo.gov/fdsys/pkg/CREC-2012-08-01/html/CREC-2012-08-01-pt1-PgH5599-3.htm> accessed 28 July 2013.

US Department of Commerce, 2012. *Department of Commerce Approves Verisign-ICANN .com Registry Renewal Agreement, Press Release*, 30 November 30, 2012 <http://www.ntia.doc.gov/press-release/2012/department-commerce-approves-verisign-icann-com-registry-renewal-agreement> accessed 8 June 2013.

US Energy and Commerce Committee, 2012. US House of Representatives, *Hearing on International Proposals to Regulate the Internet,* 31 May 2012 <http://energycommerce.house.gov/hearing/international-proposals-regulate-internet> accessed 6 October 2013.

US Energy and Commerce Committee, 2013. US House of Representatives, *Hearing: Fighting for Internet Freedom, Dubai and Beyond*, 5 February 2013 <http://energycommerce.house.gov/hearing/fighting-for-internet-freedom-dubai-and-beyond> accessed 11 March 2013.

US FCC, 2011. "In the Matter of International Settlements Policy Reform," notice of proposed rulemaking in IB Docket No. 11-80, (FCC 11-75), 13 May 2011.

US Majority Committee Staff, 2012. "Hearing on International Proposals to Regulate the Internet", *Memorandum to the Committee on Energy and Commerce,* 29 May 2012 <http://energycommerce.house.gov/sites/republicans.energycommerce.house.gov/files/Hearings/CT/20120531/HMTG-112-HHRG-IF16-20120531-SD001.pdf> accessed 28 July 2013.

US National Security Agency, 2013. *The National Security Agency: Missions, Authorities, Oversight and Partnerships*, 9 August 2013 <http://www.nsa.gov/public_info/_files/speeches_testimonies/2013_08_09_the_nsa_story.pdf> accessed 13 August 2013.

US White House Press Office, 2013. *Joint Statement by the Presidents of the United States of America and the Russian Federation on a New Field of Cooperation in Confidence Building*, The White House, 17 June 2013 <http://www.whitehouse.gov/the-press-office/2013/06/17/joint-statement-on-a-new-field-of-cooperation-in-confidence-building> accessed 18 June 2013.

van Gelder, Stéphane "Is WCIT Failure the Start of a Digital Cold War?" *CircleID*, 14 December 2012 <http://www.circleid.com/posts/20121214_is_wcit_failure_the_start_of_a_digital_cold_war/> accessed 11 March 2013.

Walden, Ian (ed.), 2009. *Telecommunications Law and Regulation,* Oxford University Press.

Weber, Rolf H., 2010. "New Sovereignty Concepts in the Age of Internet?", *Journal of Internet Law,* August 2010, p. 12.

Weber, Rolf H, 2011. "Politics Through Social Networks and Politics by Government Blocking: Do We Need New Rules?", *International Journal of Communications*, vol. 5, p. 1190 <http://ijoc.org/index.php/ijoc/article/view/1167/605> accessed 28 July 2013.

Weller, David and Woodcock, Bill, 2013. "Internet Traffic Exchange: Market Developments and Policy Challenges", *OECD Digital Economy Papers*, No. 207, OECD Publishing <http://www.oecd-ilibrary.org/science-and-technology/internet-traffic-exchange_5k918gpt130q-en> accessed 8 August 2013.

Westby, Jody, 2012. "Google's Media Campaign Against the UN Slapped Down", *Forbes,* 4 December 2012 <http://www.forbes.com/sites/jodywestby/2012/12/04/googles-media-campaign-against-the-un-slapped-down/> accessed 11 March 2013.

Winsek, Dwayne, 2012. "The ITU and the Real Threats to the Internet, Part IV: the Triumph of State Security and Proposed Changes to the ITRs", *Mediamorphis,* 19 June 2012 <https://dwmw.wordpress.com/2012/06/19/the-itu-and-the-real-threats-to-the-internet-part-iv-the-triumph-of-state-security-and-proposed-changes-to-the-itrs/> accessed 10 March 2013.

Wong. Cynthia, 2012. "ITU Gives a Nod Towards Transparency; Still a Long Road to Full Civil Society Participation", Center for Democracy and Technology, 16 July 2012 <https://www.cdt.org/blogs/cynthia-wong/1607itu-gives-nod-towards-transparency-still-long-road-full-civil-society-partici> accessed 6 October 2013.

Working Group on Internet Governance, 2005. *Report* <http://www.wgig.org/docs/WGIGREPORT.pdf> accessed 6 October 2013.

WTO, 1994. *Annex on Telecommunications* <http://www.wto.org/english/tratop_e/serv_e/12-tel_e.htm> accessed 6 October 2013.

WTO, 1996. *Telecommunications Services: Reference Paper* <http://www.wto.org/english/tratop_e/serv_e/telecom_e/tel23_e.htm> accessed 6 October 2013.

Wu, Tim, 2010. *The Master Switch: The Rise and Fall of Information Empires*, Knopf.

Yu, Peter K., 2008. "Access to Medicines, BRICS Alliances, and Collective Action", *American Journal of Law and Medicine*, vol. 3, pp. 345-394 <http://papers.ssrn.com/sol3/papers.cfm?abstract_id=1088893> accessed 28 July 2013.

Index

Publikationen aus dem Zentrum für Informations- und Kommunikationsrecht der Universität Zürich

erschienen bei Schulthess Juristische Medien AG, Zürich

Band 1 **Neues Fernmelderecht – Erste Orientierung**
WEBER ROLF H. (Hrsg.),
mit Beiträgen von Fischer Peter R., Geiser Jean-Maurice, Gunter Pierre-Yves, Haag Marcel, Hoffet Franz, Maurer François, Ramsauer Matthias, Rieder Pierre, Stampfli Katharina und Weber Rolf H., Zürich 1998

Band 2 **Symposium Schluep – Querbezüge zwischen Kommunikations- und Wettbewerbsrecht**
WEBER ROLF H. (Hrsg.),
in Zusammenarbeit mit von der Crone Hans Caspar, Forstmoser Peter, Zäch Roger und Zobl Dieter,
mit Beiträgen von von der Crone Hans Caspar / Groner Roger, Mestmäcker Ernst-Joachim, Nobel Peter, Schwarz Mathias / Klingner Norbert und Weber Rolf H., Zürich 1998

Band 3 **Informatik und Jahr 2000 – Risiken und Vorsorgemöglichkeiten aus rechtlicher Sicht**
WEBER ROLF H.
Zürich 1998

Band 4 **Daten und Datenbanken – Rechtsfragen zu Schutz und Nutzung**
WEBER ROLF H. / HILTY RETO M. (Hrsg.),
mit Beiträgen von Druey Jean Nicolas, Gaster Jens-L., Hilty Reto M., Kemper Kurt, Sieber Ulrich und Weber Rolf H., Zürich 1998

Band 5 **Neustrukturierung der Rundfunkordnung**
WEBER ROLF H.
Zürich 1999

Band 6 **Rechtsschutz von Datenbanken (EU – USA – Schweiz)**
KÜBLER PHILIP
Zürich 1999

Band 7 **Informationsqualität – Ein Beitrag zur journalistischen Qualitätsdebatte aus der Sicht des Informationsrechts**
ZULAUF RENA
Zürich 2000

Band 8 **Werbung im Internet – Rechtsvergleichende, lauterkeitsrechtliche Beurteilung von Werbeformen**
JÖHRI YVONNE
Zürich 2000

Band 9 **Rechtlicher Regelungsrahmen von raumbezogenen Daten**
WEBER ROLF H.
Zürich 2000

Band 10 **Geschäftsplattform Internet – Rechtliche und praktische Aspekte**
Weber Rolf H./Hilty Reto M./Auf der Maur Rolf (Hrsg.)
Zürich 2000

Band 11 **Finanzierung der Rundfunkordnung**
Weber Rolf H.
Zürich 2000

Band 12 **Der Softwarepflegevertrag**
Widmer Michael
Zürich 2000

Band 13 **Datenschutzrecht vor neuen Herausforderungen**
Marketing – E-Commerce – Virtuelle Bank – Sachdaten
Weber Rolf H.
Zürich 2000

Band 14 **Geschäftsplattform Internet II – Rechtliche und praktische Aspekte**
Weber Rolf H./Hilty Reto M./Auf der Maur Rolf (Hrsg.)
Zürich 2001

Band 15 **Digitale Verbreitung von Rundfunkprogrammen**
und Meinungsvielfalt – Entwicklungen, Probleme, Lösungen
Weber Rolf H./Dörr Bianka S.
Zürich 2001

Band 16 **Die Übernahme von Allgemeinen Geschäftsbedingungen in**
elektronisch abgeschlossene Verträge
Schwab Karin
Zürich 2001

Band 17 **Geschäftsplattform Internet III – Kapitalmarkt – Marktauftritt – Besteuerung**
Weber Rolf H./Hilty Reto M./Auf der Maur Rolf (Hrsg.)
Zürich 2002

Band 18 **Rechtliche Rahmenbedingungen für verwaltungsunabhängige**
Behördenkommissionen – Untersuchung am Beispiel der geplanten
Fernmelde- und Medienkommission
Weber Rolf H./Biaggini Giovanni
Mitarbeit: Dörr Bianka S./Peduzzi Roberto
Zürich 2002

Band 19 **Elektronische Signaturen**
Schlauri Simon
Zürich 2002

Band 20 **Zugang zu Kabelnetzen – Spannungsfeld zwischen**
Netzbetreiberfreiheit und offenem Zugang
Weber Rolf H.
Zürich 2003

Band 21 **Elektronische Signaturen und Haftung der Anbieter von Zertifizierungsdiensten – Eine Darstellung am Beispiel der Regelungen in der EU, Deutschland, Grossbritannien und der Schweiz**
Dörr Bianka S.
Zürich 2003

Band 22 **Geschäftsplattform Internet IV**
Weber Rolf H./Berger Mathis/Auf der Maur Rolf (Hrsg.)
Zürich 2003

Band 23 **IT-Outsourcing**
ICT: Rechtspraxis I
Weber Rolf H./Berger Mathis/Auf der Maur Rolf (Hrsg.)
Zürich 2003

Band 24 **Rechtsfragen rund um Suchmaschinen**
Weber Rolf H.
Mitarbeit: Spacek Dirk
Zürich 2003

Band 25 **Schweizerisches Filmrecht**
Weber Rolf H./Unternährer Roland/Zulauf Rena
Zürich 2003

Band 26 **Kinofilmverwertung in der Schweiz**
Unternährer Roland
Zürich 2003

Band 27 **E-Health und Datenschutz**
Berger Kurzen Brigitte
Zürich 2004

Band 28 **Unternehmensinformation und Recht – Eine Übersicht**
Stückelberger Balz
Zürich 2004

Band 29 **Schutz von TV-Formaten – Eine rechtliche und ökonomische Betrachtung**
Spacek Dirk
Zürich 2005

Band 30 **Kulturquoten im Rundfunk**
Weber Rolf H./Rossnagel Alexander/Osterwalder Simon/Scheuer Alexander/Wüst Sonia
Zürich 2006

Band 31 **Zugang zu Premium Content**
Weber Rolf H./Osterwalder Simon
Zürich 2006

Band 32 **Sorgfaltspflichten bei der Datenübertragung**
Favre Katia
Zürich 2006

Band 33 **IT-Sicherheit und Recht – Grundlagen eines integrativen Gestaltungskonzepts**
WEBER ROLF H. / WILLI ANNETTE
Zürich 2006

Band 34 **Privatvervielfältigung im digitalen Umfeld**
BAUMGARTNER TOBIAS
Zürich 2006

Band 35 **Das Recht der personenbezogenen Information**
WEBER ROLF H. / SOMMERHALDER MARKUS
Zürich 2007

Band 36 **Staatliche Massnahmen gegen Medienkonzentration**
KELLERMÜLLER HANSPETER
Zürich 2007

Band 37 **Der Mehrwertdienst im Fernmelderecht**
HUBER KARIN
Zürich 2007

Band 38 **Telecommunications Competition and Its Driving Force**
WU JUN
Zürich 2008

Band 39 **Media Governance und Service Public**
WEBER ROLF H.
Zürich 2007

Band 40 **The Information Society and the Digital Divide Legal Strategies to Finance Global Access**
WEBER ROLF H. / MENOUD VALÉRIE A.
Zürich 2008

Band 41 **Netzzugang in der Telekommunikation**
AMGWERD MATTHIAS
Zürich 2008

Band 42 **IT-Governance als Aufgabe des Verwaltungsrates – Kriterien einer sorgfältigen Pflichterfüllung unter Berücksichtigung der strategischen Rolle der IT im Unternehmen**
WILLI ANNETTE
Zürich 2008

Band 43 **Der ASP-Vertrag**
CHRISTIAN M. IMHOF
Zürich 2008

Band 44 **Zivilrechtliche Haftung von Internet-Providern bei Rechtsverletzungen durch ihre Kunden**
FRECH PHILIPP
Zürich 2009

Band 45 **Public Key Infrastructure**
MARKWALDER DANIEL
Zürich 2009

Band 46 **Shaping Internet Governance: Regulatory Challenges**
WEBER ROLF H.
Zürich 2009

Band 47 **Rundfunkübertragungsrechte an den Olympischen Spielen im europäischen Kartellrecht**
Medienmärkte, gemeinsamer Erwerb durch die European Broadcasting Union und Exklusivvergabe
HELLWIG IRENE
Zürich 2009

Band 48 **Spyware**
Rechtliche Würdigung ausgewählter Fragen sowie Empfehlungen an die Praxis unter besonderer Berücksichtigung des Eidgenössischen Datenschutzgesetzes
BUCHER MANUEL
Zürich 2010

Band 49 **Internet of Things**
Legal Perspectives
WEBER ROLF H./WEBER ROMANA
Zürich 2010

Band 50 **Datenschutz v. Öffentlichkeitsprinzip**
Erläuterungen zu den Spannungsfeldern am Beispiel des Zürcher Informations- und Datenschutzgesetzes
WEBER ROLF H.
Zürich 2010

Band 51 **Online Marketing und Wettbewerbsrecht**
WEBER ROLF H./VOLZ STEPHANIE
Zürich 2011

Band 52 **Internet-Access-Providing-Verträge mit geschäftlichen und privaten Endkunden**
Eine vertragsrechtliche Analyse nach schweizerischem Recht unter besonderer Berücksichtigung des Rechts der Europäischen Union
ORSOLYA FERCSIK SCHNYDER
Zürich 2012

Band 53 **Classification of Services in the Digital Economy**
WEBER ROLF H.
Zürich 2012

Band 54 **Neuer Regulierungsschub im Datenschutzrecht?**
WEBER ROLF H. / THOUVENIN FLORENT
Zürich 2012

Band 55 **Die Erzwingung unangemessener Preise im Kartell- und Fernmelderecht – Eine rechtsvergleichende Untersuchung**
VLCEK MICHAEL
Zürich 2013

Band 56 **The Evolution of Global Internet Governance**
Principles and Policies in the Making
ROXANA RADU / JEAN-MARIE CHENOU / ROLF. H. WEBER
Zürich 2013

Band 57 **The New International Telecommunication Regulations and the Internet**
A Commentray and Legislative History
RICHARD HILL
Zürich 2013

Band 58 **Trennungsgebot und Internet**
STEPHANIE VOLZ
Zürich 2013

Ausserdem erschienen:

Regulatory Models for the Online World
WEBER ROLF H.
Zürich 2002

Towards a Legal Framework for the Information Society
WEBER ROLF H.
in collaboration with Roduner Xenia
Zürich 2003

MIX
Papier aus verantwortungsvollen Quellen
Paper from responsible sources
FSC® C105338

If you have any concerns about our products,
you can contact us on
ProductSafety@springernature.com

In case Publisher is established outside the EU,
the EU authorized representative is:
Springer Nature Customer Service Center GmbH
Europaplatz 3, 69115 Heidelberg, Germany

Printed by Libri Plureos GmbH
in Hamburg, Germany